Rex Barney's *THANK Youuuu*

REX EDWARD BARNEY

Rex Barney (signature)

Pitching Record

		W	L	PCT	ERA	G	GS	CG	IP	H	BB	SO	ShO
1943	Durham	4	6	.400	3.00	11	10	7	81	70	51	71	1
1943	Montreal	0	1	.000	2.45	4	2	1	22	19	18	18	0
1943	BKN N	2	2	.500	6.35	9	8	1	45.1	36	41	23	0
1946		2	5	.286	5.87	16	9	1	53.2	46	51	36	0
1947		5	2	.714	4.98	28	9	0	77.2	66	59	36	0
1948		15	13	.536	3.10	44	34	12	246.2	193	122	138	4
1949		9	8	.529	4.41	38	20	6	140.2	108	89	80	2
1950		2	1	.667	6.42	20	1	0	33.2	25	48	23	0
	ML Totals	35	31	.530	4.34	155	81	20	597.2	474	410	336	4
WORLD SERIES RECORD													
1947	BKN N	0	1	.000	2.70	3	1	0	6.2	4	10	3	0
1949		0	1	.000	16.88	1	1	0	2.2	3	6	2	0
	2 years	0	2	.000	6.75	4	2	0	9.1	7	16	5	0

Batting Record

		G	AB	H	2B	3B	HR	HR %	R	RBI	BB	SO	SB	BA
1943	BKN N	9	18	1	0	0	0	0.0	0	0	1	5	0	.056
1946		16	17	4	0	0	0	0.0	1	0	2	5	0	.235
1947		28	27	3	1	0	0	0.0	3	3	0	12	0	.111
1948		44	84	14	0	0	0	0.0	5	2	2	40	0	.167
1949		38	47	10	1	0	0	0.0	3	2	1	14	0	.213
1950		20	8	1	1	0	0	0.0	0	0	1	2	0	.125
	ML Totals	155	201	33	3	0	0	0.0	12	7	7	78	0	.164
WORLD SERIES RECORD														
1947	BKN N	3	1	0	0	0	0	0.0	0	0	0	0	0	.000
1949		1	0	0	0	0	0	–	0	0	0	0	0	–
	2 years	4	1	0	0	0	0	0.0	0	0	0	0	0	.000

REX BARNEY'S
THANK Youuuu

for 50 Years in Baseball
from Brooklyn to Baltimore

By
REX BARNEY

With NORMAN L. MACHT

TIDEWATER PUBLISHERS
Centreville, Maryland

Library of Congress Cataloging-in-Publication Data

Barney, Rex.
    Rex Barney's thank youuuu for 50 years in baseball from Brooklyn
to Baltimore / by Rex Barney with Norman L. Macht. — 1st ed.
        p.   cm.
    Includes index.
    ISBN 0-87033-443-3
    1. Barney, Rex.   2. Baseball players—United States—Biography.
3. Sportscasters—United States—Biography.   I. Macht, Norman L.
(Norman Lee) , 1929-   . II. Title.
GV865.B28A3   1993
796.357′092—dc20
[B]   92–44664
                                                                   CIP

Manufactured in the United States of America
First edition

To my father and mother,
Eugene and Marie Barney

*Nothing flatters me more than to have it assumed
that I could write prose—unless it be to have it
assumed that I once pitched baseball with distinction.*
— *Robert Frost*

Baseball has given me a life of joy.
— *Branch Rickey*

Contents

Foreword

ТODAY, baseball is very much into measurements. It seems like they have electronic devices to measure everything. Let Jose Canseco hit a home run and the announcer no longer says, "It's a real tape measure job," because all he has to do is look at the electronic scoreboard and chances are the distance the home run traveled is up there.

A Nolan Ryan grunts and fires his best fastball and a radar gun is there to measure the speed. To me, for the most part, things like that aren't that important. If the ball travels 330 or 530 feet, once it clears the fence, it doesn't matter anymore. The same is true of the velocity of a pitch.

When you walk up to the plate to face a Sandy Koufax, a Sudden Sam McDowell, a Bob Gibson, a Bob Feller, or a Nolan Ryan, you don't care whether the pitch comes in at 93, or 96, or 196 miles an hour. It's like the weatherman's wind chill factor. I'm already cold, so I don't need to know it's even colder. If I'm not going to hit a pitcher anyhow, I don't need to know how fast the pitch was that got me out.

Rex Barney's fastball belonged in the company of Koufax, Gibson, and the rest of that group. The fact that Rex had that kind of speed, plus problems with his control, did nothing for a batter's peace of mind. Rex Barney on the mound made an impression, and I mean that in more ways than one.

Ted Williams says, "Hitting a baseball is the single most difficult thing in sports." I'm living proof of that. But when Rex

Barney was pitching, then the catcher could have some problems. I'm proof of that, too.

I go back a long way with Rex: We were in the army together during World War II, stationed at Fort Riley, Kansas. He could throw that overpowering fastball even then, but since we were teammates, I didn't have to bat against him, so I had nothing to worry about. Right? Wrong!

We were playing one night in Junction City, Kansas, and the lights were not very good. Rex was tough in daylight, but he was almost impossible to hit under those lights. It was about the same light you would get from three guys holding cigarette lighters. On this night the batters weren't the only ones who had trouble seeing. It turned out that Rex was having trouble seeing, too.

I put down two fingers for the curve ball, but Rex only saw one finger and here comes his fastball. Catchers wear chest protectors so that mistakes like this don't hurt them, but this was Rex Barney's fastball. I woke up in the infirmary and had perfect seam imprints on my chest. I felt like a blocked kick.

Rex Barney was an army buddy, then an opponent when he was with the Dodgers and I was with the Cardinals, but always a friend. Since he works for the Baltimore Orioles as the PA announcer, I still get a chance to visit and talk about his fastball. You're lucky because you will be able to read about it. I tried to hit it and catch it. I saw it and I heard it. Yes, I mean heard it. You could be sitting in the last row in the bleachers and when that ball hit the mitt you heard it. Rex made it sound like they were stacking two-by-fours at the lumberyard.

You always feel better after a visit with Rex. I'll bet that when you're through reading this book, you'll feel the same way.

Joe Garagiola

Preface

THE BALTIMORE ORIOLES were playing in New York one day in the early 1970s, and Brooks Robinson and I got into a cab to go to Yankee Stadium. The driver was an older man who spoke English. On the way, Brooks and I talked about the game the night before, and when we arrived the driver turned to me and said, "Are you Rex Barney?"

"Yes."

"I've been a fan of yours from your playing days in Brooklyn. Can I have your autograph for my grandson?" He handed me back the ten dollar bill I had just given him and said, "Sign that. I'll give it to him."

So I signed it and said, "Don't you want Brooks Robinson's autograph, too?"

The cabbie shrugged and said, "Well, I guess so, if he wants to sign it."

When we got out, Brooks said to me, "I'll be a sonofabitch. I'm supposed to be the star around here."

"Well," I said, "now you know how it is when you're on my turf."

Recently a friend of mine from Baltimore told me he was in Grand Central Station in New York getting a shoeshine. The shine man and another customer were talking baseball, and my friend said, "I'm from Baltimore. Did you ever hear of Rex Barney?"

The shoeshine man snapped his polishing rag and grinned. "Oh, yeah! Rex Barney. I'll never forget how hard he threw and, boy, was he wild."

This was more than forty years after I threw my last wild pitch. Despite my short career and mediocre record, why am I still remembered, while so many players who were up there a lot longer and put up much better numbers than mine are forgotten? It is a question that stumps me, but in writing this book I may have uncovered a few clues.

For one thing, my name is memorable. I am not aware of any ballplayers before me named Rex; the only one I've known since is Rex Hudler of the St. Louis Cardinals.

I think, too, that hard-throwing pitchers are remembered the most graphically. The fans in Brooklyn took to me because I was a big 18-year-old fireballing right-hander who made the catcher's mitt pop like a Fourth of July cherry bomb. I was spectacular at times: striking out Joe DiMaggio with the bases loaded in the 1947 World Series; pitching a no-hitter against the hated Giants in the Polo Grounds; throwing two one-hitters. I was also spectacularly wild at times, and they remember that, too. And how they remember that.

It used to bother me when people pitched those catch phrases at me: "If home plate was high and outside, Rex Barney would be in the Hall of Fame . . . He could throw the ball through a brick wall, if he could hit the wall . . . "

When they asked me, "Were you really that wild?" I would get very defensive and say, "No." But now I just laugh and go along with it. "Wilder," I say.

I know that some people do it to needle me or put me down, as if to say, "You didn't have much of a big league career."

No, I didn't. But I was there.

I was broadcasting the Mutual Game of the Day with Bob Neal in Chicago one day and I spotted Nat "King" Cole sitting in a box seat, busily keeping score. It was a Sunday doubleheader, and Cole agreed to do an interview between games. On the air we talked a little and then I said, "With all the things you've accomplished—movies, night clubs, hit records, your own television show—what's left for you to do?"

"I'd give it all up," he said, "my whole career, to be the third baseman for the St. Louis Cardinals."

I've heard general managers say to players, "I would give anything to have played one day, one game in the major leagues." So when people try to downplay my big league career,

I know they wouldn't even mention it unless they were a little envious. And it doesn't bother me a bit.

I suppose there is something legendary about the guy who threw harder than anybody, the flame-throwing wild man, all that potential, the brief flashes of glory. It has all the elements of mythic lore. And yet, the Dodgers of the 1940s had a bunch of hard throwers: Banta, Gregg, Behrman, Taylor, Lombardi, Branca. Old Giant fans don't remember them (except Ralph Branca, of course). I was the guy they hated, the one who no-hit them in their own backyard, the only Brooklyn pitcher who ever did that to them.

Time and place are other factors in my being so well remembered. Anybody who played for the *real* Dodgers in Ebbets Field has an automatic leg up on baseball immortality. I was part of some of Brooklyn's greatest teams. From 1946 to 1955 they won five pennants and lost two tie-breaker playoffs. I was there when Jackie Robinson broke the color barrier, when Leo Durocher was suspended for a year, when Ralph Branca threw a pitch to . . .

I was only 25 when my big league career ended, the kid who had it all and fell far short of what I should have done. I visit the Hall of Fame in Cooperstown at least once a year and I cry a lot when I go there. I'm just a big dumb Irishman with a soft heart and I look at all those stars of the past and I think, boy oh boy, if I could only have been part of all this. I'm not, and it is something I have anguished over for more than forty years.

Staying in the game as a broadcaster and, for the past twenty-two years, the public address announcer for the Baltimore Orioles is also part of the reason for my longevity among fans of all ages.

I enjoy all sports, but I have always been fascinated by baseball. I consider myself the luckiest person in the world because I have been part of the game for fifty years—so far. I have seen upwards of 6,000 games and cannot wait to see the next one, which may be the greatest game of them all. When a Nolan Ryan battles a Cal Ripken one on one, I'm on the edge of my seat, raptly engrossed. I have watched scores of great players and seen "scrubinis" make some of the greatest catches. I agree with Orioles manager Johnny Oates and other baseball

men who say, "At the end of the season, let's have one day off
and start over."

And I've made more friends in and out of baseball than any
man deserves.

Over the years several people have approached me about
writing a book. I always said no. I could never get it through
my head that anybody cared that much about what I had done
or seen or felt in my lifetime. Then, on October 4, 1991, I
collapsed after a game and wound up in the hospital, missing
the last two games ever played at Memorial Stadium. Among
the more than 300 cards and letters I received, there was a note
from a teacher in Baltimore. In it she said she rushes home to
hear me every day at 4:15 on WBAL with her two small
children, and tells them they should treat people with courtesy
the way she said I do on my call-in talk shows. Then she added
that her kids go around the house imitating my trademark
sign-off, "THANK Youuuu."

When I read that and realized what I meant to her and her
family, tears rolled down my face. That is very humbling, but
rewarding at the same time, and I understood for the first time
that it was not for me to decide if anyone might be interested
in reading about my life and the baseball stories I could tell.

But the clincher came when a friend put it to me bluntly:
"There is a chance you might die someday. You've got 8,000
stories from your playing days and your twenty-five years with
the Orioles. Don't you think you should share all that while you
still can?"

And, I thought, by God, he's right.

Acknowledgments

A WISE MAN once wrote, "The older I get, the more clearly I remember things that never happened." We are all subject to slippery retrospect, especially when trying to recall dates and scores and who said what, when, and where, fifty years ago.

So I am indebted to many people for their help in researching the facts and confirming or correcting my hindsight. And if I have misplaced an error or called a curve a fastball somewhere along the way, please forgive me.

The roll of people who are due thanks is long and probably incomplete, and for that I apologize. It includes Jack Carlson and Tom Hetrick of the Society for American Baseball Research; Orioles friends Rick Vaughn, Bob Brown, Bob Miller, Helen Conklin, Lisa A. Waskiewicz, and Stephanie R. Kelly; Steve Getscheier of *The Sporting News;* my dear friends Chuck Thompson and Sam Lacy; Bob Schweppe of the Los Angeles Dodgers; Bill Miller of the Durham Bulls; Joe Garagiola; Buddy Kerr; Alvin Dark; old Dodgers Gene Mauch, Buzzie Bavasi, Don Drysdale, Tom Lasorda, and Bobby Bragan; Dr. Sheldon Goldgeier; Bill Deane of the Hall of Fame Library; Marilyn Dicey for her transcribing; Chuck McGeehan for his review of the manuscript; and Harriett Macht for her hospitality and cooking during our lengthy taping sessions.

Rex Barney's *THANK Youuuu*

ONE

No-Hitter

J IM PALMER and I were sitting at the bar in a restaurant in Key Biscayne, Florida, one day and Jim said to the bartender, "You know, there's only one bar in the entire country right this minute with two guys sitting there who pitched no-hitters in the major leagues."

Pitchers are proud of that feat; only about a hundred of them have done it in the 115-year history of the National League. And I'm one of them.

To appreciate what made my no-hitter so special, you have to know something about the two teams that were involved. New York was the only city where there were two teams in the same league. And no more intensely bitter rivalry has ever existed in any sport. Even if both teams were in last place, that intensity never flagged. There were few empty seats when the Giants and Dodgers played (how mild and innocent that word "played" seems when applied to those battles). Fights were common in the stands. New York and Brooklyn fans even fought over who had the better broadcaster.

In Ebbets Field the players had to go through a tunnel and up some steps to the dugout. If the Giants put a cap on the end of a bat and stuck it above the dugout roof, the fans would start booing. The Polo Grounds clubhouses were in deep center field. As soon as a Dodger blue cap appeared in the visitors' doorway, the hostile thunder began. All of this poured over to the players. Hatred is not too strong a word; we hated the Giants.

September 9, 1948, was only fourteen years after Giants manager Bill Terry had cracked, "Are the Dodgers still in the league?" After which the sixth-place Brooks had knocked them out of the pennant in the last week of the season. Nobody on either side had ever forgotten.

Just two months earlier Leo Durocher had struck a match to this volatile mix by leaving the Dodgers to manage the Giants, a switch that had stunned fanatics on both sides and left them confused, hurt, and angry. If I had pitched my no-hitter against the Pirates or Reds—sure, it would have been great. But to do it to the hated Giants, in their own yard, something no other Brooklyn pitcher had ever done—that's why I am still a hero in Brooklyn.

And it almost didn't happen.

It rained all day September 9. The night before, my wife had not been feeling well and I had walked the floor with my restless baby daughter until about five A.M., then slept a few hours. Orders were to report to the ballpark whatever the weather, so I went to the Polo Grounds certain we would not play that night. That upset me, because I was in a groove and raring to pitch. After a poor start that year, I had won 10 and lost 5 since July 2, including a one-hitter three weeks earlier against the Phillies. Pee Wee Reese had said to me a few days before, "If you ever pitch a no-hitter, it'll be this year."

But no pitcher goes into a game thinking no-hitter; you just go out there to win.

The Giants had virtually the same lineup that had hit a record 221 home runs in 1947: John Mize (who would lead the league with 40 home runs), Sid Gordon, Willard Marshall, Don Mueller, Walker Cooper, and Whitey Lockman, who owned me outright. They always gave me a rough time.

Game time was 8:15 and it was still raining. I sat in the clubhouse, looking out the window, fidgeting. I never could stand inactivity and I was getting nervous and tense. When it got close to 9:00 the clubhouse man, Charley Digiovanna, assured me that we wouldn't play and brought me a hot dog. Those ballpark franks would kill a snake. I tasted that one for a week. There were 36,000 people sitting there waiting—a Giant-Dodger game would draw a crowd in a typhoon. The Giants secretary, Eddie Brannick, and the umpires had decided to give it an hour before calling it off. A little after nine Brannick climbed toward the press box to make the announcement. On the way he noticed the grounds crew removing the covers from the field. He paused, changed his mind, turned around, and went down.

The rain let up and I went out to warm up. The starting catcher took over the warm-up for the last five or ten minutes. When I finished, Bruce Edwards said to me, "You sure have plenty of stuff tonight."

I knew it. But it looked like it would be a long night when I walked the leadoff man, Jack Lohrke, on four pitches; threw wildly to second trying for a double play; and walked Mize to load the bases. But Marshall hit into a double play. I didn't walk another batter.

When young pitchers ask me what it feels like to pitch a no-hitter, the first thing I say is, "Don't believe it when a pitcher says he did not know he had one going. Every pitcher knows exactly what he has or has not given up in a game. There's no way he can't know. Every time he looks at the scoreboard for the outs or the count he sees that 0-0-0 up there. But it's just another game until he gets to the sixth inning and begins to think he has a shot at it."

Leo Durocher, coaching at third base, got on me. "We're gonna get you this inning, you no-good busher." When I went up to bat, catcher Walker Cooper said, "You'll never last with that slop you're throwing." Every time I came off the mound after an inning the fans were hollering, "You know you're pitching a no-hitter." The old jinx routine.

By the seventh inning you notice that all of a sudden you're sitting alone on the bench. Nobody wants to be near you. They slide away like the Red Sea parting. Nobody speaks to you.

The Giants fans gradually began to come over to my side and I got a big ovation after every out. The score was 2 to 0, so the game was still on the line, and I had to remember that winning came first. But with each out I got a little more pumped up.

By the ninth, the tension had spread to the others on the field. Gene Hermanski, not a good fielder, still talks about how I must have been dying with him in right field that night. "I was out there praying they wouldn't hit the ball to me," he says. But the sure-handed Carl Furillo in center wasn't worried.

5

The ninth inning was one continuous deafening howl. It began to rain again as pinch-hitter Joe Lafata stepped in. I half expected him to try a bunt on the wet grass, but he struck out. I got Lohrke easily and there stood my old nemesis, Whitey Lockman, between me and glory. Bruce Edwards came out to the mound.

"You know who this is," he said.

"Yes."

"What are you going to do?"

"Just throw it as hard as I can."

I thought my first pitch was perfect, but umpire Babe Pinelli called it a ball. I yelled, "No!" Took a deep breath. Took another. Got the sign from Bruce. Wound up and threw. Lockman lifted a high foul pop-up and Edwards whipped off his mask and ran what seemed like two city blocks to the top of the dugout steps and caught it. I leaped about two feet in the air and Jackie Robinson and Pee Wee were the first to reach me. And then we were running out to the clubhouse and here was Durocher, who had been my manager until two months ago and my heckler that night, coming alongside me. "I'm proud of you, kid," he said and ran on past me.

Pinelli told reporters I was the fastest he had seen, and a fine young man, to boot. But I wasn't trying to be nice out there. I was always very competitive. I had thrown 116 pitches, only 41 out of the strike zone.

I was so worked up, I could never eat after a game. I'd drink gallons of water but it took me a few hours to settle down. There was a crowd of writers around me, and it was after midnight before I got out of there. Arch Murray of the New York *Post* asked me where I was going, and I said, "Toots Shor's, I guess." That was the popular hangout for the sporting crowd.

Shor, a fanatic Giant rooter, had been at the game. When I entered his place, everybody stood up and gave me a hand. Shor, in his booming voice, let them know the only way I could no-hit the Giants in the Polo Grounds was "in a night game with the lights out."

The next morning, photographers were at the door and the phone rang constantly. Players today ask me what I got for pitching the no-hitter—a bonus or car or what? One of the phone calls was from Brooklyn general manager Branch Rickey. "Young man," he said, "that was a great thing you did last night. You brought honor to the Brooklyn organization. You are finally accomplishing all that we believed you could do. Thank you very much." That was my bonus. But it wasn't just Mr. Rickey. That's the way baseball was in those days. It was just another win to everybody else, except to me.

I'll tell you what else I got. The next day at the Polo Grounds when I started down those twenty or thirty steps from the clubhouse door to the field, instead of the usual names and jeers and boos, I heard nothing but cheering. I felt like a million dollars on that long walk across the field, thinking, "I could do this a few times and not complain."

For weeks I was the center of attention wherever I went. In restaurants they refused to let me pay the check. Writers came to interview me. What does all that do to a 23-year-old hick from Omaha? How do you handle that? Maybe it was the worst thing that could have happened to me. But it sure felt great at the time. And I know that whatever I failed to accomplish, this is one thing I did do that nobody can deny.

Thirty-two years later, at their annual dinner, the New York Baseball Writers gave me the "You-can-look-it-up" Award for pitching the last no-hitter thrown in the Polo Grounds. Wrote Harold Rosenthal, "Singling out Rex Barney for the special honor traced not to the fact that he was the greatest Brooklyn Dodger pitcher of the post-war era, which he wasn't, but that he was their greatest mystery."

TWO

Growing Up in Omaha

I HAD THE GREATEST CHILDHOOD in the world, even though we had nothing but plenty of love and devotion and support. And discipline.

I was born on December 19, 1924, on a typical winter night in Omaha, Nebraska—twenty below zero. My father could not get the old Model T Ford started, so he called somebody to help him rush my mother to the hospital. She told me I was born in the elevator on the way up to the delivery room.

My two sisters, Beatrice and Bernice, were thirteen and eleven, and my brother Ted was nine when I came along. They always teased me that I was a mistake, and it took me a long time to understand what they meant. We were a tall family: my father was 6-2, my brother 6-1, my mother and sisters 5-8.

We were Irish Catholic on both sides—O'Haras and Barneys and McDoufeys. My name is the equivalent of three first names, Rex Edward Barney, but my mother never told me why she chose them.

My grandparents, Spencer and Theresa Barney, lived in Millard, about ten miles west of Omaha. It took an hour to get there in the old flivver. During our visits there, we kids slept in the attic, my brother and I in one big bed. There was no insulation, no electricity, no indoor plumbing. In the wintertime, we would lie there under a thick feather quilt, the moonlight coming through the window and glistening on the frost around the nailheads in the roof. In the morning we dashed down to the kitchen in our drop seat long underwear and huddled around the hot stove that was filled with burning corncobs. That was our way of life and I loved it.

Grandpa had a crystal radio set; only one person could listen at a time. You put big earphones over your head and you could hear faint voices and music before it faded out or was lost beneath the crackling static. It was great. Later we had a big radio that stood on the floor, and I would sneak into the parlor when my parents were asleep and press my ear against it, listening to whatever I could find. Occasionally, when the signal was strong and the wind was right, we heard a little of a St. Louis Cardinals or a Cubs game. That was how I first heard about Dizzy Dean and Stan Hack and Kiki Cuyler, a name that fascinated me. I used to wonder what kind of person would have a name like that.

My father, Eugene Spencer Barney, worked for the Union Pacific Railroad for forty-five years, and became a general foreman. His territory was from Omaha to Cheyenne, Wyoming. He left home on Sunday nights and was on the line until Friday night. One of my big thrills was going to the depot on Fridays to meet him. That was the home base of the U.P., a magnificent building with a grand dining room. Sometimes we would eat supper there; that was a big treat.

Once in a while during school vacation he took me on the road with him. He knew everybody on all the trains and had a gold pass that let him ride free on any railroad; I was very impressed by that. Sometimes we slept in a berth on the train, and some nights in an old railroad hotel by the tracks in a room with a bare yellow bulb hanging from the ceiling. By the time I left home to play ball I knew my way around trains. If I had gotten hurt and could not play ball, I would have worked for the railroad.

My mother, Marie, was my strongest influence because my father was away all week. She never struck me, but when she said, "Rex Edward, come here," I knew I was in some kind of trouble. She was a very polite person, and I got that from her. "The most important words in life are 'please' and 'thank you,'" she taught me. She lives on in me every time I say, "THANK Youuuu."

Mom was a stickler for proper behavior. My brother had a pal, Howie. Ted would stand outside Howie's house and holler, *"How-wee!"* the way kids do. My mother hated that. "Go to that house and knock on the door like a gentleman," she scolded him.

I was a tag-along; whenever Ted and his friends were going someplace, my mother would say, "Take Rex along," and he hated that. One day we went to get Howie and I said to Ted, "Go ahead and call him. Mother won't do anything." So he did, and out she came and marched us right back home and down the cellar steps; we didn't get out of there the whole day.

Mom preached cleanliness is godliness. The two cheapest commodities, she said, were soap and water.

Being the youngest, I said the blessing before every meal. One day my father said, "Son, don't you think you ought to take off your gloves before you come to the table?" I looked at my hands; they were filthy black. I got his message, and never sat down to eat with gloves on again.

The only time my father ever hit me was while I was going to Our Lady of Lourdes grammar school. When you misbehaved there, you held out your hands and the dear sweet nuns slapped them with a ruler. One day Sister Mary Magdalene got ready to slap me and I pulled my hands back and she almost fell.

"Turn your hands over," she ordered. Whacko! Man, that hurt.

It was a Friday and my father was home. "How was school today?"

"Not very good."

"What's the matter?"

"Sister Mary thought I was talking in class and she went to slap my hands with the ruler and I pulled them away and she almost fell."

He hit me a shot that knocked me across the room. "Don't you ever misbehave to those nuns," he said, "or to your mother or me or the cop on the beat."

"Yes, sir."

From then on, even if I did get whacked by the nuns, it was always:

"How was school today?"

"Great, just great."

My mother was a good cook, but strictly meat and potatoes. No meat on Fridays, and in Nebraska there was no such thing as fish. Friday meals might be fried mush—cornmeal with some kind of gravy on it. It was terrible, but it filled you up.

10

Macaroni and cheese was a big treat; I still love it. Another was rice with raisins and cinnamon and you poured cream over it. Sundays, if things were good, there was a big chicken. There was plenty of beef, but in the Midwest it was always very well done, to the burning point. That's all I ever knew as a kid—burnt beef.

I cannot stress enough what a good and supportive family life I had. My parents were all for me and encouraged me and let me do what I wanted to do. Sure, I had chores: wash the dishes, cut the grass, shovel snow. I dug dandelions out of the lawn and got a penny each. One day I dug up twenty of them and I was rich. One of my duties was to stack the coal furnace at night, pushing the hot coals to one end so the fire didn't go out during the night, then get up at five to rebuild the fire before everyone else was up. If that fire went out during the night, it was a dirty job to restart it.

Another chore was emptying the water from the icebox. No refrigerator—icebox. A fifty-pound chunk of ice sat in the top part and gradually melted and ran down into a container. When it was full of water I had to empty it. "And don't spill it," Mom warned every time. And of course it was a dead cinch you would spill some on her clean kitchen floor.

I loved Christmas and Thanksgiving and especially Easter, when we made little round nests with our clothes and the next morning we found colored eggs that the Easter bunny brought. I believed in Santa Claus for a long time because I did not want that fantasy to end. I remember Christmas trees with real candles on them; you had to watch them like a hawk and blow them out at night. We always got some kind of present, usually something to wear which you didn't want. Since my birthday was less than a week before Christmas, I never got two presents. Never. From anybody. It was always, "Wait 'til Christmas next week." But I never thought anything about it then. As far as I knew, that was the way of the world.

About a dozen years ago I'm in a bar down near Fells Point in Baltimore with a friend and some guy says, "Isn't your birthday soon?" and I say, "Yeah, next week," and I mention something about how I have never gotten two presents, and they laugh. The next week I'm in there again and it's my birthday, and another guy walks up to me and says, "We were

11

here last week and heard you say you never got two presents from anybody. Here's two presents." And he hands me two boxes, a long one and a little square one. "But you have to open them now," he says.

In one box there's one sock and in the other one is the mate. "Now don't say you never got two presents," he says.

So I won't anymore.

People tease me about Omaha, but I thought it was the greatest place in the world to grow up, and I still do. Anybody who has played in the college world series there remembers it fondly.

The biggest employers were the Union Pacific, Mutual of Omaha insurance, and the stockyards. Omaha is also world renowned for its Community Playhouse. I was not aware of it at the time, but Omaha actors were well regarded because they had no pronounced accent of any kind to overcome. Marlon Brando's mother and grandmother, and later his sister, Jocelyn, ran it and taught acting. Area alumni you may recognize include Johnny Carson, Dick Cavett, Henry Fonda, Fred Astaire, Sandy Dennis, and Dorothy McGuire.

President Gerald Ford was born there. Among local ballplayers who made good, spitball pitcher Clarence Mitchell and Mel Harder were our early heroes. Wahoo, the home of Hall of Famer Sam Crawford, was about twenty-five miles away. Gregg Olson, Wade Boggs, and Bob Gibson were born in Omaha, and Richie Ashburn came from nearby Tilden.

The population was about 225,000, predominantly Italian and Irish. Little Italy was near the depot. The black neighborhood was in North Omaha, but nobody called it a ghetto. It was just their section of town, and nobody ever bothered anybody.

I had a very Catholic upbringing: went to parochial schools, where we traded our terrible baloney sandwiches for the Italians' hot peppers, and served early mass every morning in the church a block from home.

One of the highlights of my life has been my association with Boys Town. My parents knew Father Flanagan when he ran a shelter for derelicts and street people in Omaha, in a building provided by a Jewish real estate man, Bozell Jacobs. One day Father Flanagan asked Mr. Jacobs to drive him out in the countryside. They were in the middle of nowhere when Father Flanagan asked him to stop.

"You see this piece of property? I want you to buy it and build me a building."

Jacobs laughed. "What for?"

"Homeless and abused boys need a place they can go to, and I think we can help them."

That original building, which held about twelve kids, is still there. Today more than 500 boys and girls live in Boys Town.

Our house was about five miles from there, and in the summer Father Flanagan let me serve mass for him. Then he'd take me to the rectory to have breakfast with him. Pitching a no-hitter and playing in the World Series and all that is great, but knowing Father Flanagan and serving mass for him is as big a thrill as I'll ever get in my life.

About that time they made a movie about Boys Town with Spencer Tracy and Mickey Rooney. (It was very accurate, by the way.) When Tracy won an Oscar for that role, he sent it to Father Flanagan with a note: "To the man who deserves this more than I do."

In 1947 Father Flanagan went to Europe to start a Boys Town there. He called me from Omaha just before the World Series. "Son, I will be in New York. Do you think you can get me a couple World Series tickets?"

"Father," I said, "you can sit where I sit, as far as I'm concerned." I told Mr. Rickey about it and he saw that Father Flanagan had the best seats. It meant a lot to me to be able to do something in return for that man.

I played sports with blacks and Jewish kids and thought nothing about it. There were a few Jewish kids at Creighton Prep, the Jesuit high school, because it was the best school in the city. We thought they were lucky; they got to play outside while we were in religion class. If somebody said anything derogatory to them, I didn't even know what it meant.

I'm not trying to say there was no prejudice. My own parents had racism and anti-Semitism bred into them. And I took some taunting. One day when I was in the second grade my brother was walking home with me. Some kids from the public school yelled at me from across the street, "Hey, you dirty catlicker."

Ted said, "Are you going to take that?"

"Take what?"

"He called you a catlicker."

"What does that mean?"

"That means you're a no-good Catholic."

"No," I said, "I'm not going to take that."

We crossed the street and this little kid and I started beating up on each other until my brother pulled us apart. I didn't understand that kind of stuff, and I still don't.

We lived in a tree-lined residential neighborhood of modest single-family homes. Ours was a one-story, three-bedroom house with one bathroom at 2114 South 34th Street, thirty-four blocks south of the main drag, Dodge Street. We had a party line telephone; when nobody else was using it, you picked it up and the operator said, "Number, please," and you told her the number. The nearest store was three blocks away. There were Irish, German, and Italian families, and nobody gave anybody a bad time. You could run across a lawn or play ball in the street and nobody got after you for anything.

There was one empty lot where we played every game imaginable. At night we played sidewalk handball or pitched pennies, and argued and yelled and carried on, but always under the streetlight on the corner so my parents could look out and see me. That may sound wimpish today, but that's the way families were run. There was no vandalism or crime; none of us gave any of that stuff a thought. We were too busy having fun.

Sure, we did some dumb kid stuff. We had two cherry trees and an apple tree in our own backyard, but we thought it was fun to go to some other neighborhood and steal cherries and apples off somebody else's trees. They tasted sweeter, I guess. Once I reached over a fence for an apple and fell into the yard and I thought I'd never get out of there alive.

A bunch of us would chip in a penny each to buy one ten-cent ticket to get into the Orpheum Theater downtown. One kid would buy the ticket, go inside, run downstairs to the door in the back, and open it. The rest of us swarmed in and ran to the men's room in search of ticket stubs in the sand where the cigarette butts were. Then, if the usher caught you, you could show him the stub. Of course, he knew what we were up to, but we didn't think he was wise to us. We believed we were really putting something over on him. We'd sit there all day in the winter, see the movie twice (plus the stage show), and keep warm.

On Sundays after mass my father would give me a quarter: a nickel for the streetcar, ten cents to get into the Orpheum, a nickel for popcorn, and a nickel to get home. In good weather I'd walk or hitch a ride home, and spend that extra five cents for candy. God, how I cherished that quarter. And I thought life was just great.

I was always looking for a way to make a few dollars. If you had a couple bucks in your pocket and the other guys had nothing, boy, you were big stuff. In the summer I pushed a lawn mower and dug dandelions. In winter I shoveled snow: fifty cents for a sidewalk, a dollar for a big job. I tried to be the first to the big Maxwell house near us because you got a buck from Mrs. Maxwell plus a cup of hot chocolate. One day I was using her shovel and it broke. She made me get it fixed; cost me two dollars. I probably shed a few tears over that, and vowed I'd never shovel that mean old lady's walk again. But next snowstorm, there I was. One thing about Omaha: it snows a lot. You could do plenty of business.

I had a paper route in the morning, and sold papers on a street corner at three cents in the afternoon. I was a pretty good pool hustler, too. (I found out later in the minor leagues you better learn to shoot pool or you're in trouble. There was only one movie house in every town and not much else to do.) I caddied at Omaha Field Club and earned a dollar for eighteen holes. If you were lucky, you could double-bag it and make two dollars. It was a very exclusive club; I could never play there.

When I got a little older I worked for the railroad from six to ten in the morning sorting mail, but I had to give my mother five dollars a month for room and board.

I was fifteen when we moved to a better house at 1221 South 52nd Street, and it was such a disruption to me, I thought I could never function again. I rode the streetcar to Creighton Prep, but sometimes in cold weather my father took me in the car. I'd freeze more in that car because he did not believe in using the heater and he drove with the windows open so they didn't frost up. I chose to ride the streetcar whenever possible.

The big bands played the Orpheum in the 1930s and 1940s, and that's when I fell in love with that kind of music. It's also what led me to skip school once and got me into a whole lot of trouble. I was at Creighton Prep on an athletic scholarship

15

because we could not afford it, when Harry James and his band came to town for a week. On weekends I was busy playing ball, so one Friday I skipped school with a few other truants and we went to the Orpheum and had a great time.

On Monday morning after mass the principal, Father Henry Sullivan, called me into his office. He waved me over to a big bay window.

"Do you see that big red building over there?"

"Yes, Father." That's the way you answered them; you never elaborated.

"What is that building?"

"Omaha Technical High School."

He said, "In that school you can learn to be a shoemaker or a mechanic or a truck driver. How would you like to go there?"

"No, Father."

"Well then, do you think you could find it in your scheme of things to attend school and not go to the Orpheum Theater to see Harry James?"

I tell you, they knew everything, those Jesuits. I had heard that before, but now I was convinced.

"Yes, Father."

I never skipped school again, and never failed a subject, because if you failed one course you didn't play any sports. And that would have killed me. They didn't have to worry about me making the grades. No, sir.

Playing every kind of sport was the most important thing in life to me. My mother never had to worry about what I was doing; I always had a ball in my hands. No cowboys and Indians or cops and robbers for me. Just give me a ball and you'd lose me for hours. I built a little nine-hole golf course in the yard around the house, digging little holes about ten feet apart. If there was nobody around for a pickup game, I'd go to the lot and kick a football and run and get it and kick it back the other way all day. We played basketball on a playground, shot marbles until our fingers were cracked and chapped, skated on the frozen pond, and played makeshift hockey with a flattened tin can.

When I was about ten I fell on the ice and hurt my knee. It swelled up, so I went to Dr. Allingham and he operated on it and took out some bone chips. I was in a cast the rest of that

16

winter. I still have a knot on my knee and a tiny scar but it never gave me any pain. That could have ended my baseball career before it started.

We played kick the can in the street and nailed cans to our heels to make noise when we ran, which tore up our shoes. I'd cut out a piece of cardboard and stick it in my shoes to cover the holes in the soles, and my mother gave me hell for that.

"You kneel at the altar when you serve mass every morning," she said. "People can see the holes in your shoes. At least put some shoe polish on the cardboard so it blends in." Then they came out with glue-on patches for your shoes and I went down to Kresge's and bought them and glued them on all crooked, but it was better than cardboard. I didn't care and I didn't complain.

The Maxwell house had wide cement steps in front of it. For hours at a time I threw a tennis ball against those steps and made up a game: if it rebounded over my head it was a home run, and so on. There were probably a million kids all over the country doing the same dumb thing, dreaming the same dream: to be a professional baseball player. In the winter I used snowballs: hit the fifth step for a single, the tenth for a double, and so on. And when it was too cold to be outside, I propped an old pillow in a corner of the sofa and threw a ball into it for hours. We lived in a very small house but my mother never said a word until many years later when she told me, "You used to drive me crazy with that thud thud thud all day long."

Once in a while I missed the pillow and broke something. One day I was playing catch with my brother in the side yard. Trying to act smart, I threw the ball real hard and it got away from me and went through a window. I had to dig a lot of dandelions to pay for it. Come to think of it, I guess I was wild from the time I was seven.

I ate Wheaties because Babe Ruth did, and I sent away three box tops and twenty-five cents for a Babe Ruth cap and I wore that cap everywhere, even to bed. I kept scrapbooks, and read the sports pages, and heard all about Bob Feller coming out of Van Meter, Iowa, when I was eleven. And my father told me I could get to the major leagues when I was eighteen, just like Feller, if I worked hard.

17

THREE

Born to Play Ball

ONE OF THE BIGGEST THRILLS of my life came when I was eight years old and I lied about my age so I could play on a Midget American Legion team for kids ten and older. But my first game was almost my last.

Legion baseball is a big thing in Nebraska, where the cold spring weather curtails the high school season. There was no Little League then, so the Midget teams were the first chance for us to play any kind of organized games. Maybe they let me play because nobody else wanted to be the catcher and I volunteered. I should have known then that I was hopelessly hooked on this game. I didn't want to be a catcher, but if that was the only way I could play, I did it.

We had no uniforms, just T-shirts with "P & C Grocery" on them. I had a crude kind of mask, no shinguards, and a borrowed catcher's mitt. My mother had driven me to the game at Riverview Park and she sat in the car behind home plate.

I was so scared, I wet my pants when I squatted behind the plate to start the game. After the inning, which seemed to take hours, I went to her, crying, and asked her to take me home.

"No," she said. "You wanted this. You started it, you finish it. Then we'll talk about it."

So I finished the game in that uncomfortable condition and never looked back. I caught for a few years until I shot up in height and became the biggest kid on the team. Our coach, Harry Williams, had played a little first base for the New York Yankees back in 1913-1914. He saw that I could throw the hardest of anybody on the team and made me the pitcher. When I was thirteen I pitched two no-hitters for the Corrigans in the Omaha Midget Legion league.

But I would do anything, play any position, just to be able to get into a game. Anywhere. Anytime. Some days we chose up teams on the empty lot. I still see some of those guys—Jack Carter and Bill McAndrews—when I go back to Omaha. We had enough players for three teams. Two teams played, then the winner played the other team and they kept playing as long as they won. I switched sides all day and played any position just to stay in the game.

One of the kids, Howie Zotzman, had polio. He couldn't walk, and rode around in a wagon. He was mean, but he could flat-out hit the ball. He'd get out of his wagon and sit in the dirt at home plate. Another kid would stand alongside home plate and run for him when Howie hit the ball. If you didn't run fast enough to suit him, he'd whack you with one of his crutches. I used to beg for that job, too, just to get in the game. We were the original designated hitter and runner.

We never had the money for a new baseball and never saw a clean white one. Even in the Midget leagues they were semiwhite at best. Sometimes we'd go to the field where the semipro teams played and hang around during batting practice. If a ball came near me I'd glove it and throw it to another kid and he'd throw it half a block to another one and we'd relay it out of the neighborhood before they could catch us. When the covers got loose we taped them with heavy black sticky electrical tape. If we got hold of a cracked bat we went to the cigar store and begged for an empty cigar box. The boxes were held together with tiny tacks, which we used to nail the splintered bats together, then wrapped the fracture with black tape.

Another source of balls was the Omaha Cardinals in the Western League. I was one of those pests always hanging around trying to be batboy or chasing foul balls. If a ball was hit over the roof and you got it, you could use it to get into the game free. Sometimes I got the ball and hit it, then sneaked into the game. That way I saw the game and had a ball to play with, too.

One day, when I was ten years old, I thought my life was over. In the fall, major league players put together barnstorming teams and traveled all over the country. That year Babe

Ruth and Lou Gehrig headed two teams that toured the Mid-west. One of their stops was Council Bluffs, Iowa, right across the Missouri River from Omaha. I just had to see that game. My mother said if my grades were good, she would take me. I saw to it that they were up to par, and we were going.

The day of the game it rained so hard they never even came to Council Bluffs. I just knew I was going to die that day; there was nothing more to live for. Can you imagine a baseball-crazy kid in Omaha, Nebraska, is going to see Babe Ruth and Lou Gehrig at the same time—and it rains? That's not supposed to happen. I cried all day.

Babe Ruth was a big supporter of Boys Town; every new boy and girl who becomes a citizen there is sworn in standing in front of a large photo of Ruth and Gehrig. In the winter of 1947 I sat next to Ruth at a sports dinner in Omaha. He had seen me pitch in the World Series and said, "Kid, you throw pretty hard. But I'd'a hit you." That was an honor for me, just to hear him say that, and I told him how my heart had been broken that day I never got to see him play. He said, "Well, you've got better things in life to look forward to."

I didn't think so that day when the skies and my eyes were weeping in Council Bluffs.

The Kansas City Monarchs and other black teams often played in Omaha and I saw Satchel Paige and Josh Gibson. Paige pitched three innings every day against local teams. When an Omaha batter got a foul off Paige, that made big headlines in the Omaha *World-Herald*. How that Paige could pitch! It's sad he never could pitch in the majors in his prime.

My father bought me my first glove when I was twelve. I convinced him that I was going to be a great pitcher, so we went downtown to Vim Sporting Goods and I picked out a Rawlings Bill Doak model. Doak, a spitball pitcher for the Cardinals, had invented the webbing for baseball mitts, and I knew that anybody who had a Bill Doak glove would be a big shot. It was real leather, about as big as your hand, and it smelled beautiful.

"That's it," Dad said. "Don't lose it."

I knew that was my glove for life. I took it to bed with me and never let it out of my sight. I strapped it on my belt when I went to a game, oiled it with neat's-foot oil, wrapped it with a ball in the pocket for the winter. My mother sewed and resewed it, and I used that glove until I signed a professional contract.

Our Lady of Lourdes was a small school; we had three classes in one room. But we had fierce rivalries on the playing fields with the local public schools. Between that and Midget Legion ball, I knew what competition was all about by the time I went to Creighton Prep. And I loved it.

At Creighton I was always on winning teams, and it never occurred to me that you were ever supposed to lose. We won the state basketball championship twice and the baseball tournament four years in a row. It was an all-boys school, maybe forty-five in the graduating class. The girls' school, St. John's, was a block away. When we had mass, the boys sat on one side of the church and the girls on the other. We thought they were the ugliest things God ever put on earth, and they thought we were the worst things ever created. But they were our cheerleaders.

I played freshman and sophomore football, basketball, and baseball. Our uniforms were hand-me-downs from Creighton University, but they were our first real uniforms and we wore them proudly. I was a skinny 6-3, which was very tall for high school kids, 'way back then. I was an end on the football team, with good hands and mobility, and played all sixty minutes, offense and defense.

I was lucky to play for one of Nebraska's greatest high school coaches, Skip Palrang. He coached every sport, managed the Legion team, and later became athletic director at Boys Town. He also prepared me for Leo Durocher.

Skip Palrang was a tough, strict disciplinarian who could yell and scream and cuss you out with the best of them. You did not want to make a mistake where he could see it. Every year during basketball season we had a school retreat; the students had to be silent for three days. We went to church and lectures. Anyone who skipped one day during retreat time was gone from that school. We had to keep quiet during basketball practice, too. But Skip went on calling us all kinds of names as usual, unless a priest wandered in to watch; then he'd clam up. For three days we prayed for the priests to come in and watch us.

After my second year, Skip said to me, "Son, you can do anything you want, but you ought to give up football. You've got

21

a chance to be a baseball player, and basketball will teach you agility and quickness." So I gave up football.

I was a bigger star on the basketball court than on the diamond, and made the all-state team my senior year. On the opening day of school the good Jesuits would announce: "If I have any athletes in this class, they should get up and leave. I don't care for sports." I found out later this was just a test. I was on a scholarship and had to toe the line. When I got to be the whole show in Omaha, the priests would tell the class, "If Rex scores twenty points tonight, no homework." You can imagine the looks the other kids gave me. This was in the days when basketball scores were something like 30 to 20. So one night when I scored 24 against Northwestern High in Lincoln, you'd have thought I conquered the world. So much adulation, and I loved every minute of it.

We played on Tuesday and Friday nights. My father always tried to get home in time for the Friday games. But on Tuesday nights my mother stayed home and lay on her bed saying her rosary until I came home.

"Rex Edward, how did you do?"

"Did fine."

"Did you win? You okay? Get hurt?"

I had to report in full. I did not think it was much fun then, but I understand it now. They cared.

As a high school pitcher you never really know if you're wild because kids swing at anything and it's nothing to strike out a bunch of them. One day I pitched a no-hitter. After the game we rushed back to the gym, where we changed clothes and found a radio to listen to the Joe Louis–Billy Conn fight. I was a great Joe Louis fan. Conn had him beaten until Louis knocked him out in the thirteenth round. The next day that was the big headline. On an inside page there was a small photo of me and a brief paragraph about my no-hitter. That fight had robbed me of the big headline.

I never went to dances or proms in high school. I was always going to play ball somewhere the next day and went to bed early. I don't think I had much interest in girls until I was eighteen. Sure, I had all that hero-worship and stuff, but we just thought we were all hot stuff at Creighton Prep and didn't want to be bothered with girls. Yes, it was another world and, yes, I do go back a long way. But that's the way it was. I still get letters from women who tell me how they idolized me when we were in high school, and that's great to hear. I did enjoy being the big star in those days. Why not?

I ran a lot in the winter, and never drank anything stronger than milk. I drank iced tea all year 'round and still do, because my father did. But my parents and coaches said that soft drinks and aspirins were drugs and no good for me and I believed all that, because they said so. And I never had a cigarette in my life.

When I was fourteen, coach Palrang let me pitch in a practice game for American Legion Post Number One, which went on to win the national title. I became a starting pitcher for the Murphy-Did-Its Legion team, pitched a no-hitter in 1941 and a four-hitter to win the state finals. I would pitch a game, then go to the Creighton University gym and shoot baskets for an hour. Duce Belford, the Creighton athletic director, followed my exploits and was the one who recommended me to the Brooklyn Dodgers.

I had never owned a pair of spikes until I became a regular. When the sponsor bought me a pair of spikes with a steel pitcher's plate on the toe, you know how high that made me feel? The day I put on that pitcher's plate was one of the proudest of my life.

In 1941 I had my first look at Yogi Berra. He and Joe Garagiola were on a St. Louis team I pitched against.

The Legion tournaments attracted scores of major league scouts and they began to take an interest in me. They were not allowed to sign anyone who was still in high school, but they could talk to us.

During the 1941 season I began getting letters from somebody named Wish Egan, a Detroit scout. One day in September we got a long-distance phone call (a big deal in those days) from Detroit. The Tigers wanted me to come and work out with the team. Wow! Hank Greenberg and Charlie Gehringer—I idolized those guys. I was only sixteen, so my brother had to go with me. We were there for five days. I pitched batting practice, which the hitters complained about, because I threw so hard and was too wild. I remember Gehringer telling me, "Kid, you throw too hard. Let up a little bit." Then we got to watch the games, the first big league games I ever saw.

Mr. Egan was a delightful, charming, older man. I could see where this guy got what he went after. There were two other kids working out at the same time. One was the future Dr. Bobby Brown, now the American League president, and the other was Art Houtteman, a fine pitcher for the Tigers for many years.

On December 7, 1941, I was ice-skating at a pond. When I got home, my parents were very somber. They sat me down and told me about the Japanese attack on Pearl Harbor. I didn't really understand what it was all about. The next day my brother joined the Marines and went away. My mother said to me, "We have to sacrifice one son, but you'll never go. The war will be over." It tore her up when I was drafted two years later.

The next year, I worked out with the Cardinals in St. Louis and the Yankees' farm team in Kansas City. During those years scouts seemed to be coming around all the time looking for my parents. They were interested in a prospect's background and how he lived. They shook hands to test your grip and measure your hand size. My father reacted the same way to all their pitches: "You mean you're going to pay this boy to play base-ball?" He could never comprehend that.

The war forced all big league teams to train in the north in 1943. The Brooklyn Dodgers invited me to their camp at Bear Mountain, New York, during Easter vacation, and my father went with me. There I saw Leo Durocher for the first time, but he didn't intimidate me; I was a product of coach Skip Palrang.

They had another pitcher, a year younger than I was, pitching batting practice, Calvin Coolidge Julius Caesar Tuska-homa McLish from Anadarko, Oklahoma. McLish could throw equally hard with either arm. One day Durocher said to me, "Sit here next to me, kid. I want you to watch something."

McLish was throwing BP right-handed and Dixie Walker, a good left-hand batter but a real prima donna, was hitting. Walker stepped out to get another bat and Durocher yelled to McLish, "Start pitching left-handed." Walker stepped back in and this kid wound up and threw lefty and whistled an inside pitch under his chin. I thought Dixie was going to lose his mind.

From there we went down to Lakewood, New Jersey, and I threw for Mel Ott, manager of the Giants. He was another hero of mine; he had gone to the Giants when he was only fifteen.

I must have caught some kind of bug from those big leaguers, because when I got back to Omaha I couldn't get the ball over the plate and lost my next two games. But then I won a couple and didn't walk hardly anybody.

Meanwhile I received offers of basketball and baseball scholarships from colleges, including Nebraska, Stanford, and Notre Dame, which was where I decided to go. But the war showed no signs of being over in a hurry, and I was eighteen and single and ripe for the draft. So I went to the draft board and asked them what would happen if I enrolled in college. They said I'd be in the army before I finished a year.

I said, "What if I go into professional baseball? Could you let me get in a full season?"

They thought that over and finally agreed. "But the day the season ends, you'll be in the army."

That's why I didn't go to college. I've often wondered whether I did the best thing. I'll never know.

About that time we got a letter from Wish Egan offering me a $3,000 bonus when I graduated. My father wrote back quickly, accepting. But Mr. Egan got sick or something and the general manager, Jack Zeller, interceded and said the Tigers would not pay me that much. I was disappointed, because I wanted to go to Detroit.

The Yankee scout, Bill Essick, was pretty intent on signing me. He sold the idea of playing for the Yankees, which was a big selling point: they were about to win their seventh pennant in eight years. Every kid in the world wanted to be a Yankee. My father used to tell me, "If you bet on anything, always bet three things to win: the Yankees, Joe Louis, and the Notre Dame football team." It was good advice in those days. I think he secretly wanted me to sign with the Yankees, but they offered us only $1,000 and we decided to wait.

I wonder sometimes: What if I had gone with the Yankees? Would I have been better off or worse? Maybe I would never have gotten out of the minor leagues. Maybe I would have won 300 games. That's one mystery I'll never solve.

Tom Greenwade was the midwestern scout for the Dodgers. He later signed such stars as Mickey Mantle, Hank Bauer, and

Elston Howard for the Yankees. He had been watching me for two years, and for a while had taken a room in a boardinghouse nearby to keep an eye on me. My father was most impressed with Tom. They were alike: tall, sincere, very strict, and very midwestern. Greenwade was honest and straightforward, explaining the chances that I might not make it to the major leagues. But I wasn't thinking that far ahead anyhow. I just wanted to see what it was all about to go away and be a professional ballplayer somewhere. Anywhere.

The Dodgers sent Branch Rickey, Jr., out to talk to my parents, but he was too overpowering for us and they did not like him at all. Tom Greenwade came back and, at the end of April, Branch Rickey, Sr., the Dodgers' general manager, flew out to Omaha. He and Tom came to the house and they sat in our kitchen and Mr. Rickey did the talking and my mother was very impressed, even though he was a Methodist or Presbyterian or something, but not a Catholic.

Mr. Rickey said, "We are willing to pay you a bonus of $2,500. However, we have checked with your draft board and we understand that you will be drafted after this season. So we will give you $500 when you sign, and the rest if we retain your contract a year from now, or whenever you come back from the army and can demonstrate that you can still play."

We had no problem with that, but it was my introduction to Mr. Rickey's shrewdness. He told me to buy a new glove and shoes and a pitcher's toeplate and the Dodgers would pay for them. We did not actually sign anything then, because I was still in high school. But they wanted me to report to Durham, North Carolina, in the Piedmont League as soon as possible. I didn't want to hang around until graduation, so I persuaded Father Schine and Father Cervantes to tutor me on weekends and let me take my exams and graduate early.

It didn't bother me to be leaving home. My mother told me not to miss mass and to keep the holy days and I assured her I would. I got on the train one afternoon in May 1943 and rode all night and arrived in Durham the next night. I still hadn't signed anything or seen any money, but I didn't care. I had a brand new pitcher's toeplate in my gear and the world was my oyster. I was a professional baseball player.

FOUR

The Ballplayer

I GOT OFF THE TRAIN in Durham, North Carolina, on a warm May evening in 1943, and soon discovered that I was in a foreign country.

After a night's sleep at the Washington Duke Hotel, I went down for breakfast and ordered ham and eggs. When the waitress put it in front of me, half the plate was covered with some white stuff.

"Excuse me," I said, "I didn't order this cream of wheat."

"Boy, don't you know what that is?" she drawled in astonishment.

"Sure. Cream of wheat."

She said, "That's grits," making it sound as if it had two syllables.

"What are grits?"

"You don't know what grits are? That's Georgia ice cream."

I surrendered and ate it, but I didn't like it. However, in Durham it was served with everything, so I learned to eat it.

Walking to the ballpark, I passed some strange signs: Colored Entrance, Colored Drinking Fountain, Colored Restroom. I had no idea what that meant; maybe they were a different color or something. When I asked, I found out quick. At the ballpark, blacks could sit only in a small section of the right field bleachers. If we walked down the sidewalk and a black man came toward us, he'd cross the street and walk on the other side. Damnedest thing I ever saw. I never did understand all that. Still don't. But it was that way wherever we played in Virginia and North Carolina.

The general manager who greeted me at the Durham ballpark was a young man named Buzzie Bavasi, who was just beginning his long, successful career. He had a contract ready for me to sign for $200 a month, and my bonus check, which I sent home. Bavasi explained the local facts of life to me: where to eat, places to avoid.

"Most of the guys eat at Walgreen's drugstore," he said. So I hung out there, too. He directed me to Ma Gregory's rooming house, where a half-dozen of the single players stayed. Ma was a Durham institution. She was in her sixties and weighed over 200 pounds, and the players who roomed with her instantly became known as "her boys." She went to all the games and her foghorn voice shook the wooden stands. Her favorite rooting cry was, "You're better than he are!"

I shared a room with another eighteen-year-old rookie who reported that day, a real California hot dog: blond, ducktail haircut, suntanned "pepper pot," like nobody I'd ever seen. His name was Gene Mauch. We paid $12.50 each per month for a huge room with two beds, bathroom down the hall, big breakfast, and a snack after the games. We walked everywhere: downtown, to the ballpark, to the hamburger joint. It was a small town, and none of us had a car.

The Durham manager was a tough, scrappy little guy, Christian Frederick Albert John Henry David Betzel, a real Prussian from Tennessee. Better known as Bruno, Betzel had been an infielder with the Cardinals during World War I. He looked like an old man to me, but he was only forty-eight. Everything he did was quick and jumpy. When he spoke, the words spat out like bursts from a machine gun. His usual words of encouragement were, "If you guys played for shit, you wouldn't get a smell."

He was not far off in his assessment. The Herd had a year-long lease on the Piedmont League cellar. They had lost their first 8 games, and were something like 7 and 27 when I left. They eventually finished 52 games out of first place in a 127-game schedule. To say we had a porous defense would be like calling the Johnstown Flood a leaky faucet. The only good hands were Mauch's and an outfielder's from Baltimore, John Sinnott, whom I see once in a while.

"Were it not so pathetic," wrote *Herald* sports editor Ed Mitchell, "the plight of the Bulls would be humorous. However, local fans and sports writers can see no humor in what's being disguised as baseball at the local park." Most of us were kids as green as May peaches, and the rest were over forty. One guy was a volunteer fireman; if the alarm went off during a game, he was gone.

But every team all the way up to the majors suffered from the player shortage during the war. One night Bavasi was on the phone with Branch Rickey, Jr., during a game. Suddenly there was a lot of noise from the stands.

"What was that?" Rickey asked.

"Hermanski just hit a home run," Bavasi said.

"Put him on the next train to Brooklyn."

The Dodgers had given one Durham player a $3,000 bonus. The kid's father showed up and wanted his son released. Bavasi talked to Mr. Rickey about it, and was told to try to get the bonus money back. Bavasi told the father he wanted the $3,000 back, plus the $300 in salary he had paid the player. The father sat down and wrote out a check.

They were so desperate for pitchers, Bavasi went on the radio one day and asked for volunteers to pitch. A big tall guy showed up and said he had pitched for Atlanta. Buzzie assumed he was referring to the Atlanta Crackers of the AA Southern Association, so he signed the guy. After he pitched a double-header one Sunday, the FBI showed up and took him away for draft evasion or something. It turned out the Atlanta team he had pitched for was the federal prison team.

The Durham Athletic Park, then as now, was dominated by that big Bull Durham sign in left field. The left field fence was a cab ride away; right field was short. The dugout was tiny, and there was one shower in the little clubhouse right behind it (they now have five showers). When Rocky Bridges played there, he stashed a cot in the clubhouse and made a deal with the security guard to let him back in after everybody had gone home. Rocky slept there for about a month before they caught him.

The penetrating odor of tobacco curing hung over the place like a shroud. The smell of fresh tobacco was tolerable, but when they burned the discarded leaves and stalks, the stench was terrible. It seemed like every ballpark in the league smelled the same.

On the night of June 4, 300 loyal fans were writhing in agony as the Norfolk Tars, a Yankees' farm team, pummeled pitcher Bob Lyle. Down 5–0 with 1 out in the second, Bruno Betzel decided to take a look at his new pitcher from Omaha. I can still hear the PA announcer's voice: "Now pitching for the Bulls, Rex Barney."

The lights were maybe 100 watts strong; that's for the entire ballpark, not for each bulb. And when I think about it now, how hard I threw—my God, it must have been devastating for those hitters.

The first batter I faced was Jack Phillips, who later played first base for the Yankees. The press box was at field level behind home plate, with a chicken wire screen in front of it. My first pitch whistled about five feet above and behind Phillips's head. The ball tore through the chicken wire and conked the sports editor in the head, knocking his glasses flying and damn' near scalping him. No wonder he reported, [Barney's] pitching was of the compass type—he threw in the general direction of the plate . . . When he did get the ball over, the Tars smacked it far and wide."

But after that first pitch some of those Tars suddenly developed aches and pains that prevented them from staying in the lineup. You think *they* were shook up? *I* was scared to death! Welcome to professional baseball.

Norfolk scored in every inning and by the time I was taken out for a pinch hitter in the fifth, I had been "touched" for 7 runs on 9 hits, walked 3, and struck out 7, with 3 wild pitches. Not impressive. "But," the forgiving sports editor acknowledged, "the lad has plenty of steam and may develop into a pitcher."

Evidently Bruno Betzel agreed. About a week after we arrived, he called Gene Mauch and me aside. "You're the only two guys on this club with a chance to go up. If you want to come out early every morning, I think I can help you."

We were out there every day, and he helped Gene with his fielding and taught me how to hold men on base and some other tricks of the pitching trade.

On the road we traveled in an old yellow school bus. On most minor league clubs a veteran player drove the bus and earned an extra $5 a day. But Buzzie Bavasi did our driving. On the long hauls to Richmond and Lynchburg, we would sleep on the floor or stretch out in the luggage racks above the seats. In Norfolk we stayed in some old broken-down barracks while we played Norfolk and Portsmouth, and rode the municipal bus to the parks. But we also stayed in some hotels, such as the Ponce de Leon in Roanoke, that seemed luxurious to us. All this and $2.50 a day cash meal money. We thought we'd died and gone to heaven.

I made my first start in Roanoke on June 12 and fared better than in my debut. But we made our usual 4 errors, and when I went out for a pinch hitter in the seventh, we were trailing, 3 to 0. In six innings I had given up 6 hits, 4 walks, struck out 6, and hit 1 batter (but no sports editors). What's more, I got my first professional hit, a double. We lost, 7 to 2, and I was 0 and 1.

A week later I hit another double off the same pitcher, a guy named DeMasters, who never made it to the big leagues. Too bad—if he had, I might have hit .300 up there. This time I had a 7–4 lead until the eighth, when 2 hits and 2 errors gave the game away, 8 to 7. Now I was 0 and 2.

I enjoyed being away from home, on my own, managing my own business, what little there was of it. I saw other players with a lot of talent who got homesick and never made it for that reason. Not me. I didn't care where I was, as long as I was in the game.

It didn't take me long to notice a pretty little blond girl who sat behind our dugout at every game. I started talking to her, then walking her home.

One day Bavasi said to me, "That little girl you've been seeing."

"What about her?"

"She's off-limits."

"What are you talking about?"

"She and her mother have screwed everybody who ever played in this town, and you're not going to be one of them."

That was the end of that romance. Later I heard she married a left-handed pitcher for the Bulls.

I liked and respected Buzzie. On Sunday mornings I went to first mass at the little ramshackle wooden Catholic church, then I sat with his little boy, Peter, while they went to second mass. When I left there, he missed his baby-sitter more than his pitcher.

I tossed a 4-hit shutout at Norfolk on June 26 for my first professional victory. A catcher named Larry Berra got one of the 4 hits. I fanned 7 and walked only 3 and felt like the king of the hill that night. But my 2-game hitting streak was stopped.

Three days later I whipped them again, 3 to 2. This time Mr. Berra was 0 for 3. Many years later somebody sent me a clipping of that box score and I showed it to Yogi. "It's a fake," he claimed. "You never held me hitless in a game." He still sticks to that story, despite the evidence.

On July 3 in Portsmouth, both the Herd and I reverted to our earlier form. We made 9 errors (including 1 by me) and I was gone in the fourth on a wave of 4 hits, 7 walks, and 2 wild pitches. I was beginning to show the "now and then, good and bad" pattern that would plague me for most of my career. Five days later I went all the way to beat Richmond, 6 to 1.

By now Ed Mitchell was beginning to rate me among the fastest pitchers ever to wear a Bulls uniform. He decided I was swifter than Johnny Vander Meer, who had won 19 games there in 1936, striking out a league record 295 in 214 innings. But in Ed's book I was not quite as fast as Ed Albosta, a wild right-hander who had two cups of coffee but no wins in the big leagues.

About that time Buzzie Bavasi called me into his office and introduced me to Bill Veeck, who owned the Milwaukee club in the American Association. Veeck was looking for players and he wanted to buy me and Mauch, but the Dodgers turned him down.

From then on I finished every game I started, but I lost my best game of the year, 1 to 0, to Norfolk, walking only 1 man.

Four days later I gave up only 4 hits and fanned 11, but I walked 9, hit a batter, and threw 2 wild pitches in a 3–1 loss.

On July 19 I took a 4–2 lead into the ninth at Roanoke, but a guy named Vance Dinges, who later played for the Phillies, beat me with a hit in the ninth. We moved on to Lynchburg, where I started against another rookie making his debut, Ned Jilton. Jilton and I were mowing down the hitters. When the Bulls loaded the bases with no outs in the third, he struck out the next 3 hitters. I fanned 9 and he whiffed 10 in 7 innings. But I also walked 7 and twice hit some poor second baseman named Kluttz with fastballs (later I was told that that experience inspired him to quit baseball), and I was behind, 4 to 0. After the umpire ejected Bruno Betzel during an argument in the seventh, the "Battling Bovines" woke up and scored 5 in the eighth. I had 2 hits that night and drove in a run.

In the last of the eighth, with our philanthropic defense in mind, Gene Mauch said to me, "If you want to win this game, you'd better strike out the last six batters." So I did.

My record was now 4 and 6 with a 3.00 ERA. I had pitched 7 complete games. In 81 innings, I struck out 71 and walked 51. But that didn't prove much; most of those hitters had no idea of the strike zone. And I was throwing harder than anybody they had ever seen.

But I guess I looked pretty good to the Dodgers, because, after that game in Lynchburg, Bruno Betzel told Gene and me, "Pack your gear. You two are going up to the Montreal club."

Gene and I looked at each other. We couldn't believe it. We had been in Class B only two months and we were going up to the AAA International League? Sure, there was a war on, and players were scarce, but I was barely two months out of high school!

Gene and I took a bus from Lynchburg to Durham to pick up our few belongings and catch a train to Baltimore, where the Montreal club was supposed to be playing. (I have not been back to Durham since I broadcast a Mutual Game of the Day from there in the 1950s.) We got off the train in Baltimore, Gene carrying a couple bats strapped to his bag, me with my glove hanging from my belt. I can understand why the manager of the Emerson Hotel did not want to let us in when we arrived.

Montreal was playing in Jersey City and they were not due in until the next day. We finally talked our way in, stowed our stuff, and went out on the street. We had the night off; what to do?

Gene said, "I wonder which way we should go to get something to eat?"

"Well," I said, "I see a lot of lights down that way."

So we headed that way and quickly found ourselves in the middle of "The Block," the strip joint area, with guys standing out front yelling things like, "Come in here . . . the only place recommended by Duncan Hines." (Hines wrote a popular restaurant guide.) But we were too young, and we couldn't go in. We wound up at Miller Brothers' restaurant, then found a pool hall.

When the Montreal club arrived, we signed contracts for $225 a month and they handed us $5 a day meal money and now we were in some kind of high cotton, let me tell you. But we didn't have any idea how to get to the ballpark, so we trailed after a couple veterans, got on the streetcar when they did, transferred when they did, got off when they did at 29th and Greenmount.

The Montreal manager was Lafayette "Fresco" Thompson, a banty rooster of an infielder with a quick wit and a sharp tongue who spent his entire life in baseball, most of it with the Dodgers.

The first game I pitched for the Royals was on Sunday, August 1, at Syracuse. In the minor leagues, the second game of a doubleheader was seven innings, and Thompson wanted to start me off easy, so he put me down for the nightcap. Gene Mauch played second base and the third baseman was a guy named Al Campanis.

Fresco claimed to his dying day that I was the only pitcher who ever got 9 men out with 1 pitch. My first pitch was a fastball that zipped behind Goody Rosen's head. It hit a steel pipe that supported the screen and rang out like a cannon shot. Fresco swore, "Those hitters were so scared after that, they didn't care if they swung or not. They just wanted out of there." At least I had kept the ball out of the press box.

At the end of seven innings, we were tied, 1–1. Both teams scored in the ninth, but they got a couple hits in the twelfth and beat me, 3 to 2. In twelve innings I gave up 12 hits, walked 6, and struck out 10. Not a bad AAA debut. In fact, Fresco called it one of the most impressive debuts he had ever witnessed.

Four days later I started in Newark, but was taken out for a pinch hitter in the sixth, trailing 4 to 2, after walking 7 and fanning 5. Montreal came back to win it. Unknown to me, Yankee manager Joe McCarthy was in the stands that night. He was probably more impressed with his Newark Bears farmhands than the kid who started against them.

When we got to Montreal, I found myself suddenly transplanted to another foreign country, a world apart from Omaha and Durham. Here, too, I saw strange signs: "We speak English here." At the ballpark, everything was announced first in French, then in English. On August 13, when I relieved to start the sixth inning, I heard the PA announcer say, "Lanceur [pitcher], Ray Bar-nay," and I remember thinking, we don't have anybody named Ray Bar-nay.

Montreal is a beautiful city. I always enjoyed seeing new places and everything there was different from anything I had ever seen. Hal Gregg had been there all season and he showed us around. And no more boardinghouses for Gene and me. We put up at the Ford Hotel.

I used to think, how could I share all this fascinating new world with my parents? But I knew that one square block in Omaha was all they really wanted. They visited me once in Brooklyn, and when my father got back home, all he could talk about was how he had actually walked on the Brooklyn Bridge.

I was sitting in the bullpen one night in Montreal with an older pitcher, Barney DeForge.

"Kid," he said, "you think you'll make it to the major leagues?"

"That's my ultimate goal," I said.

"Well, you know you gotta chew tobacco to play in the big leagues."

In those days almost every player had a chaw in his jaw, but I had never touched it.

"Really?"

"Oh, yeah. You gotta chew to be a big leaguer."

Well, I swallowed that, and that's not all I swallowed. He gave me a wad and I stuck it in my mouth and swallowed some of the juice and I have never been so sick. Must have lost everything I ate for the previous eighteen years. I never made it to the ballpark the next night and missed my start. The worst part was that, as I lay dying, I was thinking—honest to God, I thought this—I'll never make it to the major leagues 'cause I can't chew tobacco.

The closest I ever came to being one of the guys was bubble gum.

The night I became "Ray Bar-nay" I pitched four shutout innings, walked just 2, and struck out 4. I was unaware that Branch Rickey and some scouts were in the stands. After the game, Harold Parrott, the Dodgers road secretary, came to me and said Mr. Rickey had been very impressed, and I might be in the major leagues before the end of the season.

A few days later a call came for me and Hal Gregg to report to Brooklyn. I had been a professional ballplayer for less than four months and I was going to the big leagues. What's more, I was headed for yet another foreign country, in many ways the strangest of all.

FIVE

Ebbets Field

THE BROOKLYN DODGERS, Ebbets Field, and baseball was the greatest triple play God ever executed on this planet. If a player didn't fall in love with Ebbets Field, there had to be something wrong with him. And those fans—their enthusiasm for their beloved bums was overwhelming. Today they call it chemistry; I prefer to think of it as a love affair. That's what made it such a tragedy when the team left Brooklyn.

Ebbets Field had about 32,000 seats and every sound and sight was up close. They razzed us and cheered us and they knew their baseball. Hilda Chester ringing cowbells, and the Dodgers Sym-phony Band, and the organist, Gladys Gooding, playing "Three Blind Mice" when the umpires appeared—we couldn't wait to get to the ballpark. Many of the fans were as familiar to us as we were to them; they sat in the same seats every game. It took some time for me to learn the accent; I heard things that made me wonder what language was being spoken.

Even the names had a unique ring to them: Cookie and Leo, Pistol Pete and the Duke and Dixie and Preach, Frenchy and Mickey, Koiby Higgleby and Oisk, Spider and Pee Wee, yes, and Rex. And Whitlow Wyatt—what kind of a name was that for a Brooklyn pitcher? And Hugh Casey. The name alone sounds like it wants to fight you.

Brooklyn fans invented "Stan the Man" and "Swish" Nicholson. When Bill Nicholson of the Cubs took his practice swings before hitting, the fans went *swish* in time with the sweep of the bat. Sometimes he would tease them by cutting the swing short abruptly, and the fans would try to quicken their *swish* to stay in step with him.

The players entered the marble rotunda on the corner and went in through gate 26. No matter how early in the morning we arrived, there was a swarm of kids waiting, not for autographs, but for Leo Durocher. "Come on, boys," he'd say, and take them all in. "Go hide somewhere so they don't throw you out."

There were always nuns at the games and Leo would go out of his way to speak to them. If they ever heard him screaming and swearing at us during a game, they'd probably kill him.

I knew people who quit their jobs in the summer so they could go to the games. There was a little Hebrew school up the street. Every day about the fifth inning, when the ticket takers left their posts, here they came, kids wearing yarmulkes. They would watch a few innings until here came the rabbi and dragged them all out.

From the clubhouses to the first base dugout, both teams came through a tunnel to a passageway that was separated from the fans by nothing but a chain link fence. Visiting teams hugged the wall as far away from the fans as they could get, to avoid being pelted by flying objects. Some notable fights between players occurred in that runway, especially when the Giants were in town.

When autographs became more sought after, there were still no ballpoint pens; kids carried fountain pens. If you didn't sign for them, they'd open those pens and squirt ink on the back of your shirt or coat. But they also came up with an idea that I thought was a good one. They would hand a player a self-addressed postcard and say, "Please sign it when you have a chance and drop it in a mailbox." The players took them and invariably signed and mailed them.

Ebbets Field was not a pitcher's paradise, although left field was pretty expansive. It was 297 feet down the right field line to a 38-foot-high screen along Bedford Avenue atop a concrete wall. A huge scoreboard filled the wall in right center; at its base a sign read: "Hit Sign Win Suit - Abe Stark Clothier." It was a joke, because it was directly behind where the right fielder played. Nobody ever hit it, except once that I know of. I think it was Erv Dusak of the Cardinals who hit a line drive headed straight at it. The Dodgers had a big lead at the time, so Carl Furillo pretended he had slipped and the ball hit the sign and the fans went crazy. Players on both teams were laughing and cheering. I remember Furillo patting that sign at the start of every inning.

A Bulova clock crowned the big scoreboard. Any batter who hit the clock won a watch. On May 20, 1946, Braves outfielder Bama Rowell hit a double that smashed the clock and showered Dixie Walker with broken glass. Rowell never got the watch until sportswriter Bert Sugar shook one loose from the company forty-one years later.

In the clubhouse it quickly became evident that Dixie Walker was the king. He got the most attention from the trainer and clubhouse man. We all sat on long benches in front of the rows of lockers, but Dixie had a special chair at the end. He held court in that Old South drawl. "Come heah, son," he said to me, "you know you got to get another pitch before y'all can win heah in the big leagues."

But it was also Danny Comerford's kingdom. He was the boss of the clubhouse. I've seen him go through every locker during a game, looking for baseballs that players had pocketed during batting practice. If he found a clean white ball he replaced it with the dirtiest one he could find. Nobody ever said anything about it.

One day when I'm going to start the second game of a doubleheader, I'm lying on the training table listening to Red Barber doing the first game. I see Comerford with a jock strap and he's got his foot on one side of it and he's pulling and stretching it way out of shape.

"Danny, what are you doing?" I said.

"That cheap sonofabitch bought this thing at the damned dime store. I'll teach him to buy from me."

I'm a rookie; I know I'm not going to argue with him.

Danny had a great sense of humor, and if you got knocked out of the box early in the game, he'd be the first one to come over to you and comfort you. "That's okay, son, everything will work out." He must have been there forever. I loved to listen to his stories about the old Dodgers, Zack Wheat, and Dazzy Vance, and the rest. Danny Comerford, and a grand old man he was.

Leo Durocher ran everything, besides coaching third base often. He had only two coaches, Chuck Dressen and John

Corriden. Dressen loved to play the horses. Mr. Rickey had fired him in 1942 and promised to rehire him if he stayed away from the tracks and the bookies. Dressen was rehired in July of '43.

Corriden, the first base coach, was an old Irishman they called "Lolli." He'd say, "Son, let's go get a couple lollipops," which were liquid and 100 proof.

Corriden never talked about the time when he was the rookie third baseman on the St. Louis Browns in 1910 when Ty Cobb and Nap Lajoie were battling for the batting championship, and the whole league was rooting for Lajoie to win. On the last day Corriden was told to play deep on Lajoie, who proceeded to beat out 7 bunts down the third base line. There was a big furor at the time. That just shows how far into the past the links in my personal baseball chain extended.

Corriden was a beautiful person, a little guy, redfaced from too many lollipops, the guy who, when you had a bad day, was there with an arm around you and a "Hang in there, son." Always a good word when you needed it, or even when you didn't. He was the complete opposite of Leo and Chuck, and I think Leo knew he needed somebody like that. We called him John, although his nickname was Red. When Dressen went to manage the Yankees, John went with him.

Unlike today, we had only two coaches, none for hitting or running or pitching or bench strategy or body building or mind shrinking. Whatever help pitchers got came from one of the older pitchers, if they felt like helping us. Whitlow Wyatt taught me how to throw a real curve. And Hugh Casey tried to help me.

Before every game the pitchers lined up in left field. Dressen or Corriden stood by second base and hit a fungo 20 or 30 feet toward center field and one of us would run hard to catch it and we each took our turn. That was our running exercise.

I always wanted to be in the game, but I also loved the days when I could sit there watching the players' mannerisms, hearing their endless variety of cusswords, dodging the sprays of tobacco juice, and absorbing everything I could about these great players who had been nothing but names and legends to me just a short time ago.

The most fascinating of all was Paul Waner, then forty, who had made his 3,000th hit when I was pitching for American

Legion Post Number One. I knew Waner was one of the greatest hitters ever, and I had heard that he drank pretty heavily every day.

One day Johnny Cooney told me to watch Waner during batting practice. What I saw you won't believe. I know I wouldn't if I hadn't seen it. This scrawny little guy staggered out to the batting cage, head drooping, looking as if he was about to fall over. Somebody said, "Your turn to hit, Paul."

A left-hand batter, he sagged up to the plate without a bat. "Gimme a bat," he mumbled.

They could have given him the leaded bat, it wouldn't have made any difference. He hefted the bat a few times, choked up a few inches for one swing, then four inches for another, then gripped the end of the handle—didn't matter—and hit the damnedest line drives one after another I've ever seen.

Then somebody said, "Paul, let's play the game."

As soon as the pitcher released the ball, they'd yell "center field" or "right field" or "left" and he never missed. I mean, young pitchers throwing bullets out there, in on his fists, and if they yelled "left field" he hit it to left field. A human being is not supposed to be able to do that.

Late in a game Durocher might say, "Paul, get a bat." Paul would be snoozing down the end of the bench, in a stupor. I mean, guys would have to shake him awake. He'd move to the bat rack, pick up any bat, go up and hit a line shot. It might be caught, but a line drive! Most magnificent bat control I ever saw. Rod Carew came close among modern players, but not like this guy. He was 10 for 21 as a pinch hitter that year. Chuck Dressen told me that when Waner was in his prime, they would pitch him outside to stop him from pulling the ball. But he'd foul off every pitch until he got one from the middle of the plate in, then voom—line shot.

Somehow I wound up rooming with Waner once on the road. I'm in bed early. About midnight, boom, in he comes. Gets on the phone. "Send up six beers." I got one eye open, watching. The beers arrive. All night long I'm hearing "pop," then "glug, glug, glug." Next morning there's six empties. I roomed with him for three nights and every night was the same.

One day in Pittsburgh Dixie Walker was sick. Durocher said, "Paul, you're going to have to play right field."

We could see that Paul was in no shape to play right field.
"I don't know if I can, Leo."
"You gotta do it. We got nobody else."
"Okay."

He played, hit three doubles like you've never seen in your life, finished the game, walked into the clubhouse, and threw up all over everything.

Waner batted .311 in 1943. When somebody asked him for the secret of his continued success, he said, "Same as it has always been. I never drank or smoked or dissipated in any way until I was eight years old." Paul Glee "Big Poison" Waner. Unbelievable.

I knew about Billy Herman from his days with the Cubs. One of the smartest players around. "Googoo Eyes" they called him because he had great big round eyes. His reputation for mastery of the hit and run is not exaggerated. I saw pitchers hit him on the fists with a fastball as good as you can throw and he would hit it on the ground to right field. If the pitch was 10 feet over his head he got the bat on it some way. If he couldn't put it in play he would foul it off to protect the runner.

A take-charge guy, he was a comfort to see playing second base behind me. You knew he was going to be a manager someday, although he didn't like it when he tried it. He was always ready to help another player and to teach whatever he knew.

When Herman was traded to Brooklyn, he had left his horseplayer buddy, Augie Galan, behind in Chicago. But not for long. He persuaded Larry MacPhail to get Galan, too. They would walk into the clubhouse, racing form in hand, and call their bookie on the clubhouse phone. They had runners in every city to place their bets. Mr. Rickey eventually put a stop to that.

Galan was as selective a hitter as Ted Williams. He swung only at strikes. Even in batting practice, he made the pitchers throw strikes. A popular guy, he was very proud of his record of 162 games without hitting into a double play.

Herman, Galan, and Dressen were the greatest trio of sign stealers in the business. Nowadays stealing signs is considered not fair, or unethical, or something. Players get upset if they think somebody might be catching their signs. But in my time it was an art.

Dressen couldn't read a book without his glasses, but from the coach's box he could spot the pitcher changing his grip the slightest bit. Sitting on the bench, Herman watched the hitter while Galan studied their third base coach. Herman would say, "He's doing this . . . he's doing that . . . he's looking down at the coach." And Galan would say, "The coach did this . . . he did that . . . " and they'd figure out what was happening.

With Herman at bat and Dressen coaching third, Chuck would whistle to signal a curve ball coming and Billy's eyes would get a hundred times bigger. He was a good hitter to start with, but when he knew what was coming, look out. And if Galan was on second and Herman up, or vice versa, they worked together.

Some hitters wanted a tip-off and others did not. They tried it with Dixie Walker and got crossed up and Dixie almost got killed. Reese never wanted the sign, either. Billy Herman could never understand why a hitter would not want to know what's coming.

For a while, Herman, Galan, Howie Schultz, and I formed a regular bridge foursome on the trains. I've always wondered if those guys were as good at flashing signs to each other at the bridge table as they were on the field.

Mickey Owen was probably the noisiest guy in the Dodgers' clubhouse, always with something to say, a real chip off the old Gashouse Gang. Almost fifty years later I was sitting with Ralph Branca and Clyde King at an oldtimers' game and in walks bowlegged old Mickey, still bouncy as ever.

"You know," he said, "I caught the first big league pitch from all three of you."

He was right. Then he pointed to me. "You had the greatest stuff. Goddamn, you knocked my glove off. Tell 'em how I threw the ball back to you."

I said, "I don't have to tell them. They know as well as I do."

And there was Arky Vaughan among those old Dodgers of 1943, a quiet guy, another one who liked to wager on the nags. Vaughan had a peculiar stance at the plate, coiled up very tightly, so rigid he looked as if he could never get out of the way of an inside pitch. But he claimed no pitcher in the world could hit him. They knocked him down a lot but I never saw him hit by a pitch.

I mentioned that Whitlow Wyatt taught me how to throw a curve. He also suggested that I carry a ball around to get used to the feel of it. He taught me a lot about pitching. "I failed with the White Sox and Tigers," he said, "and never got my act together until I was older." Wyatt also credited Leo Durocher with making him a winning pitcher by goading him into being meaner on the mound. The rest of the time he was a grand gentleman. I can still see him sitting in a chair in center field many a morning, shirt off, eyes closed. "The sun feels good on my shoulder," he told me.

Kirby Higbe had more stuff than Wyatt, but less control on and off the field. One of those legendary characters that Ebbets Field seemed to attract, Higbe frequently led the National League in walks and tales of his escapades. He told us these stories himself, and always closed with these words of advice: "Never admit anything."

Once, he said, his wife caught him in a room with some girl. He threw on his clothes and stormed out of the place, stopped at the door and shouted back, "It wasn't me!"

Some months after he returned from the Navy in 1946, his wife found a letter in his jacket pocket from a nurse, who had apparently given him more than medical attention. She demanded an explanation. Stomping out of the house, Higbe declared, "It must be another Kirby Higbe."

Fresco Thompson's favorite Higbe story involved his attempted holdout against Larry MacPhail in 1942. "Koiby" wrote a letter to MacPhail along these lines:

> Received your contract and of course it's impossible for me to sign at those terms. My father-in-law has been after me for several years to go into business with him. He operates a chain of drugstores throughout South Carolina and my wife is concerned about my traveling so much. I think that if this is your best offer I'll have to seriously consider going in the drug business with my father-in-law. Sorry. Kirby. P.S. Please send me a thousand advance on next year's salary.

One of Higbe's favorite lines was, "I'm sicker than a mule and twice as smart."

I quickly realized there was nothing beneficial that I could learn from Mr. Higbe.

And then there was fabulous Frenchy Bordagaray, a little runt who strutted about like a cocky rooster. One of the all-time popular guys, Frenchy could liven up a ten-car funeral. One spring he had showed up with a mustache when facial hair was unheard of. They made him shave it off. He was a handyman who generally got the job done wherever he played, although he was a little scatter-armed in the infield. I mean, if you can throw a ball beyond the reach of the 6-6 Howie Schultz at first base, you're pretty far off target. Frenchy did it twice in one game. I followed him out of the ballpark one day and he was signing autographs. He wrote "F. Bordy" on a ball, explaining, "If I write my whole name, there won't be room for anybody else."

We had an infielder, Eddie Basinski, who was a symphony violinist. They called him "The Fiddler." One day he brought his violin to the clubhouse. It was a Stradivarius or some damn thing, probably cost eight billion dollars. Frenchy grabbed it, crooked it in his arm, and started playing "Turkey in the Straw"; and the clubhouse went berserk, but Basinski went crazy with fright.

Ah, those good old days. Some team bearing the name "Dodgers" has been operating out in Los Angeles for more than thirty years now, but to the people of Brooklyn, we will always remain "the *real* Dodgers."

SIX

Mr. Rickey and Leo the Lip

BRANCH RICKEY AND LEO DUROCHER were the two dominant people in my baseball career, and in fact in all of baseball in the 1940s and 1950s. No two people could have been more opposite; to me, they were the original odd couple. I don't believe they really liked each other, but they had great respect for each other. They play important roles throughout my story, but I think they deserve a special time-out for me to talk about them.

In my opinion, Mr. Rickey was the most knowledgeable, articulate near-genius baseball has ever known. Thorough, on top of every detail, two jumps ahead of everybody else, he was a preacher who would have succeeded in anything he tried. Some people said he could have been president of the United States. But he was in love with baseball.

Mr. Rickey was prime material for writers and cartoonists: bushy eyebrows, unlit cigar stuck in the corner of his mouth, ready at the drop of a question to expound on it for hours, shrewd, devious at times. Writers called him the Mahatma, his office the Cave of the Winds, his team the Flock. Cartoonists portrayed him as the miserly plantation owner and slave master.

I get kidded a lot because I often quote Mr. Rickey in reverent tones. That doesn't bother me; I have plenty of company. Baseball has been filled with Rickey disciples. Gabe Paul once went to a meeting of general managers and found that twelve of the sixteen had worked for Mr. Rickey. His admirers include Sparky Anderson, Gene Mauch, Tommy Lasorda, and

Roger Craig among managers. Earl Weaver had one sign in the Orioles' clubhouse and he said he got it from Mr. Rickey: "It's what you learn after you know it all that counts." Every clubhouse could use one of those.

Mr. Rickey never claimed to know it all. He often started a speech: "If anybody says they know baseball, they don't know what they're talking about. I've been in it all my life. There's a fascination in baseball, and I am trying to learn this game every day."

I hear young players, front office guys, writers, broadcasters who think they know it all. Nobody knows this game. Not me. Not Mr. Rickey. Some know more than others, that's all. I know I learned a lot from him. I tell young players today, "When I was 18 I was in the major leagues and I knew everything about baseball. Now I'm a whole lot older and I don't know my ass from third base. But I'm still trying to learn."

Why do I always call him Mr. Rickey? I guess it's because that's the way he addressed us players. It impressed me when this great man called me Mr. Barney.

We traveled through the South on our way home from spring training. We had so many players we were not all in uniform for every game. One day in Washington I sat in the stands behind him. A play would occur and he'd turn to me and say, "Mr. Barney, why did Reese move over that way on that play? You don't know why? I'll tell you." And he'd tell me. He could analyze six different things about a catcher just from watching him work behind one batter. His secretary, Jane Ann Jones, was always beside him, taking notes. "He shouldn't be moving to his right . . . he should go to his left . . . Judas Priest, doesn't he know that? . . . Why doesn't somebody tell him . . . Jane Ann, take this down . . . " That's how he watched a game. I walked away that day feeling like a dummy. And then I bought him a snack.

Mr. Rickey never carried any money. Our next stop was Baltimore, and we were in Union Station to get the train. We were hungry and stopped to get something to eat. Mr. Rickey sat beside me at the counter. "Mr. Barney, pay for my sandwich." I did, and got repaid by Jane Ann Jones.

The newsstand kid outside the office at 215 Montague Street in Brooklyn told me that Mr. Rickey got his newspapers from him every day but never paid him. "At the end of the week I take the bill up to the office and they pay me," he said.

Mr. Rickey had plenty of ideas but they did not always work. I don't know how long we worked on his six-man infield defense against a sacrifice bunt to move a man to third. (Gene Mauch, managing California, tried it once, successfully, in Baltimore.) We'd go to diamond number five at Vero Beach and he would enlist a few pitchers to hit against his experimental alignment. He'd sit behind the screen—I can still see those eyebrows, that floppy hat, the cold cigar—and he would say to the hitter, "Bunt . . . swing away . . . now do anything you want and let me see where this guy goes and how that guy reacts . . . " and then, "Stop!" he'd yell, and study where everybody was standing. "No, no, no, that's all wrong." Like a film director. He'd turn to a coach and say, "Judas Priest. Don't you see what I mean?"

I was the hitter when he announced on the loudspeaker, "I will bet a dollar to a dime this hitter cannot beat this defense." I took the bet. When the pitcher nearly picked off the runner at second base, Mr. Rickey announced, "Of course, the hitter loses if the runner is picked off." But I beat the defense four out of five times, and collected $3.90 from Jane Ann Jones. That's probably when Mr. Rickey abandoned the idea.

He was into the game all the way. A lot of the guys did not pay any attention to "the old goat." But I was impressed. He made mistakes and did not hesitate to tell us about them. His reputation was made when he was running the Cardinals and he created the modern farm system. His philosophy was to sign everybody who could walk, by the hundreds, and hope to get a few real players out of the crowd. At one time he controlled more than 600 players on thirty-two minor league teams. In 1937 Judge Landis, who hated the farm system, charged Mr. Rickey with violating baseball's rules and set ninety-one players free, Pete Reiser among them. The papers had a holiday equating it to the freeing of the slaves. Mr. Rickey later admitted, "I knew the rules. I just thought I could get by with it. In those days nobody paid much attention to those things." He was not alone in what he did, nor in being caught.

One of his errors was the time he met with two seventeen-year-old catchers in St. Louis. He told Joe Garagiola, "You have a chance to make the major leagues," and signed him; "You may

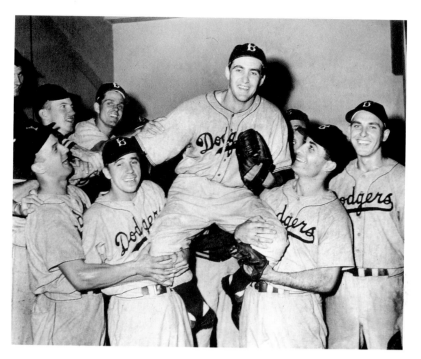

My no-hitter in 1948 gave me a big boost in more than one way. My boosters in front, from left: Gene Hermanski, Pee Wee Reese, Carl Furillo, and Gil Hodges. Back left: Preacher Roe, Jack Blaylock, Marv Rackley. In the back on the right: George Shuba. (Photo courtesy AP/ Wide World)

NUMBER OF PITCHES AND COUNT ON HITTERS										
PLAYER	INNINGS									TOTAL PITCHES
	1	2	3	4	5	6	7	8	9	
LOHRKE	4 3/0*		7 3/2			1 0/0			6 2/2	18
LOCKMAN	3 1/1		1 0/0			3 0/2			4 2/1	11
GORDON	2 1/0ˣ			5 2/2			2 0/1			9
MIZE	6 3/2*			4 1/2			6 2/2			16
MARSHALL	1 0/0			6 3/2			7 3/2			14
MUELLER		4 0/2			4 1/2			4 1/2		12
COOPER		1 0/0			3 0/2			2 1/0		6
KERR		2 0/1			4 1/2					6
KENNEDY			9 3/2*			5 2/2				14
FREY								3 1/1		3
LAFATA									7 3/2	7
TOTALS BY INNINGS	16	7	17	15	11	9	15	9	17	116

* - WALK
X - ON BASE ON ERROR

The figures on my no-hitter, September 9, 1948, showing how many pitches I threw to each batter, and the count on each before they reached first on a walk or error or made an out.

*My niche in the no-hitters'
gallery at the Hall of Fame,
Cooperstown, New York.*

Rex Barney
Brooklyn Dodgers

September 9, 1948

Brooklyn   2
New York   0

*That's me at age 2 in the middle, my brother Ted on my right, with my
sisters and cousins and other relatives.*

Durham Athletic Park, home of the Bulls since 1938, where I broke in in 1943. I loved that huge outfield. The sparse number of lights was a pitcher's pal, too. (Photo courtesy the Durham Bulls)

The building behind the Durham Athletic Park is the Liggett & Myers Tobacco Company, which produced cigarettes and the smell of tobacco that permeated the ballpark. Note the press box behind home plate, where I beaned the sports editor with an errant fastball. (Photo courtesy the Durham Bulls)

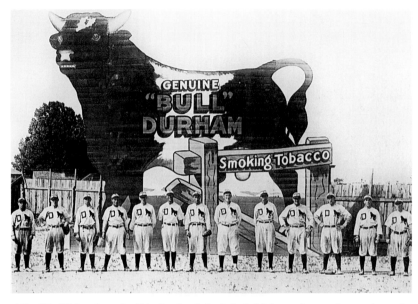

The "Bull" Durham bull in back of the left field fence: it may have given the bullpen its name. (Photo courtesy the Durham Bulls)

I was known as "Ray Bar-nay" in Montreal, August 1943.

Good old Ebbets Field. Note the similarities to the outfield of Oriole Park at Camden Yards.

Leo Durocher, always cheering us on when he wasn't riding the opposition. Note the chic wearing of the belt buckle to the side. (Photo courtesy the National Baseball Library)

Mr. Rickey in a typical pose, analyzing every-thing that's happening on the field. (Photo courtesy The Sporting News)

Five rookies at Ebbets Field, 1943. From left: *Gene Hermanski, Luis Olmo, me, Hal Gregg, and Howie Schultz. (Photo courtesy Gene Hermanski)*

Here with my parents, I'm wearing the Fort Riley Centaurs uniform. Yes, they did give us shoes.

I took some of my Fort Riley teammates to meet Father Flanagan at Boys Town when we played the Omaha All-Stars in August 1944. From left: Harry Walker, me, Father Flanagan, my high school coach Skip Palrang, a curly-haired Joe Garagiola, Pete Reiser, and Lonnie Frey. (Photo courtesy Boys Town)

Dodger teammate Cal McLish and I got together when the army put us in Linz, Austria, in June 1945.

Just out of the army in 1946, I had a brief visit with my parents before joining the Dodgers. (Photo courtesy Walter S. Craig)

The Barney family in 1946. From left: my parents Eugene and Marie, sisters Beatrice and Bernice, brother Ted, and me.

You can tell that is not Stan Musial with the bat. Musial batted left-handed.

This was the scene in the Dodgers' clubhouse between games of a morning-afternoon holiday doubleheader. Note the elegant appointments and decor. The waiter is Pete Reiser. From lower left, around the table are Joe Medwick, Ralph Branca, Gene Hermanski, Ed Stevens, me, Joe Tepsic, Bruce Edwards, Ed Head, Reiser, Ed Miksis, Rube Melton, Carl Furillo, Ed Stanky. Hank Behrman is seated at left. Standing in the back is Danny Comerford. (Photo courtesy Barney Stein)

In the fall of 1946 Chuck Dressen took a barnstorming team to Cuba, a jaunt we barely survived. From left, front row: me, Sid Gordon, Frenchy Bordagaray, Ed Stanky, Buddy Kerr, Ray Lamanno, Ralph Branca. Back row: Hugh Casey, Frank McCormick, Danny Litwhiler, Jim Russell, John Barrett, a Cuban club owner, and Dressen.

I was a two-sport pro from 1946 to 1948, when Omaha had a team in a Midwest basketball league. When the league folded, we didn't get paid for the last few months. (Photo courtesy The Sporting News*)*

Working in the sports department at A & S during the winter, I enjoyed visiting with kids. Those are cap pistols, not the real thing. (Photo courtesy the National Baseball Library)

Todd Parrott, son of Dodgers road secretary Harold Parrott, was such a big fan of mine he wore my number on his batboy's uniform.

Pee Wee Reese, me, and Gene Mauch during a break in spring training, Dominican Republic, 1948.

Leo Durocher reintroducing himself to us in spring training 1948 following his one-year suspension. The modern stadium and facilities in the Dominican Republic were great. The heat and the food were not.

Beverly, Christine, and me at home in Brooklyn.

Mr. Rickey's famous invention for the improvement of my control. The strings are still at Vero Beach. The catcher, Tim Thompson, is not. He is a scout for the Cardinals, and I still see him occasionally. (Photo courtesy The Sporting News*)*

be a triple-A player one day," he told Yogi Berra and did not sign him. Another beaut involved the most fearsome pitcher I have ever seen. Mr. Rickey thought he was too frail and doubted if Ewell Blackwell would make it.

One spring at Vero Beach he asked Ralph Branca and me to watch an intrasquad game with him, Fresco Thompson, and Buzzie Bavasi. "Young men," he said, "I'm looking at two unsigned players, the shortstop and the pitcher. What do you think?" The shortstop was Dick Howser, and the consensus was: uncertain. The pitcher was wild but looked as if he could throw as hard as I did, but the Dodgers sent Herb Score home.

Mr. Rickey looked for complete dedication in a player in addition to the five essentials: hit, hit with power, field, run, and throw. He especially liked third basemen who hit triples; to him, that meant power, speed, and a strong arm.

In the early days of Vero Beach every player had to be in uniform and through with breakfast at 8 A.M. We all crowded into the rec hall of this former Navy base—major leaguers, minor leaguers, fuzzy-cheeked kids—for Mr. Rickey's one-hour lecture. He had started his talks when he managed the St. Louis Browns and the Cardinals, but they were not universally appreciated by the players. Rogers Hornsby used to show his disdain openly by studying the racing form during the lecture. But I found it so spellbinding, I hoped he would never quit. He would analyze every position and how to play it, and talk about off-the-field behavior, too.

"Young man, you're going to Moline (or Fort Worth, or Cambridge, Maryland) and you're going to meet those very pretty little girls who are always around ballplayers, and if you think you're the first young man who ever slept with that girl, Judas Priest, you are dumber than I think you are."

He brought in the best people to teach us. George Sisler worked with pitchers and hitters and was a gold mine of good advice. Pepper Martin taught us the art of sliding and base running. Everybody reported to the sliding pits, including pitchers. They stretched a rope across the pit and you had to go in under it. Then they lowered it and you kept going in lower and lower. Feetfirst, always. None of this headfirst stuff.

Mr. Rickey devised the infamous strings for me to work on my control; they have four sets of them at Vero Beach today. He put a pole on each side of home plate and tied strings between them to form a square around the strike zone. The catcher set a target within that zone. Timmy Thompson, now a Cardinals scout, caught me every morning for hours. I would be perfect on those strings, then go into a game and be imperfect. Later Sandy Koufax inherited those strings. Many years later I stood with Sandy watching Ramon Martinez throw into them.

I commented, "Boy, Martinez throws hard for a skinny little runt."

Sandy said, "You and I threw harder. They told me your first pitch here hit the backstop of the adjacent field. Is that right?"

"I wasn't that wild," I said.

"Well, my first pitch went clear over that backstop."

Later Sandy got his act together, and then some.

Mr. Rickey brought batting helmets into the game when he was at Pittsburgh. Everybody laughed at first.

And here's the way he taught me to throw a curve: "Stand ten feet from the catcher and grip the ball the way you always do, but throw it backhanded."

I said, "That'll tear up my arm."

"Not from ten feet."

So I did it, and he kept moving me back a little after each throw. It gradually dawned on me that my arm was supposed to be in the same position after throwing a curve as it was when I started the backhand throw. They still teach it that way at Vero Beach.

Mr. Rickey's pitchers are still used by the Dodgers as standards for grading pitchers: a Rex Barney fastball, a Carl Erskine curve, a Preacher Roe slider (they don't grade spitters).

When I first got to Brooklyn, Mr. Rickey asked me, "Do you know how to gauge a pitcher?"

I said, "Sure, earned run average."

"Wrong," he said. "If you can give up fewer hits than innings pitched and strike out more than you walk, you'll be up here a long time."

I was eighteen when he told me that and I've never forgotten it. To this day, when people call in and talk about earned run average, I say, "Here's something I learned when I was eighteen," and I tell them what Mr. Rickey taught me. And when you find a pitcher whose hits and walks *combined* are fewer than innings pitched, that's really something.

From time to time, other things he said come into my mind: "There's no such thing as luck; it's the residue of design. Errors of omission cost you more than errors of commission."

Whenever he talked to a player, Jane Ann Jones was there taking notes and it all went into the file. Mr. Rickey visited each of his twenty-six minor league teams at least once a year. He would sit on the bench during batting practice and it went something like this:

"Son, come here. What's your name?"

"George Anderson."

"Oh yes, you played at Paducah last year, right? Hit .265. Made thirteen errors. I see you are hitting a little better in this league; why do you think that is? I don't think you make the double play as quickly as you can. Maybe you ought to work on that."

Then he'd go on to the next guy. "What's your name?"

"Carl Erskine."

"Yes, you pitched well last year. Now you've come up with a great curveball."

He'd go through the whole team that way.

Mr. Rickey never came into the Dodger's clubhouse; that was Leo's territory. I was astounded when I first saw a general manager in a clubhouse. Leo would tell him what the team needed and Mr. Rickey said, "If I can't get it for you, that's my weakness."

He got the best of so many deals, other general managers became wary of trading with him. His philosophy was to trade a star player just before his last good year instead of just after, and he took plenty of criticism from fans when he would swap a popular star for a group of unknowns or underachievers. And he always got a bundle of cash on the side.

In 1947 when it became obvious that Jackie Robinson would open the season with the Dodgers, Dixie Walker wrote a letter to Mr. Rickey. The gist of it was that Walker, who came from Birmingham, preferred not to play with a black man and wished to be traded. During the season Walker saw that we were going to win the pennant with Robinson, and he went to Mr. Rickey and asked to withdraw his request.

Mr. Rickey refused. "Mr. Walker, you will get your wish. When this season is over I will see to it that you are traded to a last-place team."

End of the year, he traded the "Peepul's Cherce," the most popular player ever in Brooklyn, to the last-place Pittsburgh Pirates, with Hal Gregg and Vic Lombardi. People in Brooklyn rioted. They hanged him in effigy only because they could not get to him in person. Walker played two more years. Two of the players we got for him, Preacher Roe and Billy Cox, helped us win three pennants. Neither had done anything to warrant any great hopes for them. But I believe Mr. Rickey saw things in them that nobody else did.

He was one of the first to take a personal interest in his players. If you were struggling, he inquired into your personal life, and offered to get professional help for you. "Are you having problems at home? Are you fooling around on the road? If you are, we'll learn about it, so you might as well tell the truth." He liked his players to be married and called Augie Galan, a lifelong bachelor, a "devout coward." He avoided troublemakers and rowdies and heavy drinkers.

Once in a while some player got the better of him, but not often. We had a left-hand pitcher, Joe Hatten, who was a little older than the rest of us. One day he came into the clubhouse late.

"Where you been?" I asked.

"Had to see Mr. Rickey. He wanted me to change something in my delivery. Then, as I was getting ready to leave, he said, 'Mr. Hatten, we know you have a baseball age and a real age. You are telling us that you are thirty-four, but we know you are really thirty-six.'

"I admitted it," Hatten said, laughing.

"What's so funny?" I asked.

"I still got him screwed for two years," Hatten said. "I'm thirty-eight."

Thanks to the press, Mr. Rickey is probably best remembered as a skinflint who paid his players peanuts. Jimmy Powers of the New York *Daily News* hung the "El Cheapo" tag on him. Powers did not care if it was true; he made no effort to get to know Mr. Rickey. Certainly when Mr. Rickey controlled 600 players in a farm system he didn't pay them anything, but nobody else was paying much in those days. Maybe he was a few dollars cheaper than the others, and there were some players who did not like him and thought he was cheap and conniving. To this day, Ralph Branca pointedly refers to him as "Branch." I'm not so sure Snider liked him. Nobody relished going in to see him, especially to talk contract. But, like him or not, they had to respect him. But there is another side to the story. I liked him, and I've got the floor, so I'm going to tell it.

Charlie Dressen was a devoted horse player. Mr. Rickey fired him in 1942 and promised to rehire him if Dressen quit gambling. When Dressen did lay off, Mr. Rickey not only rehired him, but paid him for the time he had been out of the game.

In 1946 the Dodgers were picked to finish in the second division. Mr. Rickey told Leo to tell us that if we won the pennant, every player and coach would get a new car. This was right after the war and most of us did not own one. The only company that was geared up to start making cars again was Studebaker.

When we heard the offer we were skeptical. How much would it cost us? Nothing. Nobody had ever heard of a deal like that.

We finished the season tied with the Cardinals and lost the playoff. But the car deal still stood. That winter we each received a certificate to present to our local Studebaker dealer. They made a car that looked the same on both ends, a radical design. I picked out a four-door black car and gave it to my parents in exchange for their beat-up old Ford. The point is that Mr. Rickey did not have to do that; we did not win. What's more, it was against the rules, and he was fined for doing it.

When we lost the World Series in 1947 he wanted to give us all National League championship rings. But the commissioner ruled no rings for the losers.

What was it like to negotiate a contract with Mr. Rickey in those pre-agent days? Red Schoendienst recalls when he first signed with the Cardinals, Mr. Rickey put his feet up on the desk so Red would be sure to see the holes in his soles.

Outfielder George Shuba went to see Mr. Rickey, intent on asking for $20,000.

"I don't think we can give you that much money," Mr. Rickey said, "but I'll think about it. Excuse me while I make a phone call. I'll be right back."

Left alone, Shuba glanced at some papers lying on the desk and he noticed a contract made out to Jackie Robinson with a salary of $20,000. Oh my God, he thought, how can I ask for the same as Jackie is getting?

Mr. Rickey returned and said, "George, you know what you're asking for is a little elevated. How about $15,000?"

Shuba jumped for the pen and signed. What he didn't notice was that the contract he saw on the desk was not signed and never would be. Jackie probably made more like $30,000 that year.

Even if there had been agents in those days, Mr. Rickey never would have talked to them. Besides, he would have known more about the player than any agent.

When I negotiated with Mr. Rickey, I was aided by some advice from Pee Wee Reese. After I won 15 games in 1948, Reese said to me, "Rex, you should get a big raise for next year. But whatever you do, don't sign until you talk to Mr. Rickey himself. He'll send out a lot of other guys to talk to you, but if you get to him, I think you'll get what you want and maybe a little more. Despite what you read about him, he is really a softer touch."

I was in Omaha that winter and Mr. Rickey sent an assistant, Arthur Mann, to see me. I asked for $20,000.

"We can't pay you that kind of money," he said.

They sent Branch, Jr., out to soften me up. I still didn't sign.

Then I got a call from Jane Ann Jones. "Mr. Rickey will be in Chicago and he would like you and your wife to join him there. We will make all the arrangements."

So we went and they treated us very well, provided us with tickets for a play with Katharine Hepburn, and invited us to Mr. Rickey's suite for lunch. Before lunch, Mr. Rickey said, "Young man, let's go into this other room and talk."

"Yes, sir."

We went into a bedroom.

"Now, why are you giving my son and Arthur Mann a problem?"

"I just think that after the year I've had and all I've done for the organization and—"

"Yes, yes, but what is it you want?"

Thinking of Pee Wee's advice, I raised my wants by $1,000.

"I want $21,000."

"Well," he said, "I don't see any problem with that."

Thank you, Pee Wee.

I have to say the Branch Rickey I knew was not the same man the writers have portrayed to the fans. But I don't think Mr. Rickey or any of his contemporaries could survive today. They ran the game. Nowadays the players run it. As Yogi Berra said—and I heard him say this one—when we played, the players were dumb. Now the owners are dumb.

The other half of this odd couple, Leo Durocher, was equally unique. My favorite writer, Red Smith, summed him up this way: "If Leo has a club that should finish third or fourth, he can move them to first better than any manager in baseball. But if he's got a club that should finish fifth or sixth, he'll finish last quicker than anybody."

I agree with that. He was not much of a driver if he did not have the horses to drive, but he did not need the best talent to bring them home in front. I played for him less than two full seasons, because he got a bum rap in 1947 and had to sit out the year. He was loud, cocky, belligerent, domineering, intimidating, forceful, and profane. There was never a dull moment around him. But everything he did was dedicated to winning.

I think most players liked him as a manager, though not as a person, but not everybody could play for him. He was like John McGraw, who had legions of devoted admirers among his players and plenty who hated him. Some players did not trust Leo. There were times when he would say something one day and deny it the next day. He got into hot water with the press by doing that.

Leo had his favorites. Pee Wee Reese was number one. Gil Hodges. Ralph Branca and me, for a while. But that did not stop him from cussing us out; in fact, he got on the players he liked more than the others. Over the years I've observed managers who tried to emulate Durocher one way or another: Gene Mauch, Alvin Dark, Bill Rigney, Eddie Stanky, Dick Williams, Earl Weaver. But there was only one Leo; if there were more, I wouldn't be talking about him this way. Like him or not, he was a special individual.

To me, Durocher was a player's manager. He gave the credit and took the blame. He'd come into the clubhouse after a loss, screaming and yelling, then say, "That was mine, guys. I never should have done what I did." A lot of managers would not say that.

At the end of the season he'd tell us, "I know a lot of you are going to be looking for raises. If you have any problems, just call me. If I think you should get more money I'll go to bat for you. But if I don't think you should get a raise, I'll tell you that, too. I won't knock you to Mr. Rickey, but if I agree with you, I'll tell him I think you deserve more money."

He was close to his players but did not mix with them. In the clubhouse he kibitzed the card games and talked to us informally. He was a great pool player and card shark, but he never played for more than a soda with another player. One year he and Luis Olmo, a Puerto Rican outfielder, had a running gin rummy game, and Olmo owed Leo about six cases of Coke before the season was over.

Leo had played the horses in his younger days. He got in deep to the bookies and they were ready to fit him for a pair of cement shoes when Judge Landis found out about it. Landis called him in and said, "We're going to pay off your debts and then collect it out of your pay, but if you ever get caught gambling again, you're out of the game for life."

Leo told us he walked out of there feeling like he was the luckiest guy in the world, and he quit betting. He would not do anything that might get him kicked out of baseball, which he loved more than anything.

Movie stars and theater people and shady characters flocked around him. Sure, he enjoyed all that stuff, but I think they were more gaga about being around the players than we were about them. Every time we got on a bus or went into a clubhouse there was some big star there. It got so we didn't pay any attention to them. Al Jolson was a big fan. Jack Benny actually made a road trip with us in 1946. He and Leo played a lot of gin rummy, and Benny thought that was one of the greatest experiences of his life. We all acted pretty cool about it, but I remember I couldn't wait to tell my mother and father about the stars I met.

Durocher's office at Ebbets Field was tiny. A door on one side led to the clubhouse, and one on the other side opened into a public gangway which he had to cross to get to the runway leading to the dugout. His visitors could use that door and not go through the clubhouse. The press was not welcome in his office; he met them in a little room off the clubhouse. Some writers felt offended by that, and they ripped Leo's managing because of it. If you think that sounds too petty to be true, I assure you the same kind of thing still happens today. On his desk Leo kept a small porcelain Cardinal as a reminder of his days with the Gashouse Gang.

Leo was a big hunch manager, not well acquainted with the playing rules, and very superstitious. Every time he walked to the third base coach's box, he picked up the third baseman's discarded glove, pounded it twice, put it down, kicked the base twice, and was ready for the inning to start. It was a ritual as dependable as the sunrise.

Leo was a very snappy, fastidious dresser, down to his silk underwear. During a winning streak, he'd wear the same clothes every day, but he'd wash them out every night. And of course he would never step on the foul line. But that makes sense. I mean, I wouldn't either. Would you?

We had a curfew on the road: midnight after day games, two hours after night games. Leo told us, "If you can't get what you're looking for by midnight, you ain't gonna get it. Go to sleep."

We were in St. Louis once and my brother came down from Omaha to see me. I asked for permission to stay out later.

"Don't lie to me," Leo said. "And if you're out with some girl, don't tell me she's your cousin. Ballplayers have more cousins than anybody. And they're all girls. And they're all good-looking."

He did not want anybody staying out late without his knowing about it because Mr. Rickey would call him and say, "I understand so and so was out until two in the morning. You know anything about it?" If Leo knew about it, he would tell Mr. Rickey. But if he didn't, somebody had left him caught off base, and that meant trouble.

Some managers did the bed checks themselves. Walter Alston did. Chuck Dressen. Billy Southworth.

Eddie Stanky tells this story:

I was managing the White Sox and we were in Baltimore and I decided to check the players in myself after a night game. I'm sitting in the lobby at two A.M. and players are strolling in. Joe Horlen, a pitcher, comes in at 2:30. I call him over and say, "Joe, breaking curfew will cost you a hundred." Joe says, "I understand." I tell him, "I'll take a check right now." Joe says, "I'll make it for two hundred because I'll be staying out late tomorrow night, too."

Not Leo. He had the trainer or clubhouse man do the dirty work. John Griffin, a big fat guy who took over for Danny Comerford, would sit in the lobby smoking a big cigar. When we came in he'd be asleep in the chair, and we'd pin notes on him: John, I came in at 12:15, stuff like that.

Charlie Dressen would give the elevator man a ball and tell him to get the autographs of every player who came in after midnight. We caught on to that one quick.

There was a telephone operator named Marge at the Schenley Hotel in Pittsburgh. She could see the entire lobby from the switchboard. If we were going to go out after midnight we'd call her up and ask: "Marge, where is John Griffin sitting?"

"By the front door."

We'd go down the freight elevator and out the back way. There was more action in that freight elevator at 12:05 than any other time of day. Before we came back, we'd call Marge again. "Where's John?"

"In the lobby."

Up the back elevator we went.

These things happened, but I don't want to give you the impression that we were a bunch of night owls. The truth is, most of us did very little running. The guys who drank usually did so quietly, in their rooms. I think we appreciated being ball players too much.

Leo was known, of course, for his arguments with umpires. But he never argued just to show them up. He believed he was helping his team by stirring things up. He would start a fight or get kicked out of a game to get the team hopped up. In a meeting he'd tell us, "If you think the ump made a bad call, I'll be right there with you. But don't embarrass me. If you know you made a mistake and the call went against you, I don't want to help you."

Among ourselves we'd say, "I wish he'd keep quiet and not argue so much," but never where he could hear us. We thought maybe the umps would give us the wrong end of the stick because of him. Later the Orioles voiced the same concern with Earl Weaver.

Dick Howser, a very close friend, was a class act, a true gentleman. His managing record was short, but successful. He often said, "I don't understand all that kicking and screaming with the umpires. If anybody can show me how that wins games, then I'll do it." On balance I don't think it has any effect one way or the other.

I asked Larry Goetz and Babe Pinelli, two umpires who were active during Leo's managing career, what it was like umpiring when Leo was managing. They said,

> He made you a little bit better. He was so far ahead of things and in the game so much, you better bear down because he never let up on you. He never yelled and got tossed but what he really believed he was right. You'd throw him out of the game and then you'd think: did I do the right thing? You knew you did the right thing for the language he used and kicking dirt on you and all that, but you wondered if you had made the right call or if his beef was justified.

Leo intimidated other teams, too, and they all hated us and wanted to beat the Dodgers more than anybody. We could not see any advantage in stirring them up to play their hearts out against us. You have to remember that this was a time when there were many bitter rivalries, when every team had fierce bench jockeys, when a player could be fined by the league and his own manager for having a friendly conversation on the field with an opposing player, even your own brother. If Leo saw one of us on the field visiting with a guy on the other team, he'd walk over and say, "Kiss the sonofabitch, and when he hits a ball out of the ballpark and beats your ass then you'll know what a friend he is." If we passed a guy we knew, we'd mutter, "How you doing," and keep moving.

Our dugout was noisy. Durocher paced up and down, cheering us on and riding the other team. "Come on, let's get these guys."

"Stick it in his ear!" he'd yell, just to plant that little bit of doubt and distraction in the hitter's mind. I never heard him tell any pitcher to deliberately hit a batter. Not once. Pitch inside. Brush him back, sure. But that didn't stop him from hollering, "Stick it in his ear!" It's all mind games. Nothing wrong with that. Everybody pitched inside. If you brushed a guy back, they didn't charge the mound. Well, maybe now and then. I dusted Peanuts Lowrey once because the guy who batted ahead of him hit a home run, and Lowrey came after me, but it didn't amount to anything. The guy who batted behind the home run hitter was always going down. That doesn't mean it made any sense, but that's the way we played the game.

Country Slaughter had been married a few times, so Leo let him have it. "Go beat up another wife, you clown!" Nothing personal; we all respected Slaughter as a player. It was just another weapon.

Marty Marion, a nice guy and great shortstop, would stand out there and make little crosses in the dirt between pitches. When Reese went out to the position, he'd rub them all out. That irked Marion; nobody knows why. He'd holler, "You little bastard, leave 'em alone out there."

Once you discovered that something really upset an opponent, you did it double. Reese never swung at a first pitch, not even a fastball down the middle. Clyde McCullough, a catcher with the Cubs and Pirates, knew that. One day he says to Reese, "How would you like a good fastball right down the middle?"

Pee Wee says, "Shut up."

Fastball right down the pipe. Strike one.

Clyde says, "Okay, I'll give you a curveball."

Pee Wee says, "Shut up."

Curveball right over the plate. Strike two.

Later Pee Wee said, "I never trusted him. I knew he was going to cross me up sometime."

Leo was like that, too. He used every weapon he had to gain an edge.

Durocher didn't fine many players, but he did it to me twice, both times to make me a better pitcher. One day he took me out of a game and I swore at him and slammed the ball on the mound and walked off. After the game he said to me, "You know all those things you called me? They don't bother me. It shows me you're really in the game. But you remember what you did with the ball?"

"Yes, I told you what you could do with it and threw it on the ground."

"That'll cost you a hundred dollars."

I said, "Leo, I'm only making five hundred a month."

"I don't give a damn what you're making. When a man comes in from the bullpen, you stand there and hand him the ball. Do you understand that? That's respect. You got him in all that goddamn trouble, hand him the ball."

"Yes, sir."

From then on, I'd stand there three days until he told me to go.

The other time, I had pitched a pretty good game but gave up a home run in the ninth to Sid Gordon that tied the game. In the clubhouse Leo said to me, "Remember that pitch Gordon hit?"

"Yes, sir."

"That pitch will cost you a hundred dollars."

"Why?"

He looked at me. "You really don't understand, do you?"

"No, sir."

"Do you know what the count was?"

"No, sir."

"No balls and 2 strikes. If you throw an 0 and 2 pitch and it's a bad pitch and he hits it, that's okay with me. Knock him down, throw a curve outside, make him go after a bad ball, as long as you're trying to do that. But when you throw it down the middle, a good hitter will kill you."

I learned quick, and I never forgot, and I never got my hundred back, either. To this day, guys in the press box know that whenever I see a pitcher groove an 0 and 2 pitch, I'll roll my eyes and shake my head and call on divine or managerial or pitching coach's intervention to set that pitcher straight. A hundred-dollar fine sure won't do it these days.

Leo always rode Pee Wee harder than anybody and I could not understand that. Pee Wee was the ultimate in what a team captain should be. One day I was sitting in the clubhouse talking to myself. Leo had been on me for something and I was mad. "Damn it," I muttered, "if he ever does that again, I'm going to smack him."

Pee Wee called me over.

"What is it, cap?"

"I don't blame you for being mad. Did you ever listen to him get on me? Remember this about Leo: as long as he's yelling at you, you're okay. But if he stops, and doesn't say anything at all to you, you're dead. You'll never play for him again. That's just the way he is."

From then on I understood.

One day I was pitching against the Giants at the Polo Grounds. Whenever I pitched, Leo didn't discuss the intricacies of pitching to the hitters. "Get the ball over the plate" was the extent of it. But this time he added, "Whatever you do, don't let Walker Cooper or Johnny Mize hit any breaking pitches. Just throw hard and make them hit fly balls to center field."

Late in the game I had a 5–0 lead and Cooper came up with a man on base. I threw him a curve and he hit it way up in the seats. We won the game and I ran across the outfield and up the steps to the clubhouse. The Polo Grounds clubhouse was on two levels, with the manager's office a few steps up from the players' area.

Everybody was congratulating me and I was pumped up even more than usual because I got a hit in the game. I looked up at Leo and I could see the veins in his neck throbbing away and I knew something was wrong. He never said a word. Next thing I knew he picked up a chair and threw it down at me. I went down and it hit in back of me and broke.

"You don't know what that's for, do you?" he yelled.

"No, sir. I just pitched a good game."

"Yeah," he snapped, "but, you little sonofabitch, you did exactly what I told you not to do."

I was so happy about winning, I didn't know what he was talking about. "What's that?" I asked.

"You threw a breaking ball to Walker Cooper and he hit it up in the seats, you dumb sonofabitch. Just do what I tell you to do. If it's a mistake I'll admit it, but let me make that decision. I'm the manager, you're the player, and if you don't do what I say I'll never pitch you again. I don't give a damn how many games you win."

That was Leo. He was doing it for me, not for himself. From then on, if he said do this, I did this. And if it was a mistake, he'd say, "I was wrong." I found nothing wrong with that.

But I made the same mistake in Pittsburgh in 1948. I was not doing too well, but this day I felt real good warming up.

"How do you feel?" Leo asked me.

"I have great stuff. I'm really throwing hard."

"Remember," he said, "don't throw any high fastballs to Kiner."

In the first inning Kiner came up with two men on and I threw him a high fastball and he hit it out of the country. I swear to God the ball hadn't even reached the fence before Durocher was standing next to me on the mound.

"Gimme the ball."

"Leo, I got great stuff."

"Gimme the ball."

I gave him the ball and stood there waiting.

"By the way, when you go into the clubhouse, do not take off your uniform and do not leave the clubhouse. Sit there and think about what happened."

We got killed in that game and he came into that clubhouse raving. "You'll never pitch for me as long as you live," he hollered at me. "I don't care what Mr. Rickey says. I'll send you so far an airmail stamp won't reach you," and all this with a string of profanity.

Boy, I was down. I went back to the Schenley Hotel with my tail between my legs. Pee Wee, Branca, Bruce Edwards all told me he'd get over it. I didn't think so. But I was wrong.

Then Leo went to the Giants and I pitched that no-hitter against him and he was riding me the whole game. But running toward the clubhouse afterward, there was Leo alongside me, telling me, "I'm proud of you, kid."

Leo could never function as a manager today. But in his day and mine, I say he was the best.

SEVEN

The Big Leagues

WHEN we were called up by the Dodgers from Montreal in 1943, Hal Gregg and I took an overnight train to New York and arrived early on the morning of August 18. We had been there before; when we played in Newark and Jersey City the team stayed at the Hotel McAlpin on 34th Street and took the train to New Jersey every day. But we had never been to Brooklyn.

With some help we found our way on the subway and located the Dodgers' offices at 215 Montague Street. When we opened the door, the first person we met was a young office boy who introduced himself as Lee MacPhail. He informed Mr. Rickey we were there, and I waited while Hal Gregg went in first. I sat there thinking, "Omaha . . . Durham . . . Montreal . . . now Brooklyn, all in one summer . . . from the Midwest to the Deep South and all that segregation stuff and then to a cultural French city and now?" All I knew about Brooklyn was the Cubs and the Cardinals played them.

Then Gregg came out and I went in. I had met Mr. Rickey when he came to our home in Omaha, and I had read about him. He was the first man I ever saw who wore a bow tie all the time. Tied it himself; that really impressed me. He always had a cigar in his mouth, but he never lit it.

In that deep sonorous voice he said, "Mr. Barney, you come from a very good family background and you're the kind of young man we want in our organization."

Here I am, an eighteen-year-old kid and he's calling me Mr. Barney, like I'm my father. I am impressed even more.

"You'll be with people like Billy Herman, Dixie Walker, Arky Vaughan, Whitlow Wyatt."

As I listened to him, I found myself staring at him. When he said, "Son, have you ever had any social diseases?" I didn't know what he was talking about.

"You're not going to pitch very much" he went on. "Hal Gregg is older and will get more work. But you are here because we know you're going into the service soon and you might gain a little experience pitching in games when we are way ahead or behind. We'll pay you $500 a month."

I thought: Five hundred a month and I don't even have to pitch. I'm really in the big leagues!

Then he called Hal Gregg back in and told us they had a room for us at the St. George Hotel, and he explained how to get to Ebbets Field on the subway. By now it's about 11 o'clock and game time is 1:30 so we went directly to Ebbets Field and found the players' entrance—gate 26.

First thing I saw in the Dodgers' clubhouse was this great big pool table in the middle of the room. Then I recognized George Raft, the movie star, sitting on an equipment trunk. Next to him sat a skinny redhaired kid with a big nose, his feet up, and big holes in his shoe soles. I found out his name was Danny Kaye. There were long benches the length of the rows of lockers; no individual chairs but one, at the end, in front of Dixie Walker's locker. A couple guys were playing cards.

Danny Comerford, the clubhouse man, was the first to speak to us.

"What's your name?" he barked.

"Rex Barney."

"There's your locker."

There was a white uniform hanging there with a big 26 on the back, and an old wrinkled and stained blue cap.

"Excuse me," I said. "Can I have another cap?"

"Who the hell do you think you are?" he snapped. "You're just a rookie. You get what I put there. And you better not ask for anything. You'll get nothing."

You think I'm making this up? Of course today's million-dollar rookies don't get treated that way. But you better believe that's how it was fifty years ago. I wore that scrungy old cap until I had pitched in a few games and then I came in one day and found a new cap in my locker.

I watched as Billy Herman, Augie Galan, Paul Waner came in and I felt like going around asking for autographs. Gene Hermanski was there. He had been in Durham briefly and was supposed to go to Montreal, but he had enlisted in the Coast Guard and there was a law prohibiting people who had registered for the service from leaving the country. So the Dodgers brought him up to Brooklyn, and that's how he got to the major leagues before we did.

Then suddenly Leo Durocher called Hal and me into his office. He said to Hal, "When did you pitch last?"

"Five days ago."

"We're playing a doubleheader against the Cubs today. You start the first game." Turning to me, he said, "You. When did you pitch last?"

"Three days ago."

"Okay, you start the second game."

We hadn't even unpacked yet. I said, "There must be some mistake. Mr. Rickey said—"

"I don't give a damn what Mr. Rickey said," he interrupted. "I'm telling you you're starting the second game."

I would have gone home to Omaha on the spot if I could have found my way out of there.

Most of the players ignored us. We were threats to somebody's job and not made to feel welcome. One I remember who was very kind was Whitlow Wyatt, a grand gentleman. And Johnny Cooney, a pitcher who had hurt his arm, gone down to the minors, and come back up as an outfielder, spoke to us.

I dressed and went out on the field and took a little batting practice and then the Cubs were hitting: Eddie Stanky, Bill Nicholson, Phil Cavarretta, and—my God! my absolute all-time hero— Stan Hack. I would actually be pitching against Stan Hack.

When I came through the tunnel into the dugout to watch the first game, Durocher stopped me. "Where do you think you're going?"

"To watch the game."

"Get back in the clubhouse and relax. Take a nap on the trainer's table."

So I didn't get to see Hal Gregg's debut. I listened to Red Barber describe it on the radio. Hal was wild—6 walks and 2 wild pitches—and was gone by the third inning. The Cubs won, 7 to 5.

Starting pitchers warmed up in front of the dugout and the game catcher always caught the last five or ten minutes of your warm-up. I started throwing to Bobby Bragan and then Mickey Owen took over. Owen had come over from the Gashouse Gang Cardinals and he was a noisy, scrappy catcher who ran the game and kept on his pitchers constantly. An excellent catcher, I'm sorry people remember him most for that missed third strike in the 1941 World Series. He deserves a better rep.

"You throw pretty hard," he said. "What else do you have?"

"I can put a little spin on it," I said. "But it's not really a curve."

I threw a few of my spinners and he said, "You're right; you don't have a curveball."

I was so scared I would have thrown whatever he called for, even if I didn't know how. The only sign I knew was one finger for a fastball. In Montreal I had learned the first inning first sign, second inning second sign system, stuff like that. When I was finished warming up, Owen started reeling off this complicated system he used. He'd flash two signs and you added them together; an even total meant fastball, odd total curve— something like that. I stopped him. "I don't know what you're talking about."

He gave me what I would call a look of sour patience and said, "Okay, I'll keep it simple. I'll give you three signs, but the first one is the only one that counts. Okay?"

Just before I went out to the mound, Whitlow Wyatt gave me a friendly warning about Owen. "Son, he throws the ball back to you real hard."

Well, I thought, not to a young guy like me. I found out different, quick. If you made a pitch Owen didn't like, he would walk a few feet in front of the plate and fire the ball back to you harder than you ever threw it to him. *Whoosh!*

The first batter I faced leading off for the Cubs was Eddie Stanky. I wound up and fired my first big league pitch and hit him square in the middle of his back. At least that was progress. Each time I moved up to a higher league, I got closer to the plate with my first pitch. Then I walked 3 guys and threw a wild pitch and 3 runs scored before I could get out of there. I gave up my first big league home run in the third, to a 5-6 .222 hitter, Dom Dallessandro. It was the only home run the little punk hit all year. That hurt.

Fortunately the Dodgers were hitting, too. When Kirby Higbe relieved me with nobody out in the fifth, the score was 6–6. I had given up 6 runs on 4 hits, walked 6, and struck out 3, plus 1 wild pitch and 1 hit batter. The Cubs roughed up Higbe and won, 15 to 6. The 12,132 paying customers, Leo Durocher, and I were not happy with the results of the day.

The Dodgers were fighting for a first division spot, but that did not stop Durocher from throwing us rookies right into the starting rotation, which in those days meant every four or five days. The following Sunday I started against the Pirates. We took a quick 4–0 lead and I was cruising along for three innings, just mowing down those big league hitters like weeds in the yard. In the fourth I walked a couple and before I knew it the bases were loaded and Vince DiMaggio was at the plate. DiMaggio knocked my fastball into the seats for a grand slam and knocked me into a state of shock. Nobody had ever done that to me. I looked into the dugout, figuring I was gone. Nobody moved. Arky Vaughan came over from shortstop. "That's all right, kid. We'll get 'em."

We scored another two, but in the eighth, DiMaggio came up again with a man on base. Durocher came out to look into my eyes, and decided I was not too scared to stay in; and I threw a called third strike past DiMaggio to nail down my first big league win. This time I struck out more than I walked. Things were looking up.

The next day Elbie Fletcher, the Pirates first baseman, said to me, "I hope your goddamn arm falls off. If you're going to be in this league, I'm getting out."

That made me feel even better.

Tommy Holmes of the Brooklyn *Eagle* gave us two kids up from Montreal mixed reviews in *The Sporting News:*

> Rex Barney, a youth out of Omaha, is only 18 years old; Hal Gregg from Anaheim is 21. Both are large and righthanded and their early performances left no doubt of their ability to

throw a ball hard. But omigosh, they were wild. Their efforts to find the plate somehow suggested the late Tad Dorgan's blind man in a dark room looking for a black hat that wasn't there.

Six days later in Philadelphia the Dodgers staked me to a 9–1 lead in the fifth, but I never got another man out. The Phils scored 6 runs on 3 hits, 4 walks, and a balk before Les Webber rescued me. Fortunately for my record, a kind official scorer gave me the win in the 14–7 game. Fortunately for my ego, the last-place Phillies drew only 1,801 fans who watched my debacle.

I've always been interested in exploring places to see every-thing. For our first few days in Brooklyn, Hal and I stayed close to Ebbets Field and the hotel. Then we got venturesome and took the subway to Times Square and ate in Jack Dempsey's restaurant. It was big-time stuff.

Our first overnight train trip was to Boston, and I got my first dose of hazing. There were no team buses; we got to the station on our own. I was waiting in the station and some players came over to me and started describing the little hammocks of netting that were in the sleeper berths.

"They're for your pitching arm," they said.

They had been pulling that gag since the beginning of time, but I knew my way around trains and said nothing. The next morning they asked me, "Your arm okay, kid?"

"Oh, I forgot to put it up there."

I've seen guys fall for that and wind up with lame arms for a week.

I had grown up wearing hand-me-downs and when it came time to go on that trip I didn't have any decent clothes. Durocher, who was a real fashion plate, saw what I wore to the ballpark and was not impressed. Everybody wore a suit and tie every day.

"Son," he said, "don't you have any better clothes?"

"No, sir."

"Go down to Buddy Lee's and get yourself a decent suit. They'll charge it to the Dodgers and we'll take it out of your pay."

So I went and bought myself a gray glen plaid suit with two pair of pants, probably cost $25. They never took it out of my pay; I don't know who paid for it. But it was the first brand-new suit I ever owned, so I guess Leo was responsible for my becoming so clothes crazy.

Another part of baseball that is gone was pepper games. You see signs in ballparks: No pepper games. The story is, a ball might go into the stands and hurt a fan. But it was fun and fans came out early to watch. Three or four guys would line up and one was the hitter and they'd toss the ball and he'd hit it and after so many catches in a row the fielder and hitter would swap places. The guy who made the most errors had to buy the Cokes. The action was quick and constant. I enjoyed playing pepper.

The Dodgers had a seven-game winning streak going and were closing in on second place when the Giants came to Ebbets Field on Saturday, September 4. A Giant-Dodger game was always intense, but this one turned out to be the most exciting game we played all year.

I was making my fourth start and had a 2–0 record, but I was still in awe of everything around me. The Giants had a veteran shortstop, Dick Bartell, a mouthy, scrappy guy, and Durocher started riding him before I threw the first pitch. Bartell always crowded the plate. In the eighth inning I hit him with a pitch and broke his wrist. That scared me. But when I got back to the bench all the guys were congratulating me, including Leo. "That's the greatest pitch you'll ever throw," and stuff like that. They confused me. Is that what I was supposed to do in the big leagues, break hitters' wrists? Charlie Dressen said, "You don't know what they're talking about, do you? Bartell's one of the most hated men in all baseball."

I was really in a groove that day. Not only did I take a 2–1 lead into the ninth, but I got my first major league hit, a single off left-hander Cliff Melton. I was even more excited about that; I was no longer batting .000. But there was no demonstration in the dugout, no high-fives or anything. That was considered showing up the other team and, boy, you do that and you'd go down on the next pitch, even if you were a pitcher.

I was 1 out away from nailing down my third win and got an 0 and 2 count on Sid Gordon. Tommy Holmes described what happened next: "At this point Rex was overbrave or didn't throw where he intended to. His fastball came down the groove and Gordon hit a home run into the left field seats to tie it."

We went ten, eleven, twelve, thirteen innings. After every one Durocher said to me, "You all right, kid?"

"Yes, sir."

I didn't want to come out. I would have stayed out there until my arm fell off.

The Giants scored in the top of the fourteenth and in the last half Augie Galan pinch-hit for me and drove in a run to knot it, 3–3. Ed Head finished the game for us and we finally won it in the seventeenth.

About forty years later some guy wrote a letter to a New York newspaper about a game he had seen just before he went overseas in 1943 and some pitcher had gone fourteen innings and who was it, and the paper said it was Rex Barney. Some of the Orioles pitchers read it and asked me if it was true.

"Sure, it's true," I said. "What about it?"

"You're crazy," they said. "Nobody pitches fourteen innings in a game."

Try to explain to them how times have changed.

Tommy Holmes called my fastball "as live as a basket of snakes." Mr. Rickey was quoted as saying when I learned to throw a change of pace I may become one of the game's greatest pitchers. I mean, that was heady stuff to read.

I started September 9 against the Phils with former president Herbert Hoover in the stands, but I didn't impress him or anybody else that day. We had a makeshift lineup, with Mickey Owen playing shortstop, but I can't blame that for my getting kayoed in the fourth. The Brooklyn bats bailed me out and we won, 7 to 6.

In Boston five days later, a .200 hitter named Chet Ross hit a home run and drove in all three runs in a 3–0 loss. That really teed me off.

Then we went on my first western trip and Durocher tried me in a relief role in St. Louis. The Cardinals were way out in front of the pack by then. The score was 2–2 when I started the fifth after Higbe was lifted for a pinch hitter. It was tied 3–3 after Musial and Cooper singled and I walked the next two batters in the sixth. When I walked Harry Walker and Musial, and Cooper singled in the seventh, Durocher had enough of me, but the damage was done and I had my second loss.

Next stop was Chicago and there they caught me on the old "We'll get it in Pittsburgh" routine. In Chicago we stayed at the Edgewater Beach Hotel. Very glamorous, high-class stuff. I remember Freddie Martin's band was appearing there, with a young singer, Merv Griffin.

Wrigley Field was a cab ride away. The standard practice was for four or five guys to take a cab and one would pay for it and get reimbursed by the traveling secretary. But I didn't know that. I tagged along with Dixie Walker, Owen, Herman, and Galan. We got to Wrigley Field and they said to me, "Take care of the cab, kid. We'll get it in Pittsburgh." I'm the big hero; I get to pay for the cab.

When we get to Pittsburgh, I'm standing on the porch of the Schenley Hotel waiting for my pals to take me to the ballpark. Here they come and I say, "Let's go, guys. It's your turn to pay for the cab."

"Follow us," Billy Herman says. We walk a block and turn the corner and there sits Forbes Field. You couldn't see it from the hotel porch.

A few years later I pulled the same trick on Eddie Miksis. That was a standard gag until they built Three Rivers Stadium in Pittsburgh.

A true highlight of my first visit to Pittsburgh was seeing Honus Wagner sitting at the end of the dugout by the runway where the players came out onto the field. He was sixty-nine then, but he was still magnificent to me, sitting there in uniform, no teeth, gumming a wad of tobacco, more bowlegged than ever. Every time we passed him, he said, "Hi, boys, how's the weather?" Maybe when he was a player it meant, "Are we going to play today?" I don't know.

Sometimes he went home before the game started; sometimes he stayed 'til the last out. He was there every time we went to Pittsburgh, for as long as I was with the Dodgers. Always in the same spot, always "How's the weather?"

I read once where he held out for $1,500, and threatened to sit out the season. Fifteen hundred dollars. The greatest player in baseball.

In that Chicago series I had made my briefest start. I walked leadoff man Stan Hack on 4 pitches and Leo yanked me for Fritz Ostermueller. In Pittsburgh I had a no-hitter going but he took me out with 1 out in the third because I had walked 5.

We finished the season in Cincinnati. I went home to Omaha, said hello and goodbye, and reported to Fort Leavenworth, Kansas. I had a new uniform, with a brand-new cap this time.

EIGHT

A New Uniform

I WAS SCARED the whole time I was overseas in World War II. Anybody who says they weren't is a liar. I went through the war with a rosary and an M1 rifle. I depended more on those beads than the rifle, but I used the M1 when I had to. And I saw things I never want to see again.

There's a man in Baltimore, Russ Niller, who pitched for a Cleveland farm club. People said he could throw as hard as anybody. During the war he bailed out of a plane and landed on his shoulder. That ended his pitching career. I mention him because he is one of many who went into the army as ballplayers and came out as ex-ballplayers, and that was my greatest fear.

I used to stand guard in below-zero weather or sit in a lookout post or huddle in a hole in the ground and pray: Whatever you do, Lord, don't make me a cripple. Either kill me or keep me whole so I can play baseball again.

I don't sit around telling war stories; I think it's boring. But the experience is locked into anyone who went through it. Since we are all the products of everything we have ever experienced, I cannot tell you my whole story without including it.

My army duty looked like a lark at the start. My pay went from $500 to $21 a month, but, like many athletes, I was assigned to special services to play basketball and baseball on camp teams. They transferred me to Fort Riley, Kansas, and skipped basic training because the basketball season was about to start. The following spring we put together a pretty good baseball team: Joe Garagiola, Lonnie Frey, Harry Walker, Pete Reiser, Alpha Brazle, Ken Heintzelman, Frank Crespi, and me. We played my old semipro team in Omaha and other camp teams, and one Sunday I arranged for the team to go to Boys Town for mass and to meet Father Flanagan, an exciting day for all of us.

My life of Riley was shattered in the summer of 1944 by the news that I was headed overseas. The National Baseball Congress has a semipro tournament every August in Wichita, Kansas, and a few companies were after me to pitch for them in the tournament. But I had my orders to ship out and a two-week leave coming. I wanted to pitch—I always wanted to pitch—but I also wanted to spend some time with my family before I went overseas. When the Coleman Company offered to pay me $50 a game and bring my father and mother to Wichita, that settled it. I pitched a three-hitter to beat Camp Livingston, and had no decision in another start, but we lost the tournament. Then I headed to Camp Shelby, Mississippi, for processing. That included going through a line where they hit you with shots in both arms. If you didn't keep moving, they'd hit you again. From there, I found myself back in New York. But this time, instead of a subway to Brooklyn, I was on a troopship to France.

It was a converted Italian luxury liner; I don't remember the name. All I know is, fourteen days on a ship crowded with scared young GIs who are trying not to show it is no luxury cruise. We were part of a twelve-ship convoy, dodging German U-boats all the way over. Four ships did not make it. The ship rocked and rolled constantly, and we were seldom allowed to go up on deck. The food was terrible. There were bunks six high, and everybody prayed for a top one. But we couldn't sleep anyhow; most of us shot craps all night. When you lost all your money, you borrowed from one of the winners and got back in the game. I hated it all.

At Fort Riley I had felt like some kind of a big shot, a former major league ballplayer. No more. The army is a great leveler. Now I was just another buck private like everybody else. Only an occasional baseball nut from Brooklyn had ever heard of me.

I didn't know what I was headed for, but I was pretty sure it was unlikely to have anything to do with baseball. By the time we landed in Le Havre, I had been assigned to a tank

74

reconnaissance group. Never mind that I was 6-3 and knew zilch about tanks. The army needed a body for the tank corps and I was it.

It was bitter cold when we landed. Le Havre was a shambles, flattened by constant German air raids. Debris and bodies floated in the harbor. We could not get to the docks, and had to wade ashore in waist-high water carrying rifles and equipment over our heads. It was cold, dirty, and muddy, with death and destruction everywhere. I don't want to remember it, but I cannot forget it.

I didn't have the vaguest idea what I was doing when I landed. But I learned quick. It's called Survival 101. I soon discovered that tank reconnaissance means that a line of alternating tanks and jeeps advances ahead of everybody else until they draw enemy fire. Then they radio back to the infantry to tell them where the enemy is. Sound like fun?

But first we had to get the tanks to the front. The first real action I saw was on a cold winter night at the Rhine River. We had to move all the heavy equipment across, but there was a German outpost on top of a hill on the other side. Somebody asked for volunteers to go across and find out what was up there. Dumb-ass me, I figure it's my first night of action—go for it. Eight of us and a sergeant got into two rubber boats, dirt smeared on our faces, carrying rifles, pistols, and grenades, watching chunks of ice floating by as we silently crossed over. We slithered around and up the hill, trying to stay out of sight. An old stone house came into view. Then suddenly we heard noises and guys talking German. The sergeant hollered, "Fire!" and we rose up and opened fire and just like that there were six dead Germans.

We slid back down the hill and raced to where we had tied up the boats. Gone. The Germans must have found them and cut them loose. I was a good swimmer, but with all that equipment and the frigid water and hunks of ice hitting me in the head, getting across that river took forever. They dragged us out and took us someplace warm and we slept the whole next day.

I was scared out of my wits, but at least I had gotten that duty out of the way. Some guys who went on later patrols got killed or wounded. We each received a Bronze Star, which was nice; more important, it earned us five extra points toward our ultimate discharge date, which was based on a point system. That was one thing about the army I had learned fast.

The houses in Germany had walls like forts and made good outposts. We occupied one near a creek and the Germans held one on the other side. We sat there watching each other. Lookout duty was on the second floor in two-man teams, two hours on, two hours off, which meant we never slept. If we saw or heard anything, we shot first and asked questions later.

There was running water in the creek. If you've ever sat near running water on a cold, dark, still night, you'd swear you could hear 8,000 troops marching right up your front walk. One night I was on duty with a big Dodger fan named Jim Eisely. He had an M1 and I had my M1 and a rosary and a brilliant idea: we rounded up all the empty tin cans we could find and threw them all over the front yard, so if anybody moved we could hear them.

In the middle of our late-night shift we were startled by a racket like a string of cans being dragged behind a newlyweds' getaway car. We opened fire and raked the place, and everything went quiet. We couldn't wait for sunup to see how many guys we got. When the dawn came, we found five stone-dead billy goats in the yard.

The tank had a four-man crew: a driver, who sat deep inside near ground level on the left; a radio operator beside him; a gunner who sat a few steps higher and operated a .50-caliber machine gun; and the tank commander, a sergeant who stood— never sat—with his head sticking out through the opening. He gave the orders and fired the 75-millimeter cannon. There was no steering wheel; the driver moved two sticks to maneuver. I never drove one; I started as a radio operator and wound up as a tank commander. The inside of a tank is cramped, hot as hell in the summer, and cold as hell in the winter. Many a night we slept in one. It was our home.

The Germans hated our cannon and took off when they heard it. They had an 88-millimeter cannon that we dreaded. Those shells had a distinctive whistle that struck icy fear in us. One night in that outpost where we decimated the billy goats we heard one coming in and I just knew we were gone. It landed in the back yard and never went off. They also had a bazooka, a one-shot gun that tore a huge hole in a tank and exploded all the ammunition inside. One day I was in the second tank and we rounded a curve in the road and heard this gun go off. The lead tank stopped and we knew right away there was nothing left of anybody in it. We bailed out of ours in a hurry. The commander dove off the top, but it took the driver a few minutes to unstrap himself and get out of there. Hairy moments, those.

The tanks and jeeps moved forward until they ran into the enemy or it got dark, whichever came first. At night we threw a net over the tank and crawled into a barn with the animals or an empty farmhouse, any place where it was warm. The whole experience was a rude awakening for me. And I don't mind telling you I hated it, absolutely despised it. I couldn't wait to get back to the life that was waiting for me. Later, after I got out of there, I could see what an education it was. If you ever think you're better than anybody else, think about your days in the army, where you'd find maybe the world's richest guy next to some bum who never had a dime, a professor in a foxhole with a guy who couldn't add two and two. I also learned that the guys who were real tough and macho in the states were the sissies and wimps under fire.

The first words of German I learned were, "Haben-sie eier?" (Have you any eggs?) We'd go to a farmhouse looking for an egg; eat it raw or cook it in our helmets. We took a bath in our helmets if we ever found water. We were filthy dirty; you could scrape the dirt off with a fingernail. Once in a while the Red Cross showed up with five-gallon cans of coffee. I poured some of that in my helmet and shaved with it. I remembered my mother preaching cleanliness and telling me, "You can always go into a gas station restroom and find soap and water," and I laughed.

We ate C rations: little packages of dehydrated something, powdered eggs, and some kind of dogmeat, and a chocolate bar. That is, when the rations caught up with us. I learned what complete hunger feels like. And if we ever saw a live chicken, it was dead in a hurry.

We were in action for thirty days at a time and then got a few days off to go back, take a shower, get deloused, and eat some decent food.

Sometimes things happened that did not seem funny at the time, but later we could look back and joke about them. Things like near misses by whistling shells, and billy goat body counts. One day we were crossing the Saar River in Germany. While we waited for the engineers to put down pontoons for the tanks to cross, we emptied a five-gallon gasoline can and filled it with some wine we had requisitioned along the way. I was sitting atop the tank when two war correspondents came up to me.

"Sergeant, you got any water?"

"Sure," I said without thinking. "Right back there. That five-gallon tank on the left."

They took a swig and said, "Dear God, this is the greatest water I ever tasted." In twenty minutes they were drunk as skunks. I guess they thought the age of miracles hadn't passed, and I had turned water into wine.

Both sides fired tracer bullets at night; we could see them flashing by. The Germans fired them high and we thought, "Okay, I can get down under that." But they were firing the invisible ones down below at the same time.

Land mines were another menace. We had to clear a path wide enough for the tank treads to get through. We'd round up all the animals we could find—pigs, cows, whatever—and send them across a field to see if they blew up. Otherwise, we were on our hands and knees, crawling gingerly yard by yard and poking bayonets ahead of us. I found some mines that way and saw friends get killed or lose some limbs beside me.

It was constantly wearing. Sometimes I would go to sleep and hope I didn't wake up for three days. I had frostbitten feet from pulling guard duty in subzero weather and was wounded twice. That earned me two purple hearts, good for ten points. But nothing major. Once I was dashing behind a barrier and machine gun fire grazed my leg. Another time the firing was pretty heavy and I was trying to dig a hole in some concrete with my fingernails and got hit in the back with some shrapnel.

I was attached to the 4th and 6th Armored Divisions of the Third Army, and had two contacts with General George S. Patton. Once he called a meeting of his tank recon commanders in the town hall of Nancy, France, which the Germans and Americans kept taking and retaking. I drove a captain to the meeting. There were a couple hundred officers there. Patton ranted and raved and cussed and screamed about how the Germans were pushing us around. He said, "From this point on, every infantryman who doesn't fire at least a hundred rounds a day at the enemy is as worthless as the prick on the Pope." And I'm thinking: here's this nice Irish Catholic altar boy sitting here listening to this, and what would my mother say?

Near the end of the war, as the SS troops fell back, they rousted out the civilians and showed them how to shoot rifles to hold us back while they retreated. One day near sunset all of a sudden I heard a big commotion from the rear and here came this jeep flying four stars. Patton was sitting behind the .50-caliber machine gun in the back. The gunner was in the passenger seat behind a thick lead windshield with little slits in it, where Patton was supposed to be. They skidded to a stop and Patton jumped out, his famous pistols on his belt. We saluted.

"Sergeant," he said, "where's the front?"

"General," I said, "the front of this tank."

"Too goddamn close for me," he said. "See you later." And off he went.

It was too goddamn close for me, too, but I couldn't go anywhere.

A recon group was not prepared to take prisoners, and that was fine with Patton. He preferred to shoot them all on the spot. One time we were trying to take some little hill, but we were pinned down by mortar and machine gun fire from the hilltop. It was midday. A couple of our guys were hit and fell dead beside me. Three of our men got around behind the Germans and captured three of them. They went behind a barn and killed them point-blank. It wasn't tough to watch at the time, but later my stomach turned a few times. I never thought I would see Americans do anything like that. I didn't do it, but I was part of it; I sanctioned it. I don't think I could have fired the shots, but I saw it, and I will never lose that sight in my mind.

We did some nasty things, but I suppose they did the same to our guys. A jeep always led the recon column, followed by the lead tank, and so on. We crept along very slowly. If we captured a German soldier, we put him on the hood of the lead jeep with his hands behind his head. Talk about a scared sonofabitch. We didn't want the Germans firing on us, but if they did—I'll tell you, I've seen some scared guys. I used to think: Damn, I'm glad I'm not up there.

And if we ever got hold of an officer and put him up there, was that fun. They'd protest that they didn't have to do that, but when it was explained to them that the alternative was to go behind a barn and get shot, they got up there. They were the bitter, deadly enemy, and we had to think of them that way at all times.

We had no way to take care of prisoners, but one day we came to a small town and the whole town surrendered to us, soldiers and everybody, white flags flying everywhere. We had to call the infantry to come and get them.

My contacts with baseball news were sparse. My radio operator had picked up some bits of the 1944 World Series through the BBC. It was against regulations to use the radio for that, but we managed it. We got to see *The Stars and Stripes* once in a while, and all during the war *The Sporting News* sent a free subscription for a scaled-down edition to every professional ballplayer in the service. When they caught up with me I caught up on the baseball news.

We were sitting in the tank one night in April 1945 and the radio operator picked up some music on the BBC. I was juking around to the music and suddenly a bulletin came on that President Roosevelt had died. I sat there and cried. My father had said that Roosevelt was the greatest president who ever lived and if he said it, I knew it must be true.

I was never much for collecting souvenirs, and did not bring back any guns or stuff. I saw guys take watches and jewelry off German officers, but I don't care for guns at all and the other stuff never interested me.

I had one ten-day leave and went to Switzerland, which I enjoyed, except that they locked up the hotels at midnight and that was too early to call it a night for a bunch of GIs on leave. But I did buy a watch for my brother and a clock for my mother.

I'll never forget the strong stench that filled my nostrils as we got closer to something we did not know we were coming to, and then we went into Buchenwald. Bodies piled up everywhere. Walking skeletons. We didn't expect it, because when you are in the thick of war you don't really know what else is going on in the world. We knew there were prison camps, and American prisoners of war, but we never knew when or where we would happen onto something. And there was no way to be prepared for this.

They mobbed jeeps, turning them over, to get at a scrap of bread. We just had to let them go to it; you could not say no. Those who could move wanted to go to the nearest village and kill everybody. We had to stop them from doing that. Others begged us to let them go home. Just walk home. That might have been 800 miles away. I didn't want to see all that, but I think I've become a better person for having seen it.

By now the Germans were in full flight, abandoning the camps. We rolled down the beautiful autobahn, the super highway, toward Austria. But when the prisoners started telling us stories about the slave laborers from Poland and other countries who had built it, how people who collapsed or died were just buried in the concrete, we didn't know that we ever wanted to ride on it again.

It was all an eye-opener to a naive kid from Omaha.

And then the war was over in Europe and I was in Vienna and every day was like New Year's Eve and another kid athlete from Oshkosh and I got hold of a bottle of champagne and killed the bottle and I hadn't been so sick since the day I swallowed my chewing tobacco.

With Europe liberated, I was liberated from the tank corps and went back to playing basketball. Vienna was divided into French, British, Italian, American, and Russian zones. We had everything; the rest had nothing. People tried to sneak into our zone from every direction, but especially to get away from the Russians. They were mean and rough, I mean animals. If they couldn't rape a girl in the street they would just as soon shoot her. They drove tanks down into the subway and fired guns into the tunnels, just to destroy it. We took all their money selling them food and things we had on the black market. I did that, but I'm not proud of it. All we had was scrip money; I had footlockers filled with it, but I couldn't spend it anywhere else.

A lot of servicemen had used the C ration chocolate bars to trade with the German girls. A little piece went a long way. I stayed away from that action, because I knew, when I got back,

Mr. Rickey would be asking me about those social diseases. In Vienna I met a Red Cross girl from Nebraska, and we Nebraskans are pretty scarce, so we stuck together. And I'll never forget a nurse named Alice Pierce. It was October 1945 and I met her in a USO Red Cross center. We started talking about the World Series between the Tigers and the Cubs and she said there was a radio upstairs. We went up there at night and I heard bits of that series, including a Hank Greenberg home run. Bless Alice Pierce. Shows you what I had most on my mind.

There were jobs offered to us if we would stay overseas another three years, running a PX, stuff like that. Some of my friends went for it and tried to persuade me to stay. But I turned them down. "I have something to go back to," I said. "I'm going to be a famous major league baseball player." Or infamous.

I figured I would be discharged in the middle of the 1946 season. But one day that winter the Red Cross delivered a telegram to me. My father was very ill with cancer of the throat (he had smoked Camels all his life) and I was given an emergency leave. I flew home in some shaky old cargo transport by way of Iceland, then took a train to Omaha. He lived a few more years and died on my birthday in 1948.

Since I was due to return to the states in a few months anyhow, there wasn't much point in sending me back to Vienna. So they kept me at Fort Riley for another month and discharged me. Ed Head pitched a no-hitter for the Dodgers on April 23, and a few days later I was back in a Dodger uniform. But I soon learned that I was happier to see them than they were to see me.

NINE

Back in Brooklyn

THERE WERE MANY DIFFERENT FACES in the Brooklyn clubhouse when I returned in 1946. I had missed spring training,
so Leo Durocher took me around and introduced me. When we
got to Eddie Stanky, who had come from the Cubs in 1944,
Stanky said, "I know the sonofabitch. He hit me right in the
middle of the back three years ago and I still got the mark. I
know how hard he can throw."

Reese, Lavagetto, Furillo, Reiser, Edwards, Ed Stevens
were all new to me. And Eddie Miksis, one of those guys who
was going to take Pee Wee's job every year. Fast and an
excellent fielder, he played fourteen years in the big leagues
and got into at least 100 games in only four of them. One year
at the baseball writers' dinner in New York, one of the skits
included this ditty: "Miksis will fix us, said Rickey the boss;
Miksis played, chalk up another loss."

And there was Joe Medwick. I had been reading about
Medwick for years when he was with the Cardinals. A tough,
unfriendly guy, he was a loner who held himself a little above
everybody else and was more interested in his own stats than
in what the team did. Mr. Rickey was not sure he wanted
Medwick on a team of green youngsters; Joe helped some
hitters but I would not want him as a batting coach. He used
all kinds of stances, held the bat every which way from one time
to the next, ignored the strike zone, and could hit the ball off
his ear, in the dirt, anywhere. Nobody intimidated Medwick.
He'd yell at our pitcher, "Knock the sonofabitch down!" then go

up to bat himself not caring if they threw at him. Which they did. He set a good example in some ways, not in other ways, but I was fascinated by him.

I recognized a few of the pitchers: Joe Hatten, Hugh Casey, Kirby Higbe. But there was a slew of young ones, too. Baseball people have always looked for youngsters who can throw hard, figuring they can teach everything else, but not that. There have been some exceptions, pitchers who made it and never threw hard: Roe, Lopat, Boddicker, McGregor. But Mr. Rickey hoped that out of every half-dozen hard throwers he might get one real pitcher. During the next few years the parade included Branca, Banta, Behrman, Taylor, Barney, and the best of the bunch, Carl Erskine.

To this day the philosophy is the same. When Jim Frey took over as the Cubs manager in 1984, he called the general manager, Dallas Green, and said, "Get me the five hardest-throwing pitchers in the organization. I don't care if they are in Class D or wherever, I want to see them." Green told him, "We don't have five. The best I can do for you is two or three."

I met Ralph Branca in 1946 and we became close friends and roommates on the road. Later we became godfathers to each other's daughters.

There was less card playing among the postwar Dodgers, too. Durocher put a ban on poker and set a low limit on pinochle, gin rummy, casino, hearts, and other games.

Since I had missed spring training, I had to work out for a few weeks and prove that I was healthy and could still throw hard before I received the rest of my original signing bonus. But I was clearly not ready for the big leagues and I knew it.

There was one catch: a law requiring employers to take men coming back from the service and give them their former jobs. In baseball, that meant if you had been on a major league roster when you went into the army, they had to keep you for a year when you returned. If they tried to send you down to the minors, they had to get waivers from the other teams, and Mr. Rickey was sure some team would claim me. I knew I needed some work but I just sat doing nothing. When I asked Mr. Rickey to send me somewhere so I could work every four days, he told me he had no choice but to keep me. So Durocher and the Dodgers were stuck with me taking up one of the twenty-five places on the team.

The Dodgers were in one of those "rebuilding" years, and were not expected to figure in the pennant race. As it turned out, we wound up in the thick of it and I became even more of an albatross. Durocher had to go with the guys who were doing the job, but when he was in need of a starter, he gave me the ball, and I was always eager to take it. Sometimes I was terrible, but a few times I was downright brilliant.

I suppose my first two games illustrate the inconsistency that characterized the year for me. I sat around for more than a month before I got into a game. On May 30 against Boston I came in from the bullpen to relieve Hank Behrman with 1 out in the second of a 2–2 game, walked 4 straight batters, and Durocher, disgusted, waved in Art Herring, but it was too late. Five days later at Pittsburgh I pitched two scoreless innings and walked only 2 in an eleven-inning Brooklyn win, but I had no decision.

On June 8 in Chicago I made my first start a good but losing one, 2 to 0. Lavagetto pinch-hit for me in the seventh; I had walked 5 but struck out 7 and even got a base hit myself.

Four days later I started against the first-place Cardinals in St. Louis and held them hitless for six innings before the roof caved in in the seventh. I was rescued with 1 out, having given up 3 hits and 9 walks. The Dodgers won it, 10 to 7, cutting the Cards' lead to one game.

And that's the way it went: one day knocked out by the Pirates in the third, the next time holding St. Louis scoreless for six brilliant innings, then opening a cloudburst of walks and hits.

The first inning on June 26 sums up the season; I walked 3 and struck out 3 Reds. I lasted into the eighth and won, 4 to 2. Dixie Walker hit 2 triples, Pete Reiser had 2 hits and 2 stolen bases, the Dodgers had a three-game lead, and I had my first W. Branch Rickey was quoted as saying, "How can you give up on a kid like that?"

But Leo Durocher wasn't so sure, and neither were many of my mates. A story in *Sports Illustrated* said, "Barney fiddles while Durocher burned . . . His monogrammed shirts, expensive suits and snazzy cuff links, his ties with flawless Windsor knots meant more to him than pitching . . . "

I can rationalize that today, but I can't rebut it. When Leo had sent me to buy my first new suit in 1943, I fell in love with clothes. I didn't have long to enjoy them before I had an all-khaki wardrobe, so when I got back to civilian life I went a little berserk. I probably did change my clothes two or three times a day. Carl Furillo, who didn't understand that, called me a hot dog to the press. Forty-five years later I saw Gene Hermanski at a banquet. He admired my spiffy outfit and commented, "You never let up." But when they wrote that my wardrobe meant more to me than my pitching, that was out of line. Nothing superseded baseball.

I was also very taken up with the oohs and aahs I would hear when I warmed up before a game. We were right in front of the dugout within close range of the fans. My fastball made the catcher's mitt bang, not just pop, and I could hear the fans' reactions and I admit I ate up all that stuff. Catchers told me I wasn't really concentrating on the business at hand all the time and they were probably right.

But things also happened when I was warming up that were not my fault. One day in Pittsburgh I was warming up before a game and all of a sudden a guy fell out of the upper deck. There was a big commotion and it turned out the guy was so drunk he was not hurt, but the man he fell on suffered two broken legs and happened to be his brother-in-law.

In the Polo Grounds for a holiday doubleheader I was walking in from the clubhouse to warm up with Clyde Sukeforth when a big hubbub broke out in the stands. Fights were common at those events so we didn't pay much attention to it. But the next day we read that an old man was sitting there with his grandson and he suddenly slumped over, like he'd had a heart attack. But some guy standing on Coogan's Bluff had shot a gun in the air and the bullet came down and hit this man. I tell you, things happened when I warmed up to pitch.

Four days after my first victory of the year, I got my second and last of the year in my best outing and only complete game. I beat Mort Cooper and the Braves, 4 to 1, and the Dodgers led the league by 6½ games. But like the little girl with the curl, when I was bad I was horrible. On the night of July 5 at the

Polo Grounds I was breezing along until a barrage of hits and walks buried me in a 5-run sixth and we lost, 7 to 6. Then we headed west.

About the only thing that has not changed in the big leagues is payday; it is still the first and fifteenth of each month. If we were on the road we did not get paid until we got home. Today the player can have his paycheck if he wants it on the fifteenth no matter where the team is playing, although many of them have their checks deposited directly.

We got $7.50 a day meal money but we never saw it. They were afraid too many guys would stash the cash and not eat right, so we had to sign the checks in the hotel dining room. And if we went over the limit, likely as not it would be deducted from our next pay. Today the players get $59 a day in cash, payable for the entire road trip on the first day out.

When the Dodgers played at the Polo Grounds, we carpooled or rode the subway. Technically it was a road game but we never got any meal money for those days. The players' association would love that today.

The longest train ride was Boston to St. Louis, about twenty hours. Invariably the air-conditioning broke down; if we opened the windows we were buried in soot from the engine. Train berths were too small for me and I had to fold up to sleep. Later we had compartments, two to a cubbyhole with an upper and lower and a little sink in the corner which you could get to only by flipping up the lower berth. I roomed with Branca and sometimes with Bruce Edwards and we'd flip to see who got the lower. The manager had a big compartment at the end of the car. We had a private dining car and Pullman, and our own porters. Players usually called the colored porters "boy." They were more likely to call a white conductor "mister" but the term "boy" was common. I have always used "pal" because I prefer it to "boy" or "hey, you." I heard "hey, you" so much in the army I began to think that was my name. To me, the word "pal" tells someone that I like them. (I'm also a toucher when I greet people.)

Major league players have long had a reputation for being tightfisted tippers. It's not true of all of them, but there were enough to give us all that stigma. But everybody liked to work for the Dodgers because Durocher was a lavish tipper and we learned from him. Leo was the type of guy, if he made $100,000, he'd spend $150,000.

The close confinement on the trains made us feel more like a family than any club can know today, but closeness did not guarantee congeniality. There were occasional fights and arguments, and a caustic writer like Dick Young might touch off somebody's temper. Gene Hermanski, a good hitter, couldn't catch you running by him. We kidded him, called him Fistsbliski and Handsmanski. One day Young called him a charging clown. Gene took exception and hauled off and poked him. So the atmosphere was not always fun and games on the trains.

Every clubhouse had a swindle sheet on the wall, with all the players listed. If you took a sandwich or candy bar or tobacco or soda, you marked it down, and when you left after a series or a home stand you paid what you owed, plus a buck or two tip. There was seldom beer in the clubhouse and if there was you paid for it. Charlie Dressen had a rule: no beer if we lost. But free food? Forget it. Nothing was free. In the Brooklyn clubhouse John Griffin or Danny Comerford would come around with a bat in hand: "Let's go. Pay up. And no checks." Clubhouse dues on the road cost $2.50 a day.

So we headed west in July. On the twelfth in Chicago I started, got 1 man out, walked 2, gave up 2 hits, and took the loss.

Cardinal-Dodger games were always great chess matches. One day Durocher sent Ralph Branca out to warm up, intending for him to pitch to one batter, while the lefty Vic Lombardi warmed up under the stands. Ralph struck out the first batter. Leo signaled to Dressen to wait on the change. Pop-up. Strikeout. Leo, a devout hunch player, said, "I think we better wait." Branca went all the way and beat them.

Desperate for pitching, Durocher made a starter out of Hugh Casey for the first time that year on July 15. It didn't work. Casey got 1 man out. I relieved him and contributed to the 10–4 loss by walking 3. We lost our sixth in a row and fell out of first place.

I didn't see any more action for two weeks, then started against the Pirates and got knocked out in the fourth. My record was now 2 and 5 and that's the way it stayed. I mopped up now and then in 10–0 and 14–8 losses, walking about 1 per inning, sometimes walking the only 2 or 3 men I faced. On September 11 the Reds and Dodgers played a nineteen-inning 0–0 tie. We used 4 pitchers, but understandably I was not one of them.

In September the fans in Durham raised the money to send Ma Gregory to Brooklyn to see the Dodgers, many of whom had stayed at her rooming house when they played for the Bulls. Ferrell Anderson presented her with a basket of flowers from six of "her boys." With her enthusiasm and foghorn voice, she fit right in at Ebbets Field.

Down the stretch, neither the Cardinals nor the Dodgers could pull away. Both teams lost on the last day of the season to finish in the first tie since 1908. Then the Cardinals won two straight in the playoff and our season was over.

At the start of the season Branch Rickey had promised everyone connected with the team a new car if we won the pennant. After the last playoff game Mr. Rickey showed up in Leo's office (he would never come into the clubhouse). We were told the two of them were in tears during that meeting. It was then that Mr. Rickey said we would get the cars despite our defeat. He told Leo, "Don't let the team think about this defeat, or think of themselves as losers; you are going to win next year and for a long time to come."

Mr. Rickey was also very upset over a column written by Joe Williams, who claimed Mr. Rickey had traded Billy Herman so the Dodgers would not win the pennant. Williams accused Rickey of preferring to finish a close second as that was good for attendance but would keep the players from demanding big raises. Mr. Rickey asked Leo to make it clear to us that he wanted nothing except to win every day. Durocher and Arthur Mann, Mr. Rickey's assistant, came into the clubhouse and passed along those messages to us. It helped to make me feel a part of the team even though I had made such a meager contribution.

During the season I had become friendly with a girl named Beverly Feinberg. That summer my parents had made their first and only visit to Brooklyn to see me pitch. I warned Beverly about my parents' views, and she understood. When I introduced her to my parents, my mother said, "What did you say her last name is?" Everything was fine until we got back to the hotel, then she started in on me. "How can you do that, a nice Irish Catholic boy like you, and this Jewish girl . . . " I'll never forget that. I loved my parents dearly, but I could never understand what that was all about. Nothing came of Beverly and me, but that had nothing to do with it. What would my mother think now if she had been here to see me made an honorary Jew by Temple Har Sinai in Baltimore in 1991, with my own handmade yarmulke, in appreciation of the many times I have appeared there as a speaker?

In the fall Chuck Dressen put together a barnstorming team: Ralph Branca, Eddie Stanky, Frenchy Bordagaray, and me, Buddy Kerr, Sid Gordon, and Willard Marshall from the Giants, and some players from other teams. We played some black teams in Brooklyn and Newark; that was my first look at Roy Campanella and Monte Irvin.

Dressen had arranged some games for us in Cuba, so we got on this DC-3 with two little propellers beating the wind and headed right into a hurricane off South Carolina. We were supposed to land in Miami. No way. We turned around and landed in Jacksonville. It was the most violent flight I ever had. We were all sick, white as sheets when we got off, swearing never to leave the ground again. And then, on top of all that, when we taxied out to take off again, both the engines quit, right there on the runway.

When we finally got to Cuba, the island was a mess from the hurricane. But absolutely nothing on earth will keep the Cubans from a baseball game. We played some amateur teams and beat them every game. It was boring, so, to liven things up, Frenchy decided to start a fight with the home plate umpire. It was just a joke. He fussed and raved and pushed the poor ump back toward the stands. Well, you just don't treat umpires that way in Cuba. The fans went berserk. They were climbing the screen and pouring out of the stands bent on tearing us apart. We needed a police escort to get out of there alive.

When we trained in Cuba the next spring, the umps could call my perfect pitches a ball every time and they wouldn't hear a peep out of me. I had discovered there were actually places in this world where they took their baseball as seriously as they did in Ebbets Field.

TEN

Baseball's Noisiest Year

I SPENT THE WINTER of 1946–47 in Omaha, taking some courses at Creighton University and working in the post office, but mostly just existing until I could go to my first spring training.

I had spent no time with my family after my discharge, and this was the first chance we had to visit. When I told my war stories about my minor wounds, my brother, who had enlisted in the Marines, sat there and listened. Then when he started talking I felt like an idiot. He had been in the South Pacific, got shot up at Guadalcanal, had malaria and jungle rot. He had come back and gone to work for the railroad and settled into a quiet life in Omaha. Later, when I pitched in the World Series and became a big local hero, it tore us apart. Maybe there was some jealousy; I don't know. But in recent years we have become closer, and we visit in Florida during spring training every year.

Right after the first of the year I took the train to New York and the Dodgers flew us to Havana, Cuba. In those days flying was an adventure, a rough ride on a prop plane. But I was on my way to heaven. That was the first time we had reason to thank Jackie Robinson for something. Robinson was still on the Montreal roster, but Mr. Rickey did not want him exposed to the segregation laws of Florida, so both Brooklyn and Montreal trained in Cuba. We stayed at the magnificent Nacional Hotel, first class all the way. The Montreal club trained at a military school nearby. We played some practice games against them and a Cuban team, and the Yankees dropped in for a few games. We flew to Puerto Rico, Panama, and the Dominican Republic to play exhibition games. It was our visit to the Dominican Republic that helped to spark the big interest in baseball in that country.

I was determined to make the team, because now I could be sent down to the minor leagues without waivers, and I did not want to go down. Hall of Famer George Sisler worked long hours with me. He knew pitching and hitting equally well. A quiet, patient, perfect gentleman at all times, he must have been an oddity in the rough days when he played.

One of the things we worked on was instilling in the pitcher an instinctive reaction to break toward first base on any ball hit to the first base side of the infield, even a pop fly, in case he had to cover the base or back up a play. A game might be lost by a pitcher failing to cover first promptly, and when you'd been in a pennant race that ended in a a dead heat, you appreciated the difference one game—one play—can make.

We practiced the daylight pickoff play: If the pitcher saw the shortstop had edged to the right of a base runner leading off second, he turned and threw to the base.

We worked on this play that Eddie Stanky designed: If a batter singles to right and makes a big turn at first base, the pitcher circles behind him to first base while the first baseman goes into short right field, lulling the batter into making a wider turn. Furillo would throw to the pitcher covering first instead of throwing to second, which the hitter expected him to do. One day Alvin Dark got a hit and I followed behind him to first. Furillo threw a bullet to me and I tagged Dark out when he made the turn toward second. He moaned, "Oh, no."

It takes a right fielder with a rifle arm and a deceptive move to complete that play. Jesse Barfield could do it today. Dwight Evans could have done it.

Here's another Stanky innovation: With runners on first and second and no outs, a double play grounder to short, the throw to second for one—and instead of relaying to first as expected, Stanky would throw to third and catch the runner rounding third in anticipation of a throw to first. He might use it three or four times a year, but I heard him called more names than you can imagine when it worked. I have rarely seen anyone else make that play.

When Eddie Stanky was on your team, you loved him. When he played against you, you hated him. Mr. Rickey summed him up perfectly: "He can't run, he can't throw, he can't hit. He just beats you."

Stanky played on championship teams in Brooklyn, Boston, and New York. A feisty bantam rooster, he would do anything to win. If he saw you looking into the stands, waving to your wife, game not even started yet, he'd snarl, "The game's out here. You only got two hours. Give it all you got." It didn't matter if you were a big star or a nothing. "The game's out here. Give it all you got."

Once Jackie Robinson popped up to the pitcher for the third out in an inning, and he started to walk to his position at first base. Stanky gave him hell. "No wonder it took you so long to get to the major leagues. You don't even know how to play the game. Run to your position."

At the plate he bent over in a severe crouch, pulled his pants up so the belt was high, trying to finagle a base on balls. If he drew a walk, without looking he threw the bat down on the catcher's feet and ran to first base. That hurts. He did it to any catcher; he didn't care who it was. The next year Stanky was traded to Boston and Bruce Edwards was catching and I was pitching against him and I walked him. Stanky threw the bat down on Bruce's feet. Nice, quiet Bruce never said a word. He waited until Stanky got halfway to first base, picked up the bat, and sailed it as hard as he could. It hit Stanky behind the knees and down he went. "Don't ever do that again," Bruce yelled. From then on, whenever Bruce was catching and Eddie walked, that bat went fifty feet over everything, as far from Bruce's feet as he could throw it.

Sliding gloves had not been invented, so players used to pick up handfuls of dirt to remind them not to put their hands down when they slid. After they slid into a base they dropped the dirt. Not Stanky. He would slide into second and throw the dirt up into the second baseman's or shortstop's eyes. Connie Ryan punched him out one night for doing that.

In the field Stanky would stand behind second base doing calisthenics to break the hitter's concentration. They passed a rule to stop that activity.

That was Eddie Stanky. Do anything to beat you. A good guy to have on your side, but you hated him when he was against you. A real winner.

One of the daily observers at our training camp in Havana was Ernest Hemingway, who owned a palatial estate nearby. He often invited a bunch of us to his mansion for dinner, where he would get roaring drunk and tell us about his bullfighting and boxing exploits. A big, blustery guy, he loved Leo Durocher and was a gracious, generous host, but he seemed to me to go overboard with everything. One night he wanted to put on boxing gloves and spar with Hugh Casey, but he was too drunk to spar with anybody.

During one intrasquad game I struck out nine in a row. Eight of the nine said to Leo, "This guy's really got it." But one guy said, "I'd like to make a living hitting against him." That one was Duke Snider, a brash kid who made a pretty good living hitting big league pitching.

Jackie Robinson did not work out with us; he was still on the Montreal roster. But we began to hear rumors that he would be joining us. We could not imagine where he would play; he was a second baseman and a shortstop, and there was no way he could replace either Reese or Stanky.

Near the end of spring training Durocher decided that Jackie would join the Dodgers and play first base, a new position for him. That impressed me greatly; I have a lot of respect for any player who can make an adjustment like that, especially in his first season in the major leagues.

Some individuals griped about playing with a black man— Stanky, Bragan, Dixie Walker—but there has been a lot of exaggeration about dissension and team meetings and votes and all that protest and conspiracy stuff. Walker was the only one who wrote a letter to Mr. Rickey asking to be traded, a request he later tried to rescind. Mr. Rickey promised to trade him to a last-place club after the season, and he kept that promise.

And then a bigger bombshell hit us. Commissioner Happy Chandler suspended Durocher for a year for associating with gamblers. Not gambling, mind you, not betting on games, or anything else. Sure, we knew of gamblers hanging around the clubhouse. But Leo had disassociated himself from them after

Chandler had warned him about it. Then it came out that it was Larry MacPhail of the Yankees who had arranged for the box seats for some gamblers at an exhibition game we played with them in Havana, and not Leo. That was supposedly the big evidence and it was a bum rap all the way and we knew it. Even the guys who did not like Leo agreed that he did not deserve what he got.

But this all happened at the tail end of spring training and we didn't even hear about it until we were back in Brooklyn. The Dodgers held an annual banquet at the St. George Hotel the night before opening day. Leo and his wife, Laraine Day, were there. Mr. Rickey stood up and defended Leo. "Let he who is without sin cast the first stone," he said.

Leo, devastated, met with us and tearfully swore that he had never gambled. We were his team, no matter who took over his office. At the end of the year we voted him a full World Series share, but Chandler vetoed it.

Jackie Robinson had not traveled north with us. He made his debut at Ebbets Field on April 11 in our city series with the Yankees. Our clubhouse man didn't even give him a locker at first, just hammered a nail in the wall for him to hang his clothes. It was pathetic. In the clubhouse before the game, I went over to Jackie and said, "I wish you a lot of luck. I'm glad you joined us." That's all. Nothing profound. I did that with every new player. Others did it, too. We didn't think anything more about it.

Pete Reiser remembered seeing Jackie watching our team practice when we were all stationed at Fort Riley in 1943. Jackie had tried to join the team but was denied a chance because of his color. I did not recall seeing him there.

Mr. Rickey had arranged for Sam Lacy, a sportswriter for the Baltimore *Afro-American*, to travel with us and room with Jackie in private homes in some cities. Later Lacy told me that I had been the first player to go to Jackie and give him a warm welcome. Sam also told me that the Red Sox could have signed Jackie, but Tom Yawkey did not want him.

When we walked into the clubhouse on opening day, we had no manager. Clyde Sukeforth ran the team for the first two games, which we won. We did not know who Burt Shotton was until Sukey told us about him: an outfielder with the St.

Louis Browns when Mr. Rickey managed that team, later a coach at Cleveland, then a scout. As our manager, Shotton, like Connie Mack and a few others, did not wear a uniform.

Some of us really missed Leo. We felt sorry for Sukeforth having to do all the dirty work for Shotton. As far as I was concerned, there was a sort of vacuum. I never cottoned to kindly old Burt. We just never got along. I didn't like him and he didn't like me. I needed the Durocher type of fire-eating manager. That's no excuse for how things turned out. It's just the way things were.

One day I was pitching and Johnny Mize was the batter and Sukeforth came out to the mound.

"Shotton says to pitch him high and outside."

"Last time up I struck him out pitching him low."

"Well, *he* says to pitch him high."

I threw a low fastball and Mize popped it up.

After the game Shotton called me into his office. "What did Sukeforth say to you when he went out to the mound with Mize at bat?"

I said something flip, like, "Oh, was Sukeforth out there?"

Of course I knew he'd been out there, and I would never have spoken to Leo Durocher that way. That's what I mean about something missing between us.

Another thing that was missing from the clubhouse was the pool table. A piano replaced it. Bobby Bragan banged that old upright and we had singalongs instead of cue sticks.

That spring was the first time I saw the old joke pulled, asking a new batboy to get the key to the batter's box so we could begin batting practice. It might have been Cookie Lavagetto who did it, and I think the batboy was Stanley Strull, who later became an FBI agent. They still pull that joke at some ballpark every spring.

I started that season with great expectations. I had a full year in the big leagues behind me, worked hard in my first spring training; and I just knew I was going to have a big year. I did not get to pitch much during the first month, but it quickly became evident that 1947 would be an unbelievable year. I saw some things that opened my eyes, and it was not very pleasant.

Everywhere we went there were throngs of people. The hero worship of Jackie Robinson by blacks was unreal. Jackie was totally embarrassed when they crowded around trying to get close to him. He would wait for all of us to get on the team bus, then dash out to get on. If a group of black fans at a game started to make a lot of noise, he wanted to hide. He was happy when that first season was over and he could be perceived as a player and not as a freak, as he put it.

Many players came from the South, where their upbringing dictated their attitudes. Jackie took a fierce riding in every city. The Phillies, led by their manager, Ben Chapman, were the first barrage we ran into. Chapman had been a speedy outfielder with the Yankees and a base stealer. He was the kind of guy who got on everybody. He did not usually coach third base, as many managers did, but when we came to town, he was out there. He'd get on me: "I'd like to be running against you. Christ sake, I'd be on third base before you could turn around." Stuff like that. I never heard a good word about him from any of his players.

So when we showed up with Jackie, that was like pouring gasoline on an already blazing fire. Chapman had the whole team, even Maje McDonald, the batting practice pitcher, calling Jackie every name in the world. When Chapman called Pee Wee Reese a nigger lover, Pee Wee put his arm around Jackie and said to Ben, "This is my boy," and all hell broke loose. But Jackie, who had promised Mr. Rickey he would keep his temper under wraps, kept quiet, and we never worried about Pee Wee being able to handle anything.

In Pittsburgh the Pirates refused to go on the field for a game against us, until they were given five minutes to get out there or forfeit the game.

In St. Louis, Country Slaughter was said to be the leader of the Cardinals who did not want to take the field. Stan Musial ended that revolt when he said, "I don't know about you guys, but I'm going out to play." That still didn't stop Slaughter. He hit a ground ball and was out at first easily. But crossing the bag he stepped on Jackie's calf and cut him. It was absolutely intentional.

Jackie was fuming, and when he got on base he said to Musial, "I'm going to get somebody."

Musial said, "I don't blame you; you ought to." Well, that took some of the steam out of Jackie.

A couple years later Jackie got even. Slaughter slid into second and Jackie tagged him in the mouth with the ball so hard it cost Country a few teeth.

The Cubs showed some meanness, too. Their first base coach, Roy "Hardrock" Johnson, was an antiblack Oklahoman who happened to wear number 42, the same as Jackie. You think we didn't remind him of that? "Hey, Roy, nice to see you're wearing Jackie's number!" We could see him boiling mad, the veins in his neck bulging.

They had a big right-hand sidearm pitcher, Paul Erickson, the kind of guy who would throw at Jackie every time at bat, and call him every negative black name from the mound. That type of thing turned me off.

Russ Meyer, now a Yankees coach, was pitching for the Cubs one day. Jackie was on third, dancing up and down the line like he always did. I heard Meyer yell, "You black sonofabitch, you'll never steal home against me." Next pitch Jackie lit out and made it easily. He was not the fastest runner, but he was the quickest, unlike Reiser, who was both fast and quick.

There used to be microphones hanging on the screen back of home plate to pick up crowd noise for radio. When they started riding Jackie with all that nasty language, the mikes picked it up and that was the end of the crowd noise mikes.

In the spring of 1992 I appeared before a state legislature committee in Maryland to lobby for money for the Babe Ruth Museum in Baltimore. But the black legislators, and some white ones too, were more interested in hearing about Jackie Robinson. Occasionally a black player asks me what it was like. What can I tell them? How can I describe what it was like?

I use my war experience as a metaphor. I was overseas like a lot of guys, got shot a couple times, saw things I never wanted to see. You come back when it's over and your family and friends want to know what you went through. You tell them, but they don't understand.

There's a town in France called St. Lo. The Germans and Americans captured and recaptured it back and forth. By the time I rode through it in a tank there wasn't a single building left standing except for a lone church steeple. All the rest was absolute rubble. You tell people and they say, "That must have been terrible." But they don't really understand.

You can't explain sleeping in mud, scared to death the whole time. There's no way anybody can grasp those things unless they've been there. And so there is no way anybody can really know or understand what Jackie Robinson experienced. All I can say is, we learned more from Jackie about being a man than he ever learned from us.

The only problem I ever had with Jackie was when I picked up one of his bats. He was one of the first I saw who had a batting practice bat and a game bat. Woe to anybody who touched that game bat. Pitchers never had their own bats and the hitters hated it when a pitcher used one of their bats to take BP. I've seen players chase pitchers all over the field for breaking a favorite bat. It was all in fun but it was half-serious, too.

About a month after the season started, when Jackie was not in the clubhouse, Pee Wee said to us, "Guys, we finished close in '46. With this guy, we can win."

Reese was a real captain in its true meaning. We all went to him for everything and looked up to him for his leadership. He played sick and he played hurt. He knew there were a bunch of guys trying to take his job every spring, but they never had a chance. Every year he would give one of us pitchers a new glove to use and break in for him, and the next year he would use that glove. It was an honor and a privilege to perform that service for him.

Before I got into my first game in 1947 I got married. I had known Beverly Duda since high school in Omaha, and our families knew each other. During the winter I had spent some time with her, and I asked her to come to New York with her mother. We were married on May 1 in a Catholic church in Brooklyn. Some of the players had a party for us at an Italian restaurant, the Gondola, and they gave us a silver bowl. We rented a small efficiency apartment with a bed that unfolded out of a couch. Like me, she soon got caught up in all the excitement and nightlife of New York.

The Dodgers were a confident, winning team: Robinson, Stanky, Reese, Spider Jorgensen, and Arky Vaughan in the infield; Walker, Furillo, Reiser, and Gene Hermanski in the outfield. Bruce Edwards did most of the catching. A rookie catcher, Gil Hodges, spent most of the season sitting in the bullpen with me, and caught a few of my games. Ralph Branca was winning 21 games, and Joe Hatten, Vic Lombardi, and Harry Taylor did most of the pitching.

A word about Carl Furillo is in order. Carl threw all-out every time and had the strongest and most accurate arm I ever saw. Infielders would catch his throws backing up. But he was a strange fellow. One day I was in the clubhouse when he came in late. I said, "How come you're so late?"

"Mr. Rickey wanted to see me."

"What about?"

"Promise you won't tell anybody. He gave me a $1,500 bonus. Do you think I have to tell the IRS about it?"

I told him he had to claim everything on his tax return.

"But Mr. Rickey told me not to tell anybody. And I promised I wouldn't. So why do I have to tell them?"

I don't know if he ever declared it, but he is beyond their reach now.

I did not make a big contribution to the team that year, doing mostly mop-up relief, but I did start 9 games and was 3–2 in them, and picked up 2 more wins in relief.

On May 12 I was thrown out of a game for the first time, but only as part of a mass bench-clearing by umpire George Magerkurth. We were all over him for his work behind the plate; when he had enough he swept the dugout clean. Generally I had a good reputation with the umps and got thrown out on my own just twice. The first time I had Peanuts Lowrey picked off at second base on one of those daylight plays and ump Beans Reardon called him safe. I ran at Reardon and accidentally ran into him and almost knocked him over. I was gone immediately for that.

The other time I was pitching against Hank Greenberg at Ebbets Field with the bases loaded and 2 outs. On a 3 and 2 count I threw my best curve right over the plate and ump Lou Jorda called it a ball. Hank told me later he was fooled by the pitch and it was a strike. Well, I called Jorda every cussword I had learned from Durocher and got the thumb.

I pitched three scoreless innings in relief on May 23 and got my first win as the Dodgers rallied to beat the Phillies, 5 to 4. That earned me a start on May 30 in Boston against Warren

Spahn. Although I got knocked out in a 4-run seventh and lost the game, I got the biggest hit of my career when I doubled to drive in a run in the second, then scored to tie the game at 2–2. I still kid Spahn about that double, but I assure him that it has nothing to do with my ranking him as the greatest pitcher I ever saw.

Actually, we pitchers were not the automatic outs that advocates of the designated hitter make us out to be. I got some hits off some pretty good pitchers—Cooper, Blackwell, Spahn— and drove in a few runs. I had been a pretty good hitter in high school and Legion ball. I tell people as a home run hitter I was 3 for 9. What I don't tell them is, that means I hit 3 home runs in nine years.

We loved our batting practice as much as the hitters, but it is true that as hitters we did not get much respect. One day I was at the plate in a game and Beans Reardon was the umpire. Beans was a colorful guy; in a slow monotone he would call balls and strikes: "Ball one, gentlemen . . . two balls, two strikes, gentlemen, let's go, hurry it up . . . " always in the same flat tone. Well, on this occasion he called, "Strike three, you're out," in that monotone, on a pitch that was two feet outside.

I said, "Beans, Christ sake, if you gave me those pitches I'd throw nothing but strikes."

He said, "What difference does it make? If it was down the middle, you couldn't hit it anyway. Go sit down."

Those umpires had an answer for everything.

The weirdest day I ever saw in baseball was June 3, 1947. The Pirates were at Brooklyn for a doubleheader. We won, 11 to 6 and 8 to 7, and I was the winning pitcher in both games. There were 32 runs scored, 45 hits for 68 total bases—and it took only 5 hours 16 minutes to complete *both* games.

I started the first game and went out for a pinch hitter in the sixth with a 6–4 lead. Hugh Casey finished up. In those days you took a shower after pitching the first game and put on a clean uniform and came back to the bench.

Shotton said to me, "Can you give me an inning or a couple hitters if I need it?"

I said, "Sure."

Preacher Roe started the second game for Pittsburgh against Hal Gregg. In the second we loaded the bases with 2

outs and Gregg lifted a pop fly near third base. Whitey Wietel-
mann dropped it; with 2 outs everybody was running and
everybody scored. (No wonder Preacher worshiped the Dodgers'
defense when we got him a year later.) Then, when Billy Cox
doubled for the Pirates, Duke Snider's throw from the outfield
hit Cox on the head as he slid into second base. He was so dazed
he failed to score on Greenberg's single. (Cox was happy to come
to Brooklyn with Roe.)

After Gregg, Rube Melton, and Clyde King were roughed
up, Shotton sent me to the mound. I pitched the last four
innings, gave up 1 run, and was credited with the win.

It's hard for young pitchers today to believe that we worked
like that. But we didn't think anything of it.

When I started a game, I would often breeze along for five,
six, seven innings, then hit a wild streak or get clobbered. The
farthest I went was into the eighth at Philadelphia on June 30,
working on a shutout until I blew up and 4 runs scored before
I could get anybody out. I escaped with my fifth and last win,
7 to 4.

Later *Sports Illustrated* ran a big story about me, quoting
Bobby Bragan about my attitude: "[Rex] would hold them to
maybe two hits for six innings, then walk three or four and out
he came. Do you think it bothered him? After the game he'd be
standing there combing his hair and admiring his tie and say,
'I had a pretty good day, didn't I?'"

Well, I can understand that. I probably did say something
like that. If you go from doing nothing to pitching six good
innings, you're bound to feel pretty good about it. Of course, in
those days, it didn't mean anything if you didn't win. Nobody
had ever heard of "quality starts."

And then there were days like June 22, when I started against
Ewell Blackwell of the Reds, who had just pitched a no-hitter. I
was gone in the second inning; his bid for a second straight
no-hitter survived until he gave up 2 singles in the ninth.

Again Bragan on Barney: "[One day] I was warming up Rex
and he threw the ball a dozen feet over my head. He was looking
at some friends in the stands and thinking about some new
clothes or something. I walked over to him and said, 'Rex, I
could throw at you all day and I wouldn't miss you like that.'
Rex said, 'Aw, I was just not bearing down.'"

That sounds as if I wasn't working hard or taking my pitching seriously, and I don't buy that. I was always the first on the field and the last off. I ran miles, worked with anybody who tried to help me. But I can understand how somebody would get that impression of me by seeing me pitch that year.

The Dodgers' lead stretched to 7 games by the end of July. One day about that time Shotton called me into his office.

"You can go home for the rest of the year if you want to," he said.

I was stunned. The words went through me like a knife in my heart. I didn't know what he meant.

"Take the rest of the year off," he went on, "and report in the spring. The club will pay you for the whole year."

I said nothing. Except for Reese, I think I was the oldest player in point of service on the team. When I walked out of there I was confused, shocked, disheartened. How would you feel if your team was winning and the manager told you to get lost, we don't need you?

My wife and I talked it over, but we did not know what to do. I went to Dixie Walker and asked his advice. He told me to stay put, just do nothing, and see what happened.

What happened was, for the rest of the season I resembled a spear carrier in an opera, except that I was carrying a mop, cleaning up in 12–4 and 16–2 losses. So it came as a genuine shock to me and to the rest of the caring world when Shotton picked me to start Game 5 of the World Series against the Yankees.

ELEVEN

1947 World Series

WE DID NOT ACTUALLY WIN A GAME to clinch the 1947 pennant. The Dodgers had a day off while St. Louis split a doubleheader that eliminated them. But even if we had clinched it on the field, there would not have been any champagne pouring over people's heads, which I think is an idiotic, asinine thing to do. I blame television for all that stuff. Sure, we celebrated, and maybe there was some champagne, and maybe we took a swig, but that was all.

In those days the first four teams in each league shared in the World Series receipts, with the two winners of course getting the biggest pot to split. The voting on World Series shares took place in a closed meeting, no coaches or manager allowed. Pee Wee Reese ran our meetings each year in the tiny manager's office, players squatting on the floor, sitting on the furniture, standing wherever they could find room. The league office sent us printed ballots, listing all the regulars who were entitled to automatic full shares. We could vote full or fractional shares for players who had been with us part of the season: batboys, clubhouse men, trainers, the road secretary, guys like that. Every vote had to be unanimous. Most of the players who had been with us for a few months got at least a three-quarters share. The kids might get a quarter- or half-share.

One thing was certain in a Dodgers' meeting. No matter who was being discussed, we'd hear Carl Furillo from the back of the room: "Give 'em ugatz." Give 'em nothing. We had to do some persuading to get him to change his mind, but every discussion began with, "Give 'em ugatz."

What a thrill it is just to be on a team in a World Series. Anybody who tells you it's just another ball game is a liar. The Series opened at Yankee Stadium on September 30. We met at Ebbets Field and carpooled behind a police escort through Brooklyn, over the bridge to Manhattan, and up to the Bronx. We dressed and had a big meeting with Wid Matthews, our advance scout. I remember one thing he said, "You can run and take the extra base on Joe DiMaggio. I've been watching the way he throws; he must have a bad arm." Well, we soon found out he had the arm when he needed it.

Then we walked through the tunnel to the dugout and I saw the sky and came out into that magnificent ballpark and all of a sudden there was a lot of noise and cheering by the vendors and ushers, as Joe DiMaggio strode majestically to the batting cage. We hung around it watching him hit, not saying a word.

Every hitter hitches a little bit. A slight dip, something. Not him. He had that wide right-hand stance and hardly moved his left foot before he swung. He must have been very strong, to need so little momentum. Tommy Henrich told me that during spring training they'd put a dime on the end of his bat and bet that the dime would drop straight to the ground every time he swung. Every hitter has some triggering or cocking movement before the pitch. Watch them. They all do. But not DiMaggio.

He was magnificent to watch, the smoothest player I have ever seen. Red Smith wrote: "People should pay to watch him run to and from his position."

Yogi Berra told me when he first came up to New York and was playing right field, he struck out to end an inning. Head down, he was walking out to right field and he felt somebody brush by him. It was DiMaggio. As he jogged by, Joe said to Yogi, "Kid, in the major leagues we run; we don't walk." Class.

A few of our guys had been in a World Series before, but most had not. We walked around Yankee Stadium thinking: This is where Babe Ruth stood; this is where Lou Gehrig played; this is where Lefty Gomez stood on this mound. Awesome experience.

105

It turned out to be one of the weirdest, most memorable of all World Series, and not because it went seven games. They won two, then we won two, they won one, then we won one, and they won the last. Hugh Casey worked in six of them and got two wins. Lefty Joe Page relieved in four for the Yankees, and shut us down with one hit over the last five innings to win the deciding game. Floyd Bevens's no-hitter blew up in his face and the impassive DiMaggio kicked the dirt in disgust when he was robbed of a home run. And the 22-year-old kid from Omaha got into three games.

In the opener my buddy Ralph Branca was shelled for 5 runs in the fifth and took the 5–3 loss. The next day the Yankees ripped Lombardi, Gregg, and Behrman for 10 runs before Shotton sent me in with 1 out in the seventh. I gave up a hit and a walk in 1⅔ innings and was the only pitcher who was not scored on in the 10–3 loss.

Back in Brooklyn we gave Joe Hatten a 6–0 lead after two, but he couldn't hold it and Casey picked up the victory, 9 to 8.

Harry Taylor started Game 4 for us, pitched to 4 men, and got none of them out. Hal Gregg took over and pitched seven innings and left trailing, 2 to 1. Ralph Branca and I were sitting on the bench. We knew Bevens had a no-hitter going, but he had walked 8, 2 of them leading to our 1 run. With 1 out in the last of the ninth, Furillo walked. Jorgensen fouled out, and Bevens was 1 out away from the first World Series no-hitter in history. Al Gionfriddo went in to run for Furillo and Shotton sent Pete Reiser up to hit for Casey. Pete had hurt his ankle and could hardly walk, and it showed. As he took a pitch, Gionfriddo dashed for second. Rizzuto caught the throw just above his waist and made the tag as Al slid in safely. If the throw is down, Al is out and the game is over. Just that split second made all the difference in the world on that play and in the outcome. That's why this game is so marvelous.

With first base open now, Yankees manager Bucky Harris ordered Reiser walked intentionally. On the bench we were saying, "What's he doing?" We couldn't figure it out. We knew Pete couldn't run and it was obvious, but we also knew he would do anything he had to, to win. He was the kind of guy who would get hit by a pitch—"take one for the team"—if it would help.

Harris was also criticized later for breaking one of the so-called baseball commandments: Never put the winning run on base.

As the wide pitches were made to Pete, Shotton got Eddie Miksis up to run for Reiser, then said to Sukeforth, "Get Lavagetto."

Sukey yelled down the bench, "Get Cookie ready; he's going to hit next." Meanwhile, Stanky, who was about to be pinch-hit for, was screaming in protest. But he yelled a lot anyhow, so nobody paid any attention.

Now, to fully appreciate this scene, you have to know something about Cookie Lavagetto. We all loved Cookie very much, but he was the sloppiest man I have ever known. His white uniform would be covered with polka dots of tobacco juice within five minutes. His feet always bothered him and he sat with his shoes off, pants legs drooping. At this point he was sitting down in the runway in back of the dugout, shoes off, feet up, half asleep.

So when Sukeforth yelled, "Get Cookie ready," Branca and I jumped up and said, "Come on, Cookie, you're gonna hit."

"What?" he asked.

"Let's go, Cookie," and Ralph and I and a couple other guys put him together, tucked in his shirt, got his shoes on his feet.

Then Cookie walked up to the plate and hit a double off the right field wall and Gionfriddo and Miksis raced home and the no-hitter went up in smoke and the game was ours. Cookie's hit was one of my biggest thrills, and the celebration that followed in the clubhouse was the biggest and most jubilant I ever saw as a player. We hoisted Cookie on our shoulders a half dozen times for the photographers, but it was genuine, not staged.

We had used fourteen pitchers in the first four games and our arm supply was exhausted. I suppose that had a lot to do with Shotton's decision, which I knew nothing about until I showed up at Ebbets Field on the morning of the fifth game. Sukeforth came over to me and said, "You okay?"

"Sure, I'm fine. Why?"

"You're starting today."

"Oh."

The newspapers had reported Vic Lombardi as the probable pitcher, and in fact we both took batting practice that day. Before the game I popped off to Arthur Daley of *The New York*

Times: "Walks don't always murder you. We had one game with St. Louis where Howie Pollet allowed 10 hits and gave 9 walks and he still won, 3 to 1."

I remember warming up that day and hearing people yelling, "Get that wild bum out of there." That's a real confidence builder. Then I was standing on the mound with my cap off and somebody sang "The Star-Spangled Banner" and I wound up and walked the leadoff man, Snuffy Stirnweiss. Henrich doubled off the right field wall and I walked Johnny Lindell on 4 pitches. Bases loaded, nobody out. Then Sukeforth was coming out of the dugout and here came Bruce Edwards toward me and I thought sure I was gone. But Sukey said, "We're going to leave you in. Nothing to worry about. Just strike out this bum and get the next one on a double play." I was too scared to say anything.

And Edwards said, "Let's start out this guy with a curve; you'll never get it over the plate anyhow."

This bum, this guy was only Joe DiMaggio.

Well, I did it. Struck him out swinging with pure speed. Then George McQuinn hit a comebacker to me and I threw home to force Stirnweiss, and I struck out Billy Johnson. The fans in Ebbets Field went berserk. All that cheering—for me—is still ringing in my ears.

In the second inning I walked Phil Rizzuto with one out, wild pitched him to second, but he was out trying to steal third. No damage.

In the third with 1 out I walked Henrich and Lindell and there stood the statuesque Yankee Clipper again. The count went to 3 and 1 and I may have been a wide one away from being yanked. But I got it over and DiMaggio grounded into a 6–4–3 double play.

In the fourth I walked 3 more and Spec Shea, the pitcher, scored one of them with a single, but Henrich grounded out to end the inning with only 1 run scored.

In the fifth I tried to throw another fastball by DiMaggio but he hit that one into the upper deck. When I gave up my ninth base on balls with 2 out, Shotton decided this was not the day to try for the record and sent Joe Hatten in to relieve me. We managed 1 run and that was the game, 2 to 1. If the Dodgers had done some hitting, I might have had a World Series victory and a world championship ring—*if.* But Floyd Bevens could use the same word, with a capital I.

The highlight of Game 6 was Al Gionfriddo's catch over the low bullpen fence that cost DiMaggio a home run with 2 on in the sixth. As often happens, a sensational catch resulted from a fielder's misjudging a ball. When the ball was hit, Gionfriddo started the wrong way and had to turn around. If he had been right-handed, his glove hand could not have reached the ball when he got to it. The fence was only three feet high and he was going to his right and stuck out the glove over it to make the catch. The film clip of DiMaggio kicking the dirt after the catch as he neared second base is probably shown more than any other photo of Joe. It was a rare display of emotion from the deadpan DiMag.

I pitched to one batter and got him out in the sixth inning of the final game, which we lost, 5 to 2, as Joe Page shut us down for five innings. Page, a lefty, was a fun-loving playboy who was the Yankees' ace reliever for a few years. The Yankees had detectives trailing him on the road, but Joe would spot them and get them drunk. Once they sent a lady detective to follow him and he wound up bedding her. Bill Roeder, a writer for the New York *World-Telegram,* told me he was with Page once when they returned from a trip and got off the train in New York. Joe's wife met him at the station. He said, "Honey, I want you to meet my friend, Bill Roeder. Bill, this is, ummmm, Mrs. Page." He had forgotten her name.

The losers' share of the World Series money came to $4,081.19 each. I bought my wife a mink jacket, and we bought a Chrysler convertible. I've never been a great one for holding onto money. We weren't exactly going Hollywood, but we sure went New York.

Here I was only 22 and already I had been in a World Series. In December *The Sporting News* sent me a biographical questionnaire for their files. After the question concerning my outstanding moments in baseball, I mentioned pitching in the Series, then added, "Just being in the major leagues is an everyday thrill."

But I felt terrible. I read where Joe DiMaggio said, "Rex Barney is the fastest pitcher I've ever seen, faster than Feller." Tommy Henrich said I belonged on another planet. Billy Johnson said, "He should be a much better pitcher than he is." Old-time first baseman Jacques Fournier, a scout for the St. Louis Browns who had been eager to sign me in 1943, said, "Rex Barney is faster than Feller and just about as fast as Walter Johnson."

I chewed on that stuff all winter. If guys of that magnitude think I'm that good, why am I not that good? And I concluded: It must be me.

TWELVE

That Wonderful Year: 1948

ONE NIGHT on my WBAL talk show a caller commented that players come to spring training in much better shape today than we did in the 1940s. I agreed, and went on to explain that players earning a million dollars or more with long-term contracts don't have to work during the winter. They can spend their time in backyard batting cages or weight rooms or cavorting on their private indoor basketball courts. Conditioning theories change, too. We were not allowed to go bowling, or to play golf during the season. Today you see golf clubs going to spring training with the rest of the equipment. As for weight lifting, we were taught that heavy muscles hindered free and easy swinging and throwing. An ideal pitcher's build was long, flat arm muscles. I believe that heavy muscles tear rotator cuffs, bones, and tendons when a player swings a bat or throws a pitch.

A few years ago I asked a player a dumb question in an interview: "What work do you do during the off-season?"

He said, "I work out."

In 1948 we sold clothes or cars or insurance or did public relations work selling season tickets or pumped gas to earn a living. All of us, including the big stars. When we finally got a $5,000 minimum salary passed, that meant a raise for a lot of players. And that's exactly what I signed for that year.

Nothing could drag my wife and me away from New York that winter. I got a job working in the sports department of Abraham & Strauss, a big department store in Brooklyn. I also made speaking appearances for them and for the Dodgers, and

I enjoyed that, meeting people and signing autographs. I have never minded signing as long as people are polite. It's a big ego booster as far as I'm concerned.

My job at A & S inspired one of Fresco Thompson's quips: "If they ever called a strike Rex Barney wouldn't know what they were talking about." It was Fresco, too, who said Brooklyn fans appreciated the papers announcing when I was going to pitch, so they could move their cars from Bedford Avenue back of the right field screen to save their windshields from being broken by home runs. Fresco was funny, but he really knew how to hurt a guy.

I earned $1,000 for appearing in a full-page ad for Chesterfield cigarettes on the back of *Life* magazine. I never smoked a cigarette in my life; the photographer smoked it down for me and stuck it in my hand.

Bowman bubble gum paid me $100 for putting me on a baseball card; it was black and white and little bigger than a postage stamp. People see it and say, "My God, you're so old, they didn't even have color." It's true. I'm not a souvenir collector, and I don't have any of them.

In January we flew to Ciudad Trujillo, the capital of the Dominican Republic, for spring training. Mr. Rickey wanted to spare Jackie Robinson and Don Newcombe, who was with the Montreal club, the indignities of Florida's treatment of blacks. The hotel was magnificent and the playing field was good, but the food was atrocious. The milk was warm, probably right out of the cow or goat or whatever. Mr. Rickey solved that by flying our food in from Miami. It was so hot we had to work out only in the morning and quit at noon.

Leo was married to Laraine Day; when we complained that there was no entertainment in the evening, she arranged with her Hollywood friends to have movies flown in for us. There were no players' wives allowed; when Pete Reiser's wife showed up, Mr. Rickey fixed that by sending Pete to the minor league camp at Vero Beach. He sent Duke Snider there, too, to learn the strike zone with George Sisler's help. At that time, if you got two strikes on Snider, he'd swing at anything.

Some players got sick; Eddie Stanky was in bed when they traded him to Boston for Ray Sanders. Stanky had never really adapted to playing alongside Jackie Robinson.

As for Jackie, he showed up fat and out of shape, and Durocher blew a gasket and was on him all the time. Jackie resented it, but there was no racial aspect to it. It was just a case of a great player reporting way out of shape, and Leo wouldn't stand for that from anybody.

My wife was in Omaha expecting our first child and I was determined to be the pitcher I should be. I asked Bobby Bragan to turn out early each morning to work with me. Cookie Lavagetto and Arky Vaughan offered to join us. They'd stand at the plate while I threw, making suggestions. I had all the help I wanted.

Mr. Rickey did not stand pat after winning the pennant in 1947. Far from it. The most important additions were Billy Cox and Preacher Roe, who came from Pittsburgh in the Dixie Walker deal. It looked like Preston Ward would solve our first base problem. A handsome kid with plenty of talent and a good glove, he did not do the job. The catching career of Gil Hodges ended when they handed him a first baseman's mitt and the job. Duke Snider was still a year away, but Roy Campanella came up from St. Paul in July when Bruce Edwards went out with a bad arm.

Preacher Roe was the epitome of a pitcher, just as Bret Saberhagen is today. He just flat-out knew how to pitch. A skinny guy, 6-1 and maybe 140 pounds, he couldn't throw hard enough to blacken your eye. He pitched like throwing darts: a little here, a little there, maybe throw 90–95 pitches in nine innings. All us big guys would go out there and throw hard and wear ourselves out throwing 140 pitches. He was fun to watch.

Roe had never been a winner, couldn't break into the Cardinals' lineup, and had a lousy team behind him in Pittsburgh. "When I got to Brooklyn," he said, "I couldn't believe all those line drives were being caught behind me." Shows you how a good defense can have as much to do with making a pitcher a twenty-game winner as a split-finger fastball.

A veteran catcher had taught Preacher how to throw the slider and the spitter while they sat in the Pirates' bullpen. The catcher was Al Lopez, and Preach became a very artful spitball pitcher.

But one guy who owned Roe was Stan Musial. One day Musial had been hitting everything Preacher threw up there, so when Stan came up to bat with the bases loaded and the count went to 3 and 2, Preach wound up and just lobbed the ball like a little girl. Musial's timing was thrown off so much he hitched and hitched and could not pull the trigger and took a called strike three.

Many a time I heard Preacher say, "If I get a guy 3 and 2, he's mine."

He was pitching in the Polo Grounds one day and I was sitting on the bench beside him and he said, "If we get to the ninth and I'm ahead and I get Mize 3 and 2, he belongs to me." And he gets Mize 3 and 2 and strikes him out. I'm listening to this stuff day after day and thinking: one pitch! I need all I can get and he's hoping to run the count to 3 and 2 so he can fan the guy on one pitch.

A hillbilly from the Ozarks, Roe played that role to the hilt. During the other team's batting practice, he'd stand behind the cage and you'd hear that southern drawl: "Get your bats ready, boys. Ol' Preach is pitchin' today. You know how you like to hit against Preach." He had nothing, and they all knew it and licked their chops, but at the end of the day he'd beat them and give up 4 or 5 hits.

I thought Crosley Field in Cincinnati was the hottest ballpark in the league. Others gave the honor to Sportsmans Park in St. Louis. We wore those heavy flannel uniforms. One day somebody weighed one after a doubleheader in St. Louis. Sweat-soaked, it weighed eighteen pounds. We were in Cincinnati one day and it was well over 100 degrees. People were passing out from the heat. Pee Wee soaked his shoes after every inning. Roe was pitching and it was 0–0 after nine and the Reds had used a few pitchers, but Preacher never broke a sweat. After every inning, Leo would say, "Hang in there, Preach, we'll get you a run." We go ten, eleven, twelve innings and Leo is still saying, "Hang in there, Preach, we'll get you a run." Finally Preach said, "You know something, Leo? I think you're shittin' me. We're never gonna get a run." But we eventually won it for him.

Billy Cox was another marvel. An introverted, emaciated little guy, he had been a good shortstop at Pittsburgh, but Mr. Rickey moved him to third base. Reese had been wearing himself out covering all the territory between second and third when

Cookie Lavagetto was there. But with Cox, Pee Wee was practically semiretired; he didn't have to go to his right for anything:

Cox had the most unbelievable arm you've ever seen. He threw out everybody—from Richie Ashburn to Ernie Lombardi—by one step. He'd stand there with the ball and drive everybody nuts, especially the pitchers. Hodges at first base would be yelling, "Throw the ball!" And Cox would stand there looking at it in his hand, counting the stitches, then shoot the runner out by that one step. And he never missed.

But Billy Cox had suffered some sort of shell shock in the army. He had terrible problems and seemed close to a nervous breakdown all the time. He could not play a day game after a night game, nor a doubleheader. He had a drinking problem but concealed it. He hung out with Preacher more than anybody, but was essentially a loner.

At the plate Cox looked the exact opposite of what you'd expect a major league player to look like: a hunched-over, frail, skinny guy. He had good power but swung at a lot of bad pitches. I guess the best way I can sum up Billy Cox for you is by saying that I have been teasing Brooks Robinson about him for twenty-five years. When Brooks was making all those marvelous plays in the 1970 World Series, he'd say to me, "Billy Cox is the only third baseman people compare me to. You played with him—what do you think?"

I'd tell Brooks, "Well, you might become as good as he was someday, if you practice."

After one of those games Brooks was surrounded by writers and he called me over. "Hey, Rex, how about my performance today? Was that as good as Billy Cox?"

I said, "No, Brooks, Billy Cox never dove for a ball. He'd catch them all standing up."

Then one day Pee Wee Reese was at the ballpark and Brooks asked him, "Say, Pee Wee, this guy Barney gives me a hard time about Cox. Was he really that good?"

Pee Wee said, "He wasn't the all-around player that you are, but he was some kind of fielder."

Billy and Brooks were different: built different, played different styles. Cox never threw a ball softly in his life. He gunned it. Brooks did not have a a strong arm; his throw might resemble a rainbow, but it got there in time. Brooks had quicker hands and first-step reflexes. But Billy Cox could fly, and he had more range. At the plate, Brooks had more consistent power. The first time you saw either of them, neither one looked anything like a big league ballplayer; Brooks a big lumbering guy, Billy a frail little fellow.

After his playing days, Billy Cox went back to Pennsylvania and worked as a bartender in an Elks Club in Harrisburg, lived upstairs over the bar, and died an alcoholic at fifty-nine. Can you imagine what kind of existence that was? Those things are tragic.

Gil Hodges and I became close while sharing space in the bullpen before he became a first baseman. We were two of the half-dozen Catholics on the club. We were flying from New York to Chicago on a Friday and Gil and I were sitting next to each other and they served us all steak dinners. I started to dig in and Gil said, "Are you gonna eat that?"

"Yeah, why not?"

"It's Friday."

"Gil, the priests will tell you that in an emergency, if meat is all the food you have, you can eat it."

"Yeah, I know, but I'm not going to eat it."

"Why not?"

He looked up toward the top of the plane. "We're too close to the head man, and He may not like it, and if you're going to eat it, I think I'll move."

He didn't eat any dinner that day.

As big and strong as he was, it's a good thing Gil Hodges was such a nice human being. Gentle and sensitive as they come. One day Branca was pitching and Bobby Adams, a little infielder, was on first. Ralph threw over to first and Adams slid back in headfirst. Hodges caught the ball, slapped the tag on Adams, hit him on the head, and knocked him cold. It probably hurt Gil more than Bobby.

When Gil was managing the Mets, he wanted to take left fielder Cleon Jones out of the game one day. He waved to Jones to come in and Jones shook his head. Hodges slowly walked out to left field and clamped a hand on Jones's arm and led him back to the dugout.

Gil was forty-seven when a heart attack killed him.

Carl Erskine broke in in '48; he was a little guy with a sharp overhand curve. A beautiful man, he bordered on being a hypchondriac. Something was always hurting him, but he'd go out and pitch us a great game. We thought if he was feeling good, it was better not to start him.

Erv Palica was another young hard-throwing pitcher who had enough basic stuff to win. But if a slider pitcher beat us one day, the next day Palica would be working on a slider. If a knuckle-baller beat us, Palica started fooling around with that. He should have stuck to the basics, but he had only one good year.

Bruce Edwards had been my favorite catcher in 1947, but he hurt his arm in an exhibition game at Folsom Prison in California. A stumpy little guy, he was built like Hack Wilson. I had confidence in him and the way he handled the game. You can tell when a catcher is not sure of himself. Some will give you a target, but when you start to wind up they'll relax and you lose the focus. The pitcher is not looking at the hitter, but at his catcher's target. Bruce was disciplined and would not let you shake him off. I'm glad Bruce got to catch my no-hitter.

I was lucky to have Roy Campanella come along to take Bruce's place during the season. There was nobody better with a catcher's mitt. Roy chewed tobacco during the game and spat that brown juice right through the mask. What a mess it was by the end of the game. And soon as the game was over, before he did anything else, he got rid of that chew and brushed his teeth. Then he took off his chest protector and shin guards. Darnedest thing I ever saw. Funny how you remember little things like that.

On the road I had trouble picking up Campy's signs, especially at night. The color of his fingers blended in with the dark road uniform. He understood, and told me in the Negro Leagues he used to put white tape on his fingers so the pitchers could read the signs. But he solved the problem for me this way: "Forget the fingers. I'll still put them down, but you ignore them. The last thing I touch with my hand will be your sign."

He might touch his mask, or chest, or his leg and each one meant a fastball, curve, or change-up. It worked.

The only knock I ever heard against Campy was that he was a curveball catcher. In a pinch he'd always call for a curve.

As a hitter he was quick and powerful. He used to say, "I hate that local (curveball), but when they throw me the express

I can get all over it. Nobody can throw the express by me, including you."

I asked him once, "What did you hit in the Negro leagues?" He said, ".365."

"How do you know you hit .365?"

He said, "We all did. We kept our own records."

These were the guys who formed the nucleus of the Dodgers pennant winners that followed.

From the Dominican Republic we went to Vero Beach for the first time. It was just a bunch of rundown barracks, an abandoned naval training base that Mr. Rickey paid the government one dollar or something to take off their hands. It was spartan living after those fancy hotels and we did not like it. But from that beginning grew the best spring training facility in the world.

We played our way north as usual, but with Jackie on the team this time it was *not* usual. He got all kinds of hate mail and there were some rough experiences. Our reception in Macon, Georgia, was typical. We dressed at the hotel and rode a bus to the park. Jackie and Sam Lacy, of course, had to stay somewhere else. They arrived in a car just as we pulled up. We all started to walk through the gate together and a big red-necked policeman stopped Jackie and Sam. "You two guys can't go in this gate. Can't you read?" He pointed to a "Whites Only" sign.

Durocher said to the cop, "How many people you expect here today?"

"A record crowd. Yes, sir, biggest ever in the state."

Leo said, "It won't be if those two guys don't come in with us. There won't be any game."

The cop backed down. Jackie and Sam walked past the "Whites Only" sign, and the walls did not come tumbling down.

Pee Wee Reese helped to ease the tension with a touch of humor. We were playing catch in front of the dugout before the game, Branca and I at one end, Pee Wee and Jackie at the other end. As the stands filled with people, Pee Wee said, "Jackie, how about going down there and trading places with Rex. When these people shoot and miss, I don't want to be near you."

We won twenty-five straight games that spring before the Yankees beat us in the opener of the city series. On Saturday,

April 17, at Ebbets Field I pitched the last two innings against them after Casey and Roe had worked. I struck out Joe Page, Stirnweiss, and Henrich in the eighth, walked Keller, then fanned DiMaggio in the ninth. Afterward, Henrich told a writer, "That young man throws like he's from another league. He shouldn't even be allowed here."

In *The New York Times,* Lou Effrat wrote: "Rex Barney has been Brooklyn's outstanding moundsman throughout the spring." Those things impressed me. I guess I impressed Leo enough for him to hand me the ball on opening day. All the more reason my early effort proved so disappointing to both of us.

We opened at the Polo Grounds on April 20 before 48, 130 fans. The Dodgers and Giants often drew a full house. They once packed 41,209 people into Ebbets Field, and the official capacity was 32,111. I always loved to pitch in the Polo Grounds with that endless center field. They could hit fly balls out there all day and never hurt me. After six innings I had given up 6 hits and walked 5 and was behind 3 to 1 when Leo lifted me for a pinch hitter during a 4-run rally that gave us the lead. Hugh Casey trudged in and we managed a 7–6 win for my first and last opening day victory.

Even more exhilarating was my first hit of the season. One of my big anxieties was getting that first base hit each year so I'd at least have an average, instead of being .000. It wasn't just the row of zeroes; we pitchers took a riding from our own bench. If I struck out, I'd hear it from Branca and Roe and the rest: "Jesus Christ, what a great swing you had," just dripping with sarcasm. Sure, I joined in and let them have it, too. If a fan gets on a player, the other players get upset and defend the target of the fan's abuse. But they can be brutal to each other.

One day Ralph Kiner hit a home run off me way up in the deepest part of Ebbets Field. When the inning was over, Branca and the rest were laughing. "Hey, you just broke a record for the longest home run in the history of Ebbets Field."

The next night Mr. Branca was pitching and Mr. Kiner hit a ball that just missed going over the roof. When Ralph came back to the bench, I said, "Well, my record didn't last long, did it?"

He threw his glove at me. "Shut up."

Younger American League fans who have never seen a pitcher swing a bat in a game except for a few World Series games may not understand this, but in my day pitchers loved to hit. We came out early and took our own batting practice, pitching to each other with kids shagging in the outfield. We worked on our hitting, especially bunting, and considered ourselves complete players. That feel of the bat making contact with the ball is something special. Today some American League pitchers enjoy coming out early and taking some cuts. But most of them never know the experience.

Talk about the strange things you remember; here's one that gave me a big thrill. Dumb thing, but it still stands out in my mind. I'm pitching against the Boston Braves one day at home and I come up with a couple men on base and I hear their manager, Billy Southworth, yell, "Don't forget, he's a pretty good hitter."

You know what that does for a pitcher's ego? No, you can't know unless you're a pitcher—in the National League. We had no-name pitchers' bats so we wouldn't break the real hitters' bats. Later I had my own model bat with my name on it. One year I won the Brooklyn pitchers' home run championship; hit 70 into the seats, all before noon.

I think the main reason pitchers can't hit better is that they don't have the time or the opportunity to hit every day against good batting practice pitchers throwing good stuff, or to see good pitching every day in games. But pitchers did and still do get hits that help win games, and they lay down key bunts or hit long fly balls to score a man from third. And once in a while a Dave McNally hits a grand slam in a World Series or a Mike Cuellar hits one in a playoff.

I hated to strike out, which I did 78 times while drawing 7 walks. Now, those would have been great pitching stats. But I hit .235 one year, .213 another. Guys today make a million for doing that. You can look it up.

Following my opening day high, things got a little rocky. In my next start I walked the first three batters in the third, then Lefty Sloat and Erv Palica walked four more, handing the Phillies four runs on no hits and Leo the symptoms of an ulcer. I lost, 3 to 2, in Boston, then on May 2 at Philadelphia I was coasting along with a 6–0 lead until the fourth, when it began to look as if I was going to walk everybody in the lineup and the telephone book, too.

Things looked brighter a week later when I worked four innings without a base on balls, went out for a pinch hitter, and had no decision. Then on May 15 I started against Warren Spahn, gave up a first inning home run to Jim Russell, and that was the game, 1 to 0. Twice they loaded the bases against me and I pitched out of it.

When you feel like you have great stuff and you go out there and right away some guy hits one out of the park, the first thing you think is maybe you don't have such good stuff after all. But you have to regroup and tell yourself, okay, that's one run. Now let's go to work on the next batter. I have warmed up thinking I had great stuff and been shelled in the first inning. When that happens, your pride tells you they must be getting the signs; they can't be teeing off like that on *me*. And I've pitched complete games when I had nothing. Don't tell me there's anybody who really knows this game.

On May 26 my daughter, Christine Louise, was born in Omaha, and Leo gave me 24 hours to go home to see her and my wife. At that point I thought I had it all together, but four days later the Cardinals kayoed me at Ebbets Field in a 14–7 slugfest. Stan Musial was his usual 5 for 5 that night, but not all of them were off me.

After another two-inning disaster against the Pirates, I didn't work for ten days, then pitched my best game 'til then, an eleven-inning 4–4 tie against the Giants that was called so both teams could catch trains to head west. It was my first complete game since 1946, and I would have won it except for my old nemesis, Whitey Lockman, who hit two home runs and drove in all four runs. The book on Whitey was to pitch him low, and I had gotten the ball up. Leo accused me of trying to pitch Whitey my way and just blow the ball by him, but I had just made two mistakes on those pitches. That's all. Still, I was in Durocher's doghouse.

About this time Hugh Casey tried to help me. Casey was the top relief pitcher of my era. He didn't have great stuff: a good sinker, sometimes a spitter, but great control, and he would knock you down as soon as look at you. He was the only pitcher Leo would allow to call all his own pitches. Bruce Edwards didn't care if Casey even saw the signs. He would infuriate Casey by telling him, "That stuff you throw isn't going to fool anybody, including me, even that spitter. So just go ahead and throw whatever you want, and I'll catch it."

After the sixth inning those of us in the bullpen would say, "Time for Hugh," and here he'd come out of the dugout, pushing that big fat belly. He owned the last three innings.

I was working out early one morning and he showed up. All he talked about to me was my feet. "I watch all you kids pitch," he said. "Your front foot never lands in the same place twice. Watch mine when I work. It never varies a fraction of an inch." I didn't believe it until I started watching him closely; he was right. Then I became aware that when I pitched, my front foot sometimes landed to the left, sometimes straight in front of me, sometimes to the right.

Another time he said to me, "I see you one inning pitching from the third base end of the rubber, and the next inning you're in the middle or the other end, all over the place. Find out what's most comfortable where you can throw strikes and stay there."

I didn't work for eight days, then started in Pittsburgh, walked two men, and Kiner hit a home run on a high fastball that brought Durocher on the run to the mound.

But when I was good I was at least pretty good, for a while. I gave up 1 hit in six innings against the Cubs, then blew up in the seventh, but escaped the loss. The same thing happened a week later when I took a 6–0 lead against the Pirates into the seventh, then lost the map to home plate. But this time I got the win.

I've often wondered how much I might have been responsible for the most momentous, astounding, unbelievable week in Brooklyn baseball history. One thing for sure, I was not contributing to the team or to Leo Durocher's physical or mental health.

We had pregame meetings to go over how the pitcher was going to pitch against certain hitters. For example, if Preacher Roe was starting, Leo would say, "We want you to pitch Musial outside. Stop him from pulling. Make him hit to the opposite field and we'll play him that way." And Preacher might say, "No, I'm going to pitch him inside. I want him to pull the ball. Swing around to right on him." And if Preacher said he was going to do that, he did it. Leo would listen to him. Do you think Leo would listen to me? Not in a hundred years. If I was starting, the meeting would go: "Rex is pitching. Get the ball over the plate." End of meeting. No inside, outside, up or down stuff. I just didn't think about that.

I had a good curveball, hardly any change-up, and a fastball that never went straight in its life. It exploded up and in on a right-hand batter. Gene Mauch says my fastball traveled the most explosive last six feet he ever saw, as if an afterburner kicked in just before it reached the plate. And because I was "conveniently wild," as Mr. Rickey put it, hitters hated to dig in against me. Somewhere along the line Bob Feller and I threw through a primitive timing device; it clocked both of us at more than 100 mph. Both Edwards and Campanella said I threw too hard. "Pitch like you do in batting practice," they said. But I thought if I did that in a game, the hitters would kill me. Try it, they said. But I guess it was difficult for me to do.

So Leo had just about given up on me, but Mr. Rickey had not. I did some mopping up, and then, on July 2, the Giants came to Ebbets Field. We had lost five in a row and were in last place, but only 10 games out of first. Durocher put three catchers in the lineup: Edwards at third, Hodges at first, and Campanella catching. We scored two in the eighth to take a 4–3 lead, and who does Durocher wave in from the bullpen to pitch the ninth? Me.

The first batter I faced was slugger Willard Marshall. I threw him a slow curve and he hit it into the seats to tie the game. A couple more hits and an intentional walk and I was out and Joe Hatten was in. Another run scored and we lost 6 to 4 and in the clubhouse Durocher was having a fit. "Throwing a slow curve to Marshall, with all the stuff that kid has!" plus assorted embellishments. He swore I would never pitch for him again. My record stood at 2 and 5, and as far as Durocher was concerned, it would stay that way.

Pee Wee tried to console me. "Hang in there. He changes his mind a lot. He's a big hunch man."

"Yeah," I said, "but you heard him." When Leo put you down, he did it in front of everybody.

Pee Wee was right. Three days later, in Philadelphia to play two, Leo said to me, "I don't want to do it, but I got nobody else, so you're starting the second game."

I pitched a complete game and won, 10 to 1, gave up 5 hits, walked only 4, and struck out 5. What's more, I was 2 for 4 and drove in a run. It was my first 2-hit game as a hitter.

Four days later I pitched a four-hitter in the Polo Grounds and won, 10 to 3, walking just 2 before a crowd of 50,819. The Giants could not hit me after the fourth inning.

The next day we beat them again and moved into fourth place, 2½ games out of third. But my—and the team's—revival apparently came too late to save Leo. Other forces were at work.

During the all-star game break we went to Montreal to play an exhibition game, while Durocher went to St. Louis to manage the National League team. Burt Shotton, then a scout for the Dodgers, was invited to throw out the first ball as the previous year's pennant winner.

Leo rejoined us in Cleveland, where we played the Indians before a packed house that came out to see Satchel Paige pitch for Cleveland. After the game, Leo announced that he was going to Montreal "to look over some players who might help the Dodgers." When we opened a western swing on July 15 in Cincinnati, coach Ray Blades was the acting manager.

Mel Ott was in Pittsburgh with the Giants, Leo was in Montreal, and Shotton was in St. Paul scouting a player. Leo flew to New York and, while I was beating Vander Meer, 5 to 3, for my third straight win, meetings were going on in New York that would shock the baseball world. There had been rumors for weeks that both Ott and Durocher were on the spot; as usual, the rumors were denied, and when it happened, it happened swiftly.

The next day Mr. Rickey flew to Cincinnati and the news came out. Mr. Rickey claimed that he never intended to fire Leo, but he had the impression that Leo had lost confidence in the team, and he was ready to accept Leo's "voluntary resignation." Leo and Jackie Robinson had never gotten along. It was nothing racial; their personalities clashed, and Jackie resented Leo's constant needling. Mr. Rickey saw that they would never get along, but he had to find a graceful way to resolve the situation. He knew that Horace Stoneham, the Giants' owner, wanted to dump Ott, so he offered to "make Durocher available" to the Giants.

Shotton flew to Cincinnati to take over the Dodgers, Durocher flew to Pittsburgh to join the Giants, Mel Ott flew away for a month-long vacation, and Mr. Rickey flew to Beaumont to look at a player.

There is no way I can put into words how earthshaking the news was in New York. People today cannot imagine how big a deal it was for Durocher, beloved in Brooklyn, to go to the Giants, the *Giants* of all people. It was as unthinkable as General Eisenhower jumping to the Germans, or President Bush switching to the Democrats, or George Will campaigning for Teddy Kennedy. But it happened. Giant fans, who looked down on Leo as the biggest, dirtiest bum in the world, swore they'd never go near the Polo Grounds again. Of course, Leo could charm a snake, and we all knew it was just a matter of time before that all changed.

Some of the Dodgers were glad to see him go, but I was devastated. I cried when he left. I was used to tough managers and I felt that I had begun to turn things around for him and now he was gone.

When Leo went, Laraine Day went with him. She had traveled with the team and often sat in on the hearts games as my partner against Jake Pitler and Pee Wee Reese. She and I cheated with signals and stuff. Later she told me the only thing she missed about the Dodgers was those card games.

Leo took over a lousy New York team and within a few years had them in two World Series. And he never said a word against the Dodgers or Mr. Rickey. Whenever I see players who change teams blasting the team they left, I cringe. Baseball is the kind of business where you never know where you might be in the future.

Suddenly I was on a roll. In Chicago I pitched my first shutout and fourth straight complete game, walking only one batter. One base on balls! I remembered what Cookie Lavagetto had told me when I came back from the army. "I never pitched," he said, "but I know it has to be the same as with everything else. The secret is getting the feel of your job, and knowing you have found the right way to do it." I was confident I had found the secret at last.

We won 16 out of 19 and moved into second place. With my teammates reminding me, "Now you're doing what we've been preaching . . . you're in a groove . . . you look the same every time you pitch . . . " I was winning just by getting the ball over the plate.

Dizzy Dean saw me pitch and said I threw hard but not as hard as Ol' Diz. He gave me this advice: "Always try to get that first out. With one out, if somebody gets on base, you've got a chance for a double play to get out of the inning. With nobody out and a man on, they're more likely to score. And get the first pitch over for a strike to every batter."

I've heard that from other pitchers over the years, but Diz was probably the first I heard it from. He also told me, "Bear down on those .220 hitters. The .300 hitters will hit .300 against you and everybody else. But if you ease up on those pesky guys, they'll kill you."

I was still far from perfect, blowing a lead in relief of Branca, and getting lifted with an 8–5 lead when I walked the first two batters in the sixth. I picked up a win in relief, then got back in the groove with two straight complete game victories. In a 4–1 three-hitter against the Reds, I rang up my career high of 9 strikeouts. I walked 1 against the Phils on August 10, then turned around and walked 8 in Boston, including one in the ninth that forced in a run in a 4–3 loss. The Braves were now four games in front of us.

And then I turned around again on August 18 in Philadelphia and beat Robin Roberts, 1 to 0, on a one-hitter. We scored the only run on an error by Roberts and a wild pitch. Early in the game Granny Hamner hit a sinking line drive and Duke Snider made a great diving catch. In the fifth, Putsy Caballero hit a little looper to shallow center and Snider ran in and made another diving try and it hit the tip of his glove and they scored it a hit. At Ebbets Field they would have called it an error. Snider always blamed himself for costing me a no-hitter. Not so. He had robbed Hamner earlier to save it at that point.

The ultimate for a pitcher is to win a 1-0 game. In that game I walked 3, and struck out the last 3 batters. Mr. Rickey always preached: finish as strong as you start and you'll be a good pitcher. Well, I wanted to do what Mr. Rickey told me to do. He was at the game, and when rain held it up for fifteen minutes after five innings, he noticed me pacing up and down in the dugout. I was antsy to get back out there. Later he reminded me that we had an official game in already and it didn't matter if it poured after that. But dumb me, all I wanted to do was pitch some more. To top it off, I got a base hit myself that night. Add Robin Roberts to my list of cousins. I mean, going back to Brooklyn on the train, I was twenty feet tall. It was five years to the day since my ignominious major league debut.

I could always sleep okay the night before a game, but I could not eat after I pitched. It didn't matter if I pitched a one-hitter or got beat, 20 to 0. I was so worked up, it took me a few hours to settle down, replaying every pitch for hours. I've never had much patience, always eager to be doing something. I am amazed that I have sat still long enough to put all this down.

I never had a sore arm or went near the trainer's room. If I had a kink I'd play catch and work it out. But if somebody tells you they pitched a complete game and it doesn't hurt, they're lying to you. It does hurt, but not while you're pitching. After you throw a hundred or more pitches and then rest overnight, try combing your hair the next morning. Walk up to anybody who has just pitched and touch the little muscle in the back of the arm; they'll jump 18,000 feet in the air.

We worked long and often and thought nothing of it. I pitched 246⅔ innings in 1948. On August 22 I started and got knocked out in the fourth, came back the next day and pitched 5⅔ innings in relief until doubles by Phil Masi and Connie Ryan beat me in the fourteenth. Then four days later I started and had the Reds shut out until Kluzewski hit a 2-run homer in the ninth and Hank Behrman saved a 3–2 win for me. Two days later I pitched 1⅓ in relief and two days after that pitched another complete game, but this time Hank Borowy threw a one-hitter at us. But that gives you some idea of how often we worked. Today my agent would never stand for that.

We had been in last place on July 3; on August 29 we went into first. Then Whitey Lockman beat me with a home run, 3 to 0, on September 4. I guess what made my no-hitter five days later so much sweeter was that it came against the Giants. I wasn't seeking revenge against Leo Durocher; the guys who had given me so much grief were Willard Marshall and Whitey Lockman. After I loaded the bases in the first inning that night, it was Marshall who hit into the double play. And it was Lockman I got for the last out.

Four days later I gained another sweet victory, beating our biggest jinx, Johnny Schmitz of the Cubs, who had beaten us six times that year.

And on September 17 I achieved another minor miracle; although I lost, 4 to 2, to the Cardinals, I actually held Stan Musial hitless at Ebbets Field. You don't think that's something? He probably hit .900 against us in that ballpark.

The better I pitched the more cocky I became. I wore my uniform pants legs down very low, like many players do today. I thought that was cool. Mr. Rickey did not. He told my wife, "If you get Rex to pull up his pants and wear them like big league ballplayers are supposed to wear them, I'll buy you a hundred-dollar dress." When she told me, I straightened up. We heard nothing more about it, until the following Christmas, when Mr. Rickey sent her a check for $100.

Everybody had a theory for my midseason turnaround: the added responsibility of a family; the arrival of Roy Campanella in July; slowing down my pace on the mound and overcoming nervousness.

In a story in *The Sporting News* I sounded very pompous for a twenty-three-year-old punk: "I wish some of the kid pitchers on this club would feel as serious about this game as I do. It doesn't kill them when they lose, like it does me. I can remember when I was that way, though; but they'll change like I did when I got married and had a baby."

The Braves pulled ahead of us and won the pennant, but I finished strong, pitching my fourth shutout on September 25, when I walked only 1 and struck out 8 to beat the Phillies, 3 to 0, for win number 15.

On the last day of the season it was my hitting, not my pitching, that got me into trouble. In the fourth inning I got a base hit off Curt Simmons to drive in a run, and when I tried to take second on the throw to the plate I slid in and hurt my ankle. I stayed in the game until the seventh and took a 4–2 loss and we finished in third place, one game back of St. Louis.

The next day I went to the clubhouse; all the equipment was gone. Doc Wendler looked at my ankle and said it was badly sprained. But I drove Beverly and the baby all the way to Omaha and it kept getting worse. Finally I went to a local osteopath who told me I had broken a bone. He operated and set it and I was in a cast for the winter. I had pitched a no-hitter, a one-hitter, a three-hitter, and a four-hitter, and three times gave up just 5 hits. After July 4, opposing batters had hit under .200 against me.

My World Series start in 1947 had catapulted me into the glaring New York spotlight. But my no-hitter against the Giants in September 1948 gave me an enduring celebrity status.

When I talk about "going New York" and the glamour and excitement of the big city—the plays, nightclubs, restaurants, and celebrities—I am talking about a scene that has all but disappeared. For older fans who will remember, and for younger fans who never knew it, I'd like to describe what it was like, so you might better understand why it so completely overwhelmed us two kids from Omaha.

Toots Shor's was the mecca for all sports and show business people in the 1940s and 1950s. Located at 51 West 51st Street, it no longer exists. Shor called his place a saloon, not a restaurant. He believed any place that served booze was a saloon. Shor was 6-5 tall and weighed maybe 300 pounds. During prohibition days he had been a bouncer for saloon keeper Texas Guinan. Always immaculately dressed, he circulated among the tables and called everybody a crumb bum. Shor was a devout Giants fan.

Anybody could go there for dinner. You entered through a small vestibule that opened into a huge room and the first thing you saw was a big circular bar. Double doors led into a large dining room with one booth on either side. These were reserved for very special VIP stars. If you arrived at about six o'clock and asked for a table, the dining room might be empty, but one of the waiters in tuxedos would say, "These tables are reserved" (which they weren't) "but have a seat at the bar and we'll see what we can do." So you'd sit at the bar and have a drink or two and about an hour later the waiter would smile and say, "Somebody didn't show up, so we have a table for you."

The food was excellent, but incidental to most of us. The bar was the focal point. Shor told me, "Bartenders can do three things to you. They can give it away, they can steal, and they can drink. If they do only one of those three, hire them. They're good."

Toots did not want his customers bothered, so there were no interviews allowed inside and nobody asked for autographs. If a tourist simply had to get an autograph from some favorite star, the proper protocol was to ask the waiter to request it on your behalf. The waiter might oblige, but never if the desired name was Joe DiMaggio. DiMag was the king, "The Big Dago" in Shor's terms. He got a big ovation whenever he showed up. It was pure adulation, the likes of which you do not see today.

There were no photos on the walls; Toots did not need them to know where he stood with his pals. But there were some upstairs in the rooms for private parties. Shor threw one party a year on Christmas night by invitation only. I got to go to a few of those parties.

Now I'm going to drop a lot of names, but I am not doing it to try to impress anybody. I'm doing it to show why I was so impressed by it all, and why I was so absolutely overwhelmed to be a part of it.

It really began in the Dodgers' clubhouse with Leo Durocher. Al Jolson, the greatest entertainer of the time, was always hanging around, and Phil Foster, the comedian, and Danny Kaye. The players were all on a first-name basis with these guys. I used to tell my brother and sisters and parents all this, but I don't think they believed me.

When Jackie Robinson joined us, Joe Louis and Bill "Bojangles" Robinson, the tap dancer, were often at Ebbets Field. They were as goggle-eyed at being with us as we were at seeing them. In those days it was customary to have a "day" for a popular player and give him a car. Bojangles Robinson was the presenter when they gave Jackie a Cadillac. A few years later Lena Horne was asked to present a car to Roy Campanella. This beautiful lady was sitting next to me in the dugout and I was telling her what a big fan of hers I am, and she says to me, "I'm so nervous; what will I do?" And I'm thinking, "You're nervous? You get up in front of all those people all alone and sing, and you're nervous about walking from here to home plate to say a few words and hand the car keys to Campanella?" She was almost trembling. I said something inane, like, "Aw, there's nothing to it."

Shor's was near the radio and television studios, in the heart of the theater district. Anytime you walked in, you might see Frank Sinatra, Spencer Tracy, Phil Silvers, Joe E. Lewis, the Ritz Brothers, Rags Ragland—people a lot of youngsters won't recognize, but who were stars at the time. Jackie Gleason was a fixture there. Steve Allen, Jack Lescoulie, Dave Garroway, Ed McMahon, Mary Healey and Peter Lind Hayes, Cab Calloway, Duke Ellington. Politicians dropped in, too, and generals and temporary heroes.

The big bands had their own baseball teams. I met Harry James there, a big Cardinals fan, and told him how I had skipped school to see him. I left tickets at Ebbets Field for Les Brown, who brought a young singer named Doris Day with him. Musicians could not get over how we performed in front of 50,000 people.

Buddy Rich, the drummer, was a big Dodger fan. I had left two tickets for him and two for the middleweight boxer, Tony Zale, on the night I pitched the no-hitter. I went to the fights at Madison Square Garden as often as I could. In one of his classic bouts with Rocky Graziano, Zale was knocked flat just before the end of one round. In the next round he came back and knocked out Graziano. Leo Durocher often cited that as an example of what you can do when you think you're beaten.

Shor didn't take to women being in his joint; they had to be avid sports fans. Dorothy Kilgallen, Faye Emerson, Tallulah Bankhead were okay with him. And, of course, when Marilyn Monroe came in with DiMaggio, or Ava Gardner with Sinatra, they were welcome.

Baseball was the only game in town. College basketball was big, but pro football and basketball were not much in those pretelevision days. Nobody knew any athletes except baseball players. Even with all their fans, players today do not know what it means to be really idolized.

When I walked into Shor's after pitching in the 1947 World Series, I was the one who drew the applause. I was the temporary hero. I was sitting at a table and a man came over to me and said, "You don't know me, but I know who you are. I saw you pitch today. My name is Pat O'Brien."

Well, my God, I mean, being an Irish Catholic and watching him play Knute Rockne in the movies and all, I was floored. Here I am, gawking at these stars and celebrities, and they're makingjust as big a fuss over me. I said it was an honor to meet him.

Then, when I pitched my no-hitter against Shor's beloved Giants, New York really accepted me. It didn't matter how much or how little I did after that, I was the object of all that attention. To a small town hick kid, that's overwhelming. When those big stars come up to you and address you by name, that's something. It has to turn your head.

One night I was in Shor's, sitting with Toots and Don Ameche. Phil Silvers was at another table with his leggy young bride. Silvers came over and said, "How long you guys gonna be here?" Toots said something like four or five A.M., which was the usual hours. Silvers took his wife home and came back. I ask you, how do you not like stuff like that?

Red Smith, in my opinion the greatest sportswriter of them all, and his pal Frank Graham were at Shor's often, as were the Broadway columnists Walter Winchell, Leonard Lyons, and Earl Wilson. Lyons took me to the Stork Club once, the really uptown joint. High society. The Cub Room was the exclusive inner sanctum. Movie stars everywhere. Lyons introduced me to the owner, Sherman Billingsley, who told me he knew all about Omaha, but not from playing in the college World Series.

"During prohibition," he said, "we ran booze into there across the river from Council Bluffs in a hearse with the whiskey stashed underneath the floor." And I'm thinking, here's this highly successful cafe society guy telling me about how he was a bootlegger. Unreal.

Shor was a friend of Jack Entratta, the front man at the Copacabana nightclub, and the guy who ran Bill Miller's Riviera in New Jersey, where all the big bands appeared. Just say the word and he'd have us a table at these places, or tickets to any show in town. One night Ralph Branca and his bride-to-be, Ann Mulvey, and my wife and I went to see Henry Fonda in *Mr. Roberts* and then we went to the Copa to see Jimmy Durante and who sits down at the next table but Fonda, William Holden, and John Forsyth. The women went berserk, but Fonda recognized me from Omaha and we visited. The only girl in that play was Marlon Brando's sister, Jocelyn, who was also from Omaha. And I have to tell you, I was impressed by all that.

Howard Cosell was always hanging around Shor's in those days. He carried his tape recorder, but Toots made him go outside to do his interviews for his radio show. I have to stick up for Howard here; people say he knew nothing about baseball. That's not true. He was at the ballpark often and he knew the game.

There were other popular sports hangouts in New York. Al Schacht had a restaurant where the bar stool legs were made of bats and the seats were oversized mitts. Dick & Harry's was a sports restaurant. My photo was on the walls of these places. But none of them exists anymore.

Looking back at it all, having been a part of that scene, I can't help but think what a lucky young man I was. There was no way I could imagine this kind of hero worship when I was the big star at Creighton Prep. I had no idea such a world as this existed. I enjoyed every minute of it. Dear God, it was fun.

Was I ready for it? No way. Could I handle it? I thought so.

THIRTEEN

The Other Side of the Hill

F ROM NOVEMBER to February I hopped around with my left leg in a cast, but that did not keep me in Omaha all winter. The siren call of New York City was too strong to resist. After my no-hitter I had been the center of attention wherever I went and I loved every minute of it. Besides, I missed the gang at Toots Shor's.

Vim, a chain of appliance stores, asked me to make some appearances for them, promoting their brand of a new gadget called television. They advertised a "big 52 square inch screen" for $325 plus installation. During the previous summer I had first seen signs in saloon and restaurant windows: "We have television . . . Ball game today on television." One day I stopped to watch it in a store window. Bob Edge was announcing the game, using one camera behind him in the booth. It was difficult to make out the players, but people were fascinated by it.

I bought one for my parents before I went to New York. It was a big piece of furniture with a little screen about six by nine inches. My mother wanted no part of it and told me to take it out. She preferred to stick with her radio, listening to "Ma Perkins." But I left it there in the sun room and she was soon hooked. Later I bought her a color TV and she didn't want that, either. I think every household in America heard the words: "Don't buy a color set, it's not perfected yet."

I went to New York in December to be best man at Gil Hodges's wedding. While I was there, my father died on my birthday. He had fought lung cancer long enough to listen to me pitching in a World Series and to hear about my no-hitter, and he was spared the pain of my rapid decline.

While Laraine Day had been traveling with us, I once told her of my fascination with Katharine Hepburn in the movies. When Leo invited me to a Christmas party I met Miss Hepburn there and we chatted briefly about baseball. Many years later Hepburn came to Baltimore in the play, *Coco*, and they had a press conference, so I went. I was near the door when she arrived; as she went by me she did a double take.

"Don't I know you?" she asked.

"I'm Rex Barney. Laraine Day introduced us one evening in New York."

"Oh, yes," she said, and began recalling the party and our chat. With all those people looking at us and wondering what I was all about, sure, I felt like a big shot.

I signed for my biggest salary—$17,500—in 1949; with my outside income I earned $28,000 that year, well above the average player salary for the time.

Mr. Rickey asked me to report to Vero Beach early to run and walk in the sand and strengthen my leg and ankle. I still had some twinges of pain when I threw and starting making adjustments in my delivery to ease the pain.

If ever a training camp was designed to get you in shape and ready to open a baseball season, Vero Beach was it. Everybody was treated the same, major leaguers to Class D rookies. In a practice game you'd see Reese at shortstop, a seventeen-year-old greenie at second base, an older minor leaguer on first. After a few weeks the sifting began.

We slept in old barracks set above the ground on concrete blocks. That was quite a comedown after those luxurious Caribbean hotels. Every morning at six o'clock Herman Levy, a retired navy man, came through blowing a whistle, then went out and raised the flag. We had to be in and out of the mess hall by 8:00, in uniform in the recreation room by 8:30 for a lecture by Mr. Rickey. Some guys hated them, but I enjoyed them. Then we all checked the giant bulletin board, looking for our names among the 600 or 700 players gathered there to get our assignments.

"Barney—sliding pits, 9:00 to 9:30; strings 9:30 to 10:00. Running . . . Red team Diamond 4 . . . " Everybody had a schedule for the day.

135

Pitchers in the sliding pits? You better believe it. Pepper Martin came in to teach us how to slide more than one way; no sliding headfirst and never slide into first base. The fans love that stuff, but the headfirst slide is dangerous and gets you to the base, especially first base, slower than running.

There was a little old guy named Beansie who squeezed fresh orange juice all day for the players and the few observers in the bleachers.

There were no wives in camp, but they could stay in the town. Mr. and Mrs. Jackie Robinson and the other black players could not get into the one movie theater in town, so Mr. Rickey brought in movies for us. We played cards in the big lobby and got to know each other. They had a swimming pool, a fishing lake, and horseshoe pits.

We could go swimming at the nearby beach, that is, until one day when a rookie, Bobby Morgan, from Oklahoma City got caught in a vicious undertow in the ocean and Gene Hermanski saved him from drowning. The beach was off limits to the Dodgers after that.

The barracks were filled with bunk beds but some of the older players shared rooms. Ralph Branca and I had a room on the end. They locked the doors at curfew time, eleven o'clock, but most of us were so worn out by then, the standard joke was: "Do we have to stay up that late?" Billy Cox and Preacher Roe went out on the town, what there was of it, and were often locked out. They knocked on our window at one or two in the morning, got up on boxes, and crawled in through the window.

The Philadelphia Athletics trained in West Palm Beach. They were our nearest big league team, so we played them often, and sometimes went down to Miami for games. Once I was going to drive to Miami for an exhibition game in 1951 and Chuck Dressen asked me to find a young pitcher on the Montreal roster and bring him with me—Tom Lasorda, a rookie curveballer, as deep-dyed Dodger blue as you can get. He was a fine minor league pitcher, but he never won a game in the major leagues. All the way to Miami he was nothing but questions for 120 miles.

A lot has changed at Vero Beach. The barracks have been replaced by motels where the players disappear into their private rooms at night. No more bulletin boards or lectures or hundreds of players. But it remains the ultimate training setup. The web of strings Mr. Rickey devised for me to pitch through in quest of the strike zone is still there. Clumps of tall evergreens still form the background for hitters at the several diamonds. When Eddie Murray signed with the Dodgers, he did not look forward to going there, but he found out if you can't get ready to start the season there, you'll never get ready anywhere. Every spring a host of former Dodgers volunteer to go there to help. That's my idea of family.

Burt Shotton was back as the manager. I always felt that Shotton did not like Branca any more than he did me. When he took Ralph out of a game in Chicago after he had hit two batters, Shotton remarked, "The nature of your nationality is a violent one, and I was afraid you were going to hit some more." He said things like that. For some reason, I believed I never really got a proper shot with him in '49.

Maybe I favored my left leg and that threw me off. Maybe I had too much coaching and too much advice. I had so much ability, everybody was eager to help me develop it. Whatever the cause, I never got into the same motion or rhythm that I had found in 1948.

At one point Mr. Rickey told me I was too laid back; I had to get mad, show more emotion. He rigged up a little ball that was moved about in a frame over home plate and had me throw at it. Then I was supposed to pretend I was throwing at that little ball in a game. For a while I had worked very slowly, and Hugh Casey said, "You ought to work faster. Don't take so much time walking off the mound. That takes energy, too. Stay up there. Don't just get the ball and throw it, but don't fool around so much."

At times I couldn't wait to throw the next pitch, and fired the ball as soon as I got it. And Branca told me, "Slow down. Step off the mound once in a while."

Cookie Lavagetto had stressed rhythm to me. "Watch good pitchers," he said. "They have the same rhythm all the time."

To this day pitching coaches tell me, "I wish I'd had you to work with; I'd have cured you."

All I know is I had a disappointing spring in '49 and began the season feeling as uncoordinated as a puppet whose strings are too loose. We had a solid team: Snider and Hodges were in place, Jackie was in good shape, and we had added Don New-combe, who had great control and no curveball. After the 1949 World Series Tommy Henrich said to me, "That Newcombe has some kind of slider." That was no slider, that's all the curve he had.

The peculiar thing about that season is that when I was good I was very, very good. In my first start on May 6 against the Cubs, I went five innings and lost, 4 to 2, but I did not walk a man. Then five days later Ralph Kiner sank me with a home run in the first, and I walked 6 in six innings. On May 14 at Boston I relieved in the ninth of a tie game. We took a 6–5 lead in the twelfth. In the last of the twelfth, Rickert singled, I walked Elliott, threw two wide ones to Russell, and Shotton brought in Paul Minner. They scored 2 runs and my record was now 0 and 3.

Pitchers and other players will debate forever who has the tougher job, the everyday player or the pitcher. Pitchers say a hitter can go 0 for 4 one day and go right back out there the next day and try to do better. Get a couple hits and everything is okay again. Position players say pitchers can lie around and do nothing for three or four days. But if a pitcher gets beat he's got to stew about it for four or five days before he can try to make up for it. It hurts. That's why I can never boo anybody. That guy out there who has made the error, struck out, or made the bad pitch is going through hell. I know. And there is nobody out there who can help you.

I took the game home with me when I lost, but I never took it out on my family. After a bad game you just want to hide, go home, and hope the phone doesn't ring. If you've made a date to go out, you try to get out of it, at least I did. I've never been able to handle losing. I felt I had let the team and my family down. I would talk about it a little, and if I couldn't sleep I'd get up and pace the floor, going over every pitch I had thrown, trying to figure out what I was doing wrong, and why I could not come out of it.

On the '49 Dodgers, I'd say Furillo and Snider and their families suffered the most when they had bad days. Not physi-cally, although Furillo was volatile. Snider could be hitting .350 and if he went 0 for 4 he'd go home and tell his wife he might be headed back to the minor leagues. Hermanski could carry on.

But Reese never got upset, probably never even read the sports pages. And Hodges was strong, silent, tough, no matter what.

And then I relieved twice, worked almost seven innings, and did not walk a man. Another funny thing: with all my speed I did not strike out a lot of hitters. Once in a while I might average more than one an inning, but many times I fanned nobody.

On May 30 I came this close to shutting out the Giants at the Polo Grounds. I started the first game of the traditional Memorial Day doubleheader before the usual packed house: 53,053. I had a 1–0 lead with 2 out in the ninth, walked Lockman and Marshall, and threw a wild pitch that scored the tying run. Erv Palica came in and we won it in the thirteenth, but that ninth inning was Heartbreak City for me.

I have to admit that Shotton did use me in close games. After I'd been kayoed by the Pirates in the third, he came right back with me the next day, bringing me in with the bases loaded and nobody out in the eighth inning of a 4–3 game. Wally Westlake hit a fly ball to tie it, then Ralph Kiner—bless him and his one dimension—hit another homer off me in the tenth to win it.

Three days later I pitched a two-hitter and beat the Cubs, 3 to 1. Four days after that I took a 5–0 lead against the Reds into the fifth, walked Johnny Wyrostek with the bases loaded, and gave up a grand slam to Grady Hatton. Talk about a lonely feeling; nobody comes over and speaks to you after that happens. Too bad I did not survive that inning; we scored 10 runs in the last of the fifth, but Paul Minner got the benefit.

On June 18 I shut out the Cubs 2 to 0 at Wrigley Field. Then on June 24 I started at Pittsburgh. Bockman walked, Restelli walked, good old Kiner hit a home run, I walked two more, and I took a hike. Talk about up and down, in and out, on and off—you figure it out. I guess I drove Shotton as crazy as I had made Durocher.

On July 8 the Giants drew the biggest night crowd of the year at Ebbets Field: 34,468. Remember, this is a ballpark with only 32,000 seats. The first two black players for the Giants, Hank Thompson and Monte Irvin, made their debuts that night. I relieved Newcombe in the fifth and got credit for the 4–3 win. My record was now 4 and 5.

After a couple weeks of inactivity I found myself back in the starting rotation in August as we seesawed back and forth with the Cardinals for the lead. I won two in a row, including my first complete game in six weeks (yes, a complete game was an important mark of success in those bygone days) and I even got a hit off Ewell Blackwell in one of them. I was starting every five to seven days that month. Then I lost two in a row: Del Ennis beat me with a home run and our old jinx, Johnny Schmitz, threw a shutout against me. On August 30 and September 4 I pitched two straight complete games and won them both. What's more, I actually struck out more guys than I walked in each game. Now, does that sound like a guy who's lost it because he broke his leg? Well, maybe that doesn't, but how about this? Four days later we took a 6–0 lead against the Giants and I got 6 outs and walked 6 before Carl Erskine came in. Maybe I was contagious; there were 22 walks in that game, 1 short of the league record. The Dodgers won, 12 to 7, and the whole wild game took three hours and twenty minutes. Today such a game would take three days.

And how's this to cap off as confused a year as any pitcher ever had: On September 19 I'm starting at Wrigley Field. The gamblers used to gather in the box seats beside the visiting dugout and we warmed up right in front of them. One guy said to me, "How you feeling today?"

I felt great, but I said, "Terrible. I won't be doing much today."

I saw him get up and go place his bets.

I walked the lead-off man in the first and I guess the guy was feeling pretty good about that, but the base runner got wiped out in a double play. I walked the lead-off man in the fifth and he went down the same way. I walked the lead-off man in the seventh and he met the same fate.

I came back to the bench and said to Branca, "I'm going to throw another no-hitter."

"Don't say that," he shuddered.

"Look," I said, "after Cavarretta's up in the eighth I know I can get the next five guys."

Came the last of the eighth and we're ahead 4 to 0 and Cavarretta's up and Campanella gives me the curveball sign and I think: that's dumb. With my reputation for being wild, he'll be taking, to try to get on base, and Campanella is known for being a curveball catcher and I want to get ahead of Phil with a fastball. So I shake off Campy and Cavarretta is thinking right along with me and when I throw the fastball he jumps on it and lines a base hit. Campy comes out to the mound and says, "Don't ever shake me off. I'm smarter than you are. Just do what I tell you." I got the message.

So I settled for my second one-hitter. As I came to the dugout after the last out, I heard from the box seats, "You rotten sonofabitch." I smiled and thought, "If you're so dumb to gamble on this game, I couldn't care less."

Another sidelight to that game illustrates my relationship with Shotton. After the game I said to him, "If you had told me to pitch a no-hitter, I wouldn't have given them the one hit."

I don't know why I said it; I was constantly stewing because I wasn't starting regularly, and I guess I thought it was funny. But, looking back, I can see that it was a stupid remark to an old man that might have hurt him.

Would you have bet then that I would never pitch another complete game, nor win more than two more games in my life? Me neither.

The Dodgers under Larry MacPhail had been among the first teams to fly. At the end of that western trip we flew home from St. Louis and were greeted by a large crowd at LaGuardia Airport. On our previous trips, four players—Eddie Miksis, Paul Minner, Billy Cox, and Preacher Roe—refused to fly and came home on the train. On this last trip, only Cox and Roe took the train.

It was common for popular players to be honored with a special day on which they were given gifts by the fans. The night after we arrived home, Cain Young, a businessman, presented Don Newcombe a two-door green Buick on behalf of the Black Brooklyn Dodgers Fan Club. I received a new car that year, too.

The pennant race went right down to the last out. We had to win one of the last two games at Philadelphia to avoid a tie and another playoff with the Cardinals. I pitched in both of those games. On October 1 we were tied 4–4 when Preacher Roe gave up a 2-run homer to Puddin' Head Jones in the eighth.

I came in and got the last 2 outs, but we were unable to score in the ninth.

In the last game we led 5 to 0 after three, but Newcombe was pummeled in the fourth. Three runs were in and men on second and third when Shotton sent me in. Richie Ashburn hit a long fly that scored the fourth run of the inning. We got back 2 in the fifth, but they scored when I walked Ennis and Bill Nicholson doubled him home to make it 7 to 5. I was unable to hold them in the sixth. Johnny Blatnik, pinch-hitting, led off with his only base hit of the year. I guess Carl Furillo was so surprised he fumbled it and Blatnik went to second. Granny Hamner singled him home and Dick Sisler singled and that was all for me. Jack Banta came in and gave up a hit to Ennis that tied the game, but then Banta held them in check until we scored 2 in the tenth for a 9–7 pennant-clinching win and it was Banta the Brooks carried on their shoulders to the clubhouse celebration.

We ran into the Yankees again in the World Series. I had been so erratic all season I did not expect to see any action except maybe in a mop-up role. It was a well-pitched Series on both sides for the first 4 games. Allie Reynolds threw a two-hitter and Tommy Henrich hit a home run in the ninth to beat Newcombe, 1 to 0, in the opener. Then Preacher Roe beat Vic Raschi by the same score. Both teams got 5 hits in Game 3 but Branca took a 4–3 loss. When Lopat beat Newcombe, 6 to 4, in the fourth game, we were down, 3 games to 1.

Nobody was more surprised than I was after that game when Shotton told me I would start the next day at Ebbets Field. I always got to the ballpark early. The next morning the cab driver asked me why I was going so early.

"I want to be sure to get a ticket," I said.

"I'm a big fan," he said, "but I wouldn't go today if it was the last game ever. Rex Barney is pitching today. The wildest guy in the world."

That's all I heard about during the entire ride. We pulled up at Ebbets Field and the kids recognized me and came running, "Hey, Rex . . . hey, Rex," asking me to sign. The driver looked at me and groaned. He got no tip from me that day.

But he hadn't been far off in his judgment. The Yankees jumped on me for 2 in the first and 3 in the third on 3 hits and 6 walks. Nobody else fared much better and we lost, 10 to 6.

That winter I saw the Series highlights movie, and I had to laugh when I heard the narrator say, "The bases are full. It looks like Barney is in trouble."

For the year I had given up 108 hits in 140 innings; that's not bad. But I had walked 89 and struck out 80; that's very bad. I had won 9 and lost 8.

Early in the year Arthur Daley had written in *The New York Times:* "Keep an eye on Rex Barney. Unless Branch Rickey and every other expert is in error, he will one day rank with the best."

After the last half of that 1948 season, why shouldn't everybody have had great expectations for me? Sure, I think about that sometimes. I should have been up there with the greats. I should have gone right up the ladder in 1949, but too many rungs were missing.

FOURTEEN

"The X Factor in Rex"

THE YEARS 1949 through 1952 were exciting for Brooklyn baseball fans. The Dodgers won two pennants and finished second twice, all by a total of 8½ games. Three times the races were decided on the last day, by the last batter.

But for me those years were a nightmare. I contributed nothing. I wish I could wake up and find it never happened, but the record books are merciless reminders of the facts.

I stayed in New York after the 1949 season and worked for A & S. Five of us—Branca, Newcombe, Miksis, Hodges, and I—formed a basketball team, augmented by three former professionals. We earned $25 each playing local semipro teams on Monday nights on the stage of the Brooklyn Paramount Theater after the feature film.

I worked out in a Brooklyn gym; headlines in *The Sporting News* screamed: "Borneo Barney Works Out." In early January 1950 I went to Vero Beach with Clyde Sukeforth and Al Campanis. I was determined to get a head start on my comeback year. But my control did not come back, and neither did I.

During spring training, Bruce Edwards tried to help me. Pee Wee talked to me. Jackie and Campy, Jake Pitler and the other coaches—they were all rooting for me and I was letting them down. Mr. Rickey never gave up on me, but the harder I tried the more screwed up I became. I can still see him, in that beat-up hat, cold cigar stuck in the corner of his mouth, standing behind the batting cage peering at me, muttering "Judas Priest" as I threw thunderbolts God knows where. He thought

I was taking my eye off the plate when I turned in my windup, and put a patch over one of my eyes, then over the other. Some wags suggested they put the covers over both eyes at the same time. Frustrated, Mr. Rickey ordered the coaches, "Teach him to control that wildness so the wildness is over the plate."

Maybe I overthrew. Maybe I had some kind of mental block. I could throw strikes through those strings all day, but not in a game. One day Bobby Bragan warmed me up to go into a game and I was throwing nothing but strikes. Then I went into the game and threw eight straight balls. Pitching against Class C and D scrubinis, I was struggling and it was embarrassing.

Many a night I lay awake anguishing. I had been on top of the world for a very brief moment, and then toppled, but I was still young, only 26, and I still had plenty of ability. Was I too conscientious? Was I overcoached? All I knew was that a leg injury should not put a pitcher out of baseball, and nobody could do the job for me.

On the way north Burt Shotton kicked my fragile confidence in the groin again. I had been demoted to the B team, but that wasn't low enough. Shotton sent me back to Vero Beach to work out with the minor leaguers. Can you imagine how it felt to be told I wasn't even good enough to stick with the B team? I can tell you it hurt, plenty, to be cut off from the guys I had played with in the World Series just five months earlier. The train ride north to rejoin the team for opening day in Philadelphia was a long, lonesome, agonizing journey.

I got into 20 games in 1950, all but one as a reliever, and sometimes I was pretty effective. On May 7 at Pittsburgh I relieved Jack Banta in the fourth of a 2–2 game and shut out the Pirates the rest of the way to earn the win, 3 to 2. But on June 10 I came in in the ninth to protect a 3–2 lead, struck out 1, walked 1, and Ted Kluszewski hit a home run to give me loss number 1. I know, the same thing happens to Dennis Eckersley and Gregg Olson. But I didn't think about that at the time.

I made one start all year, my last in the majors, in the morning game of a split Memorial Day doubleheader at Ebbets Field against the Phillies. Just to show you how much confidence Burt Shotton had in me, he had somebody warming up in the bullpen before I threw the first pitch. I don't care if you're Feller or Clemens or Ryan or whoever, a thing like that is going to eat on your mind. It was, to say the least, a discouraging day all around. I went two-plus innings, gave up 3 runs, 2 hits, and 6 walks, and hit a batter. The only "highlight" of the game was my last big league hit, a double off Robin Roberts. Boy, was I murder on those Hall of Fame pitchers at the plate!

On Sunday, July 23, at Pittsburgh I relieved Joe Landrum in the sixth as the Pirates were tying it, 6–6, and pitched two scoreless innings despite 3 walks and 2 wild pitches. The Dodgers gained the lead and Newcombe saved it for me and I had what proved to be my last major league victory.

For the rest of the year my forwarding address was Department of Lost Causes, c/o Bullpen, Ebbets Field. During that time Mr. Rickey decided to send me to a psychiatrist. It was a big secret. When I left the team during a road trip, the story was that I had a cold or something. But I was at the Menninger Clinic in Kansas. I talked with Dr. Karl Menninger for two days. His diagnosis: frustration. His prescription: relax. Big help.

One of the flakiest guys I ever met signed with the Dodgers that year. They gave Billy Loes a $25,000 bonus and before long he had lost it all playing cards with Jackie and Pee Wee. He was born with complete knowledge of pitching but no card sense. They warned him not to play cards, but he said, "If I don't play with you guys, I'll find somebody else," so they kept the money in the family.

Loes could talk pitching all day long, but nothing else. When Paul Richards managed him in Baltimore, Loes told him, "I do not run. I don't get paid to run." One morning Richards was at the park early and he looked out on the field and there was Loes, running in the outfield. Billy was out there every day, but he didn't want Richards to know it.

I mention him because many years later he told me, "Rex, the first time I came to Ebbets Field to work out, I came up those steps from the clubhouse and the diamond came into view and there was a guy throwing on the mound and I watched him and said to myself, 'What the hell am I doing here? I can't throw like that.' It was you. You almost made me turn around and go home. I'd never seen anything like it."

I'd been hearing that all my life. I knew I could still throw hard, and I never lost that. To this day Tommy Lasorda will tell you he never saw anybody throw as fast as I did, past or present. Great. What did I do with it?

Later Clyde Sukeforth made this observation about me: "Something always happened to Rex early in the game. We could see it from the bench. His jaws tightened when he got on the mound. Something would happen to him inside. What it was, nobody knows."

Looking back, I can see that I may have been guilty of that. My concentration was fierce. But that's no excuse. Most pitchers are like that. Something happens to them on the way from warming up to the first game pitch. There's a world of difference between throwing strikes in the bullpen and throwing them past a hitter. But every pitcher knows that. I see pitchers' jaws tighten and their muscles get tenser in every game.

On Monday, September 4, 1950, in the first game of a doubleheader in Boston, I threw my last pitch in the major leagues. We were losing, 10 to 4, after Tommy Brown pinch-hit for our fourth pitcher of the day in the top of the eighth. The Braves had scored in every inning but the first. Burt Shotton remembered my name just in time to bring me in to pitch the last of the eighth. My line for the day: 1 IP 1R 1H 1W 1 WP.

Then the Dodgers went on the road again and left me behind in Brooklyn to work with George Sisler and a minor league coach and a catcher. I was beginning to feel like some kind of freak, separated from the rest of the team. I got so alienated that while I was running in the outfield with the other pitchers, I'd be thinking: I'll run until they all leave the field, then I'll leave by myself. I wondered what good all this was doing me. If confidence was what I needed, this certainly wasn't giving it to me.

I finished the year with 2 wins and 1 loss, and an ERA of 6.42. In 33.2 innings, I gave up 25 hits and 48 walks and struck out 23. I wouldn't have told you, except that I know you could look it up. The only good thing that happened that year was when my son, Kevin, was born on August 21.

In the usual nailbiter of a pennant race the Phillies were in Brooklyn with a one-game lead on the last day. We had to win to force a playoff. If that happened, we had Preacher Roe ready and they had nobody. But it didn't happen. Robin Roberts pitched with two days' rest. Pee Wee Reese hit an odd home run: the ball hit the screen and landed on the top edge of the wall between the concrete and the screen and stuck there. Then Dick Sisler hit an opposite field home run that beat us. But the key play was a base hit to center field with Cal Abrams on second. Ashburn played a very shallow center field and Abrams was not fast, but third base coach Milt Stock was waving him around third and we were all on the bench yelling, "No! No!" We knew he could never make it with the winning run and he didn't.

When the 1950 season ended, Walter O'Malley gained control of the Dodgers and Mr. Rickey moved to Pittsburgh. I respected O'Malley for one thing: he admitted that he knew nothing about baseball. He promoted two people who did know the game—Buzzie Bavasi and Fresco Thompson—and never interfered, unlike some other owners I have known.

Charlie Dressen, who had been a coach with the Yankees, became the new manager, and I became his pet project in the spring of 1951. I was throwing on the mound at Vero Beach one day and Dressen asked, "Who is that?"

"Rex Barney."

"No," Dressen said, "that can't be Barney. He used to have such a smooth delivery. That guy doesn't know what he's doing."

Somewhere along the line, they had tried to change me into a sidearm pitcher, and my arm was going through more weird contortions than an Indian rubber man before I threw the ball. By this time, I had tried so many things and was so confused, I didn't know which end was up. I was blaming Mr. Rickey, because none of his experiments had worked. But I had also tried everything that anybody else had suggested, even if I knew in my heart they didn't know what they were talking about.

Charlie Dressen was determined to rehabilitate me by undoing everything and restoring my natural delivery, if we could find it again. He worked with me for weeks, and I did whatever he said. Every day I went out to the outfield, picked out a spot on the fence, and threw at it, time after time after time. And hit it. Warming up with Bruce Edwards I threw strikes. Then I'd go out to the mound to pitch batting practice and throw the ball in the dirt, over the hitter's head, behind him, everywhere but where they could reach it.

Clyde Sukeforth told a writer, "It's in his head. It can't be anywhere else. I don't think they'll stay with him much longer if he doesn't get it over. Time's running out on him."

Anybody who ever played for Dressen remembers his standard line at the end of every pregame meeting: "Hold 'em for five or six, and I'll think of something." He believed it. But try as he might, he could not think of something to cure Rex Barney.

I started an exhibition game against the Athletics and gave up 1 hit, walked 7, threw a wild pitch, and hit a batter—all in the first inning. My next outing, against the University of Miami, I threw 17 straight pitches that missed the plate and they had to take me out lest I kill one of the frightened collegians.

Some writers picked up on my teammates' frustration and their eroding patience with me. One criticized me for seeming to take it all in stride. I didn't punch lockers or snap at writers. After a terrible outing, I put on my suit, adjusted the Windsor knot in my tie, and left the ballpark. But they never saw the many times I sat and cried my eyes out after those games. I was letting down everybody, not just myself, and I knew it. Dressen had spent more time with me than with all the other pitchers combined, and they had not resented it. But I was fast degenerating from a good cause into a lost cause.

When we started north, Dressen had some health problems and had to enter a hospital. During his absence, the Dodgers sent me back to Vero Beach again. But when he returned, still hoping I could produce that "one good game" that would take me over the hump, I rejoined the team in Atlanta. Dressen planned to give me that chance on April 7 in Atlanta, but he changed his mind and decided I was not ready.

All spring the big question was, "What's wrong with Rex Barney?" In Atlanta Dick Young, the "Poison Pen" of the *Daily News,* interviewed me about my travails, then wrote:

> You listen to him, and you decide that, for the six years you've known him, you've never really known him at all. If you were

to ask most any slumping player, "What's wrong with you?" chances are he'd tell you where to go. But not Rex; he has class. He has been the butt of more newspaper jokes than Harry Truman, but doesn't write nasty letters, and he'll say hello to the newspaperman who has just beaten his brains out in print. He realizes that the reporter has a job to do. That's class.

Sure, I got sick and tired of answering the same question over and over, and sure, I felt angry and frustrated, especially when the only answer I could give was "I don't know." But I didn't take it out on the writers. They may call that class, but I know it really was the enduring influence of my father, drilling respect for everybody into me, whacking me for talking back to Sister Mary in Our Lady of Lourdes grammar school, and my mother preaching good manners to me back in Omaha.

Then we went to Asheville, North Carolina, to play our Class B farm team, the Asheville Tourists, and Dressen handed me the ball. Before the game he called me into a little office and poured me a shot of blackberry brandy and made me drink it to relax me. It was the last thing he could think of to help me come back.

"I was there the day Rex Barney died," wrote Lewis Burton in the New York *Journal-American* two weeks later.

It made a normal stomach turn flipflops. The demise of anyone isn't a pleasant sight, and here was an athlete in the full vigor of young manhood compelled to go through his death struggle in the presence of five or six thousand laughing, shrieking, exultant people, shouting their derision and impatience.

They added their vulgar torment to an inner agony they couldn't understand . . . He had been an important man in the Brooklyn scheme of things, a once good winner with a scorching fastball, until an evil spirit took hold of his control.

If it had been a cancer or a mental malady, people might have understood, but Barney passes into history an inexplicable case.

For the record, the gory details are these: 17 of my first 27 pitches were balls, not even close. In the second inning I threw 9 straight balls, including one that sailed far over Roy Campanella's head. The fans were giving me a howling fierce riding. In the third I threw 13 balls and 3 strikes. When I loaded the bases with my eleventh walk, Chuck Dressen came out to the mound. Never said a word. Waved in a new pitcher, handed him the ball, then he and I walked in silence to the dugout. There was nothing to say.

That evening I was sitting on the porch of the beautiful old resort hotel with my pal, Bruce Edwards. He had a bad arm and I had a bad head and a heavy heart. John Corriden, that priceless old coach, came up the steps and sat on the floor in front of me.

"Buddy boy," he said, "don't let them get you down."

"I'm pretty far down," I said.

"I know you are, but you can do it. I got great confidence in you."

He probably didn't, but he was the kind of man who took the time to go to the guy who was down the most. When he left, to get a lollipop, Bruce said, "That was nice of him to do that." And it was. It was one of the low points of my life, sitting there in beautiful old Asheville, and I needed all the help I could get.

In the hotel the writers were holding a wake for me. One said, "They've tried everything now, and nothing worked."

Another said, "Everything might have been all right if they hadn't tried to teach him a curve."

Somebody else allowed as how it was a shame because Barney was such a nice fellow, and they all nodded in agreement.

"The trouble was," one declared, "he had it too easy, didn't have to go through the minor league school of hard knocks."

Then one fellow had the last word: "Everybody's an expert on Rex Barney."

FIFTEEN

Down and Out in Omaha

B Y OPENING DAY of the 1951 season, it was obvious that there was no way I could help the Dodgers, so I asked them to put me on the voluntarily retired list. But they had to get waivers on me from the other teams to do that, and four teams claimed me, so they withdrew me from the waiver list. All they needed was for Mr. Rickey to claim me in Pittsburgh and find some magic cure for me. If that happened, they would have run Walter O'Malley out of Brooklyn instead of his walking out seven years later.

New York was full of so-called hardboiled newspapermen in those days. Among that group, Jimmy Cannon of the New York *Post* was a real certified twenty-minute egg. So it meant a great deal to me when he wrote:

> It's one of the saddest stories of sports and, if I break down and do a little moaning, give me a pass. This is one of the nicest kids I've ever met. It's a shame it happened to him, because no one ever liked what went with it more. This is a guy who understands what the big league is. This kid is a genuine big leaguer. But it looks like the big leagues are too much for him . . . At twenty-six Barney looks like he's had it. It's a hell of a time to be finished. Back in Omaha most guys at that age ain't even started."

So now what could the Dodgers do with me? Buzzie Bavasi offered to option me out to Fort Worth in the Texas League, where Bobby Bragan was the manager. I would still draw my major league salary, and maybe Bragan could figure out a way for me to come back. He had some movies of me taken during the 1948 season, and we studied them together. It was clear to both of us how much my mechanics had changed.

After about a week Bragan started me against Houston. I was practically unhittable, but not just because of my speed. I turned in a record-breaking performance, walking 16 batters in 7⅔ innings to break a fifty-two-year record. My record still stands. The score was only 3 to 2 when I went out; Bragan had left me in as long as I had a chance to win. Billy Hunter, who later played for the Orioles, was our shortstop that night. Once he came to the mound and said, "What are you doing, trying to make sure we set a double play record?"

As I sat alone in a hotel room after that game, the thought crossed my mind for the first of many times: death is better than this. The world is over for me. I remember thinking: what's the best way to commit suicide? Jumping out the window? I thought that. But the hope that some miracle might straighten me out, and the thought of my wife and family kept me going.

And so it went: three innings, 7 walks . . . two innings, 7 walks . . . At the end of May I had been in 3 games, pitched twelve innings, given up 16 runs, 12 hits, 30 walks. Discouraging? Destroying is more like it. The New York writers were saying, "The case of Rex Barney remains one of the mysteries of baseball." Tell me.

I worked hard. I went out to LaGrave Field in Fort Worth every day and threw at a spot on the fence, and sometimes threw the ball clear over the fence. I cried a lot. I knew what I had and I watched other guys who did not have what I had, but were throwing strikes, and I was not. Could not. Knew not why. You think that isn't frustrating?

On June 2 our game was rained out and reporters found me throwing against a brick wall under the stands, working on another new delivery Bragan had suggested. By that time I had seen more new deliveries than a midwife.

Bragan announced, "Barney is not going to pitch in another game until he and I feel he is ready." On June 15 we decided I was ready. We scored 6 in the first, but in the second a hit and 3 walks gave San Antonio a run and left the bases loaded for a reliever who served up a grand slam and we lost. Apparently we were mistaken about my being ready.

I didn't pitch for the next three weeks. The Texas League correspondent for *The Sporting News* called me " . . . the highest paid and least seen player in the Texas League."

Then, on the night of July 9, with Oklahoma City leading, 6 to 1, Bragan sent me in to start the fifth inning. My second pitch hit playing manager Tommy Tatum in the back of the neck and they carried him off on a stretcher. How far had I come since my first major league pitch that hit Eddie Stanky in the back? About six inches. I then proceeded to walk 5, hit another batter, give up a hit, throw 2 wild pitches forcing in 5 runs, before Bragan surrendered and Jack Banta rescued me. Four days later I went on the disabled list with a strained right shoulder muscle. But that is not where the real pain was.

The Dodgers recalled me in September and I was there for the historic playoff against the Giants. To this day I have never witnessed another scene like the end of that final game in the Polo Grounds. It was the quickest, most devastating turn of events I ever saw.

I was sitting on one of the bat trunks at the end of the dugout. Dick Williams was on one side of me and Bill Sharman, a good basketball player who never got into a big league game, was my other side. We had the game won. We watched Andy Pafko patting his glove like he's getting ready to catch Bobby Thomson's line drive and the game is over and we win. But the ball hits the overhanging upper deck on the way down and lands in the seats and the game is over and we lose. I'll never forget the sight of Eddie Stanky running out there and hugging Durocher. Not a word was said on our bench. Absolute silence.

Normally, when a game was over in the Polo Grounds, we all dashed to the clubhouse in center field. This time we walked very slowly. Two hours later the whole team had left and Ralph Branca was still sitting on the steps between the levels in the clubhouse, still in his uniform. The clubhouse man said, "Come on, Ralph, let's go."

Ralph said, "Okay, okay," and never moved.

When I was ready to leave, I said, "Can I do anything for you?"

"No," he said. "I'm okay."

Forty years later I saw Ralph at an oldtimers dinner. He looked at me and said, "Why me?"

I knew exactly what he was talking about. I said, "Ralph, do you do that often?"

"No," he said. "Just once in a while I'll say it to someone like you, who was there. But I've never gotten an answer."

I said, "Well, you never will. You know that, pal."

It looked as if, barring some miracle, my major league pitching career was over. My wife had no interest in bouncing around in the minor leagues, and I didn't either. I still held out some hopes of making a comeback, but she was eager to begin a new life, and she wanted to do it in California. So that fall we went to Los Angeles. She loved it and I hated it. Our life was blowing apart.

We had both been very young and impressionable during those heady days in New York. All the attention and adulation following my no-hitter had taken us by storm. And then, just like that, it was all over. Now we were pulling in different directions. So we separated; she stayed in California with the children and I returned to Omaha.

(They all still live in California. My daughter is married to a doctor, and my son and a friend own a bar and grill in Santa Monica. I now have four grandchildren, two boys and two girls. They have remained very loyal and proud of whatever I did, which wasn't all that much, and I see them whenever I am in California.)

Soon after I got a job for the winter in Omaha, Chuck Dressen wrote me a letter, asking me to come out to his home in California for a few weeks. He was sure, he said, that he could get me back to my original pitching form. But I had agreed to pay my wife $150 a month for support, and there was no way I could take the time off nor afford to pay my own way to the coast, so I had to decline. I was lower than salt as I turned down what may have been my last chance.

The Dodgers sold my contract to their St. Paul farm club in the American Association and I went to spring training with them. Clay Bryant, an old pitcher, was the manager, and he worked with me. I got into 4 games, pitched a total of 2 innings, and gave up 8 hits and 14 walks.

155

I was twenty-seven. I was finished. I get weepy thinking about it now. It's a part of my life I cannot forget, ever. When you have to face yourself with that memory every day of your life, it's not very pleasant.

They wanted to send me down to Newport News in the Piedmont League, back where I had started in 1943, but I couldn't take that and refused to report. So they put me on the suspended list and I went back to Omaha where I pitched a few semipro games. The Dodgers talked to me about managing or coaching, but I was too proud to go down to the lower minor leagues in any capacity. The only managing I ever did was a Towson Legion all-star team for a few years in the 1970s in Baltimore. I enjoyed that, but I never had any ambitions to be a manager.

The Dodgers were afraid to release me in case some other club picked me up and performed a miracle, so I remained on their restricted list until May 17, 1960, when they finally sent me my release.

In 1953 I worked in a brewery, handling beer kegs, and pitched for local semipro teams. I still had my fastball, and was still wild, but no longer conveniently so. I continued to receive sure cures from coaches, scouts, and fans, and I tried them all.

I hit another low point watching the Dodgers and Yankees in the 1953 World Series on television. There were my team-mates, and pitchers with no more ability than I had, in the World Series, and here I was, halfway across the country watching on a little picture tube before I went to work on the night shift at the brewery. At one point I broke down completely and just sat there sobbing my heart out.

I have to say that I have never really gotten over it. A couple times during the years I have been the PA announcer for the Orioles, I'd go home after the game and those flickering images would come back and haunt me and I'd almost break down. To have what I had and not fulfill it—if I could kick myself in the rear end, I'd do it. And I would trade everything I've had since for another 10 years in the major leagues.

In the spring of 1954, I was pitching for the Herman, Nebraska, semipros at $100 a game, still hoping. My friend Bill Roeder, a New York writer, and I collaborated on a plaintive piece for *Collier's* magazine. It told about my career and my sad plight; the title summed it all up: "Can't Anybody Help Me?" But I never heard from anybody. Besides, the Dodgers still owned me. In 1953 I just knew I was going to get it back. By '54 I just knew I wasn't. It was time to move on to real life.

When you were in the big leagues, there were plenty of people who told you to look them up when you quit playing and they'd have a job for you. But now I never saw any of those people. They were always out to lunch or in a meeting. I had been told that the hardest adjustment I would ever have to face was going from wartime back to civilian life. Well, that was true for a month or so; I did have violent nightmares like a lot of other guys, and couldn't sleep without sleeping pills for a while. But at that time I had my baseball career waiting for me.

Now I had nothing. Like many professional athletes, I found the hardest adjustment was going from being a ball-player—part of a team, a family—to being an outsider. Oblivion. Nobody. Nothing.

SIXTEEN

National League Wars

I WAS AN ACTIVE PARTICIPANT in the National League wars of the first five postwar years, and I retain many sharp memories and impressions of those enemy forces. Some of the people I recall most distinctly were not stars; their names may not be familiar to any but the most studious fans. They may stick in my memory because of one incident, or because of the kind of people they were, rather than their ability on the field. I do not pretend to offer a complete rundown of every lineup, but simply to share some highlights from my selective reminiscence.

In my opinion, the decade beginning in 1946 saw the best baseball in the history of the game. The intensity was ferocious. Those of us who were coming out of the service were eager to swap that khaki for a baseball uniform and to excel, because if you didn't, you'd lose it. There were only eight teams in each league and fifty-nine minor leagues filled with 9,000 guys after those 400 big league jobs. In a time of one-year contracts and no guarantees, the only way you could make any money was to stay up there and have a good year. No automatic raises for .212 hitters or pitchers with 2 and 16 records. So you know we were fighting on the field for every edge we could get. And if you were hurt you played hurt, because you might not get back into the lineup.

When the game opened its doors to the pool of black players in 1947, that just raised the level of talent and competition so much higher. The players who had been in the Negro leagues and tasted that rough existence were hungrier than anybody to get to the majors and stay there. After Jackie Robinson had been in Brooklyn for a few years and his naturally volatile competitive nature was allowed to erupt, I recall a nervous Roy Campanella telling him, "Jackie, cool it. Please don't rock the boat. We've never had it so good." Campy was not that far removed from the days of playing a doubleheader in Washington in 105-degree heat, then getting on a school bus and riding to Baltimore for a night game in the same sweaty uniform.

The St. Louis Cardinals, who dominated the wartime years, winning pennants in 1942, 1943, and 1944, were our fiercest rivals for supremacy just after the war, with the Phillies on the rise. But it seemed that every team had a few topflight pitchers to throw at you and every lineup had heavy hitters and good glove men to battle you.

The managers were smart baseball men, mostly veteran players, but not all geniuses by any means. When I came back in 1946, Frankie Frisch was the Pirates manager. A great player, and probably a good manager at one time, he had lost it by then. One of the most caustic, foulmouthed people I have ever known, he and Durocher had a love-hate relationship for years. They rode each other so much, we almost begged them to cut it out.

Frisch knocked everybody because they could not play the way he did. Rarely have star players become winning managers; you can count them on one hand. Do not include Frisch. One day I was pitching in Pittsburgh and we suddenly noticed there was nobody in their dugout but Frisch and two coaches. The rest of the team was in the bullpen, where Frisch had banished them because he was sick of looking at them, they were so bad.

If one of his players got a bloop hit, he'd yell, "Jesus Christ, I could've hit the ball farther with my prick."

If he got kicked out of a game, he'd go home and tend to his prize petunias. The bench jockeys had a field day with him. "Go water your petunias, you asshole!" Larry Goetz was a huge, tough umpire; when those veins in his neck stuck out, look out. One day in Brooklyn Frisch was in his face yelling and Goetz hollered, "Go sit down, you Nazi sonofabitch. You're staying here until this game is over. I don't care what you call me."

When Frisch got into a big argument at home plate in Ebbets Field, Durocher said to our batboy, "Go get a bunch of towels and line them from home plate to the dugout, so Mr. Frisch can walk out in style." Frisch kicked those towels six ways from Sunday on his way out.

When Leo was ejected from a game, Frisch paid him back. "Bye, bye, Leo. Go put some more of your wife's perfume on."

It was the Gashouse Gang at war with itself. Frankie Frisch. A great guy for baseball.

My old hero Billy Herman managed the Pirates in 1947 and it was a disaster. Guys would be out all night and come to the ballpark in their tuxedos. Billy said nothing. Nobody knew the game better or was more likeable, but that didn't make him a manager. And he knew it.

Mel Ott was Mr. Nice Guy, but he never grasped the helm of the Giants with any authority; just didn't know how to manage twenty-five men.

Johnny Neun, the longtime Yankee scout, was the Cincinnati manager. If anybody tried to talk baseball with him, Johnny would tell them about the unassisted triple play he made with the Tigers in 1927. Not a bad thing to talk about, but you can get bored with it when you've heard it a thousand times. As most managers did in those days, he coached at third base, and some loudmouthed guy in the stands would invariably yell, "Triple play my ass, Neun. What else can you do?" John was a Baltimore native and we often visited in the press box in his later years. We reached an agreement: he wouldn't tell me about his triple play if I wouldn't tell him about my no-hitter.

Like Bucky Walters, Neun did not last long as a manager— too nice a guy. And Jolly Cholly Grimm would not have lasted, either, if he had not been a favorite of Mr. Wrigley in Chicago. Everybody loved the banjo-playing happy-go-lucky Charlie. He'd chew out his team, then go up to each player privately and tell him, "Forget what I said. It doesn't go for you."

Charlie would have one meeting at the start of the season and that was it. Didn't matter if half the team got swapped, the signs and everything stayed the same. He was a showman and good for baseball. One day in Wrigley Field I was warming up to start a game. Charlie stood on the third base line and put his hands up to his eyes like he's looking through binoculars. He looks around and spots me warming up, pulls the lineup card out of his pocket, puts it on the ground, piles dirt over it, and blesses it.

Eddie Sawyer won a pennant with the Phillies in 1950, although some of his Whiz Kids had little use for him. I don't think he was as bad a manager as a lot of people made him out to be. He got some winning years out of them.

And then there was Billy Southworth, a quiet, kind student of the game who overcame some personal tragedies and problems. He had won those wartime pennants with the Cardinals. When his son, Billy, Jr., a good ballplayer, was killed in a plane crash during the war, Southworth started drinking. Then he took over the Boston Braves and built them into winners in one of the greatest managing jobs of the century.

Durocher considered Southworth one of the best in the business, although they were direct opposites as personalities. Southworth used psychology to boost the confidence of each of his players. He never said anything derogatory, and was liked by all his players. But—

In 1948 he rounded up all the manager-haters he could find: Bob Elliott, Sibby Sisti, Earl Torgeson, Jeff Heath, Mike McCormick, Jim Russell, Bama Rowell . . . Maybe hate is too strong a word. Some guys think they should play every day and they act like they hate the manager, but that's not it. There are some guys who won't like any manager no matter who he is. They don't like authority of any kind. A lot of players think they know more than every manager they played for. And some guys just don't like anybody.

Bob Elliott was a rednecked third baseman who turned in an MVP year.

First baseman Earl Torgeson loved to talk about his RBIs, but he was a defensive liability; we called him RLI—runs let in.

When the Braves bought Jeff Heath from the Browns in December 1947, Burt Shotton commented, "No good sonofabitch, he's not a team man." Shotton thought the Braves had made a mistake, but Heath hit .319 and led all left fielders in fielding. A big muscular guy, Heath may have been among the first players to work with weights. He had been one of the leaders of the Cleveland Crybabies in 1940, and was a loud bench jockey. I was pitching on the day in September 1948 when he broke his leg trying to score on a hit. Campanella was catching and I was backing him up behind the plate. Heath came in standing up and at the last minute decided to slide. When I heard that *Crack!* I knew what happened. Only his sock kept his foot attached to his ankle. Campy got so sick he had to leave the field.

In the middle of this hornet's nest, Southworth put the rookie Alvin Dark at shortstop and our own Eddie Stanky at second base. Dark was a complete player with real baseball sense. You knew he would be a manager someday. I was pitching against him one day and started him off with a fastball just below the letters. He swung and missed. Next pitch was another hummer, a little higher. Again he swung and missed. He stood there, thinking, "This guy is pretty smart. He's going right up the ladder with me." So he got ready for another fastball about chin high and that's where I threw it. He lined a base hit. But he had actually given me more credit than I was due. He found out later that I had not pitched him shrewdly; I was just throwing the ball and had no idea where any of those pitches were going. The shrewdness was all on his part.

Dark was the first I saw using a black bat. From Louisiana, he did his share of Jackie-bashing in those years. I guess the only black he wanted to see on the field was his bat.

Catcher Phil Masi was the opposite of most of the guys on that team, a quiet gentleman who would almost apologize to you if you struck out. Masi was an excellent receiver and clutch hitter.

Outfielder Tommy Holmes was a meek and mild little contact hitter. Any pitcher who struck him out deserved a bonus. I mean, if you fanned him, the guys on the bench gave you a standing ovation. Look it up: almost 5,000 at bats and just 122 strikeouts. Get two strikes on him and he choked up three or four inches on the bat and practically stood on home plate. No power, just a .302 hitter for eleven years. Wade Boggs is a similar type hitter.

And then there was "Spahn and Sain and two days of rain." Between them they started almost half the games that season. Spahn was the best pitcher I have ever seen, bar none.

A smooth lefty, he was the most successful at picking Jackie off first base. Spahn always credits Southworth and Sain for much of his success.

Johnny Sain is a big, tobacco-chewing, rough-looking hillbilly from Havana, Arkansas, who knows more about pitching than anybody can catalog. If you said hello to him, you might get a grunt in response on a good day. One night in Brooklyn he threw thirty-two straight curveballs from thirty-two different directions: underhand, overhand, sidearm, three-quarters, behind his back almost. The whole world knew what was coming. Didn't matter. We haven't hit one of them yet. He could drop a curve in a coffee mug. And a great hitter, not just good.

Even as a pitching coach, Sain did not believe in running, which is rare for those guys. How did he stay in shape? By throwing fifteen or twenty minutes extra every day. "I can get my legs in as good shape that way as by running," he said.

Those 1948 Boston Braves were good enough to interrupt the Dodgers' domination of the National League during my brief stay with them.

The premier player of my time—and maybe of all time— was Stan the Man Musial. A saint of a man, one of God's chosen people. I mean that. He was the most popular player with guys from other clubs and fans in every city that I have ever seen. He destroyed us in Ebbets Field, yet the Brooklyn fans gave him a day and a new car before the Cardinals' fans did. It was pure respect and love, even while he was hitting .900 against us, always with a smile and a little trace of a Polish accent.

Musial started out as a pitcher, hurt his arm, moved to the outfield, never could throw, switched to first base, and played it like he'd been born there. On one rare day when we shut him down at the plate, he beat us with four miraculous catches.

He was a skinny guy, and run?—my God, he was fast. Looked like a greyhound, sort of leaning in as he rounded the bases.

At the plate he was the strangest-looking thing you ever saw. He stood in the farthest, deepest corner away from the plate every time, coiled, bent over, peering over his right shoulder like a man looking around the corner of a building. For twenty years pitchers debated how to pitch to Musial, and the answer was always the same: "Very carefully. Just do the best you can because you're getting the best from him, and most of the time that'll be better than you."

I watched guys pitch him outside and he'd step toward the plate and—*whoom!* Then they'd say, "You know he's going to step into the pitch, so throw it inside on his hands." His stride remained the same, but he got around on the pitch before it got in on him.

If you looked at him standing there you'd swear there had to be a lot of holes in his swing. But there weren't. He looked so uncomfortable up there, Durocher would say, "Make him wait. Walk off the mound. Shake him up a little."

So I tried it. Musial never moved a muscle, never backed out. He'd stand there for three days like a statue. Then you'd throw it and duck. I tried to quick pitch him and that didn't work either. Nothing worked against Stan the Man.

Joe Garagiola is his longtime friend and business partner. One day Joe was catching and he tried to distract Musial with small talk. "Hello, Stan, how's the family?" The next thing he heard was *whack!* and Musial was standing on third with a triple. A minute later Musial scored and said, "They're all fine, Joe," as he crossed home plate.

Two confrontations with Musial stand out in my mind. I was pitching in St. Louis and Gil Hodges was playing first base. I threw my hardest fastball and Stan hit it so hard down the first base line we thought it had gone right through Hodges's body. It hit the right field wall and bounced all the way back to Gil and Musial had to stop at first.

And once in Ebbets Field Bruce Edwards called for a fastball and I threw it and ducked as a line drive went right where my head had been and Duke Snider caught it at the center field wall. Edwards came out to the mound.

"You all right?" he asked.

"Yeah, why?"

"It looked like the ball went through the middle of your head. Look at your ear."

I rubbed my fingers on my ear and there was blood on them. The ball had nicked my ear; either that or there was some vicious mosquito out there.

Even the most modest of stars have a reservoir of pride that occasionally surfaces. Jim Frey told me he was with the Cardinals at the tail end of one season and they were at Wrigley Field. The place was mobbed and Musial said to him, "Kid, you know why all these people are here? They want to see Stanley play." And that's as close to a boast as anybody has ever heard out of Stan the Man.

It's funny how some guys seem to own certain pitchers, even though they are not great hitters. I'm proud to say that not many hitters owned me, but there were some. Roy Smalley and Whitey Lockman were two I just could not get out. Alvin Dark gave me a bad time. Granny Hamner, Frankie Gustine, Red Stallcup, Frankie Baumholtz, Johnny Wyrostek . . . guys most fans never heard of. That's another reason baseball is such a great game; how do you figure why some guys hit certain pitchers and not others?

And of course there were hitters who gave every pitcher a hard time. Some defining moments of great hitters I faced stand out in my mind. I can see big Ernie Lombardi standing there waving an enormous bat, gripping it so far down at the end, his two last fingers were off the bat. One day Kirby Higbe threw him a fastball and all I heard was *crack crack*—the bat hitting the ball and the ball hitting the seats. Both cracks echoed before he even got out of the batter's box. I'd never seen anything like that, but the guys on the bench said he did it all the time.

It took Lombardi eight years to get around the bases. Pee Wee Reese said, "He runs like a turtle with arthritis." The first time we played the Giants in 1943 and Lombardi came up to bat, I couldn't believe it; there was nobody in the infield. The first baseman was down the right field line. The second baseman was in right center field. And they threw him out at first from there. But he beat the shift once, on September 5 that year. He bunted toward third and beat it out for a hit. I saw it, or I might not believe it.

Johnny Mize was one of the best-looking hitters I ever saw, a real perfectionist. Straight-up stance, squared-away feet, complete body control. If the pitch was just a fraction outside, he would go up on his tiptoes and lean and watch it go by. If it was a fraction inside, he'd go back on his heels and give it a look. The closest I've seen to Mize was Boog Powell: big, no exaggerated motion, no half-swings, pure bat control. And I'm proud to say I could get Mize out fairly often.

There are certain great hitters you can somehow do well against and you don't really think about it, then years later the guy you got out is in the Hall of Fame and you're standing there in Cooperstown looking at his plaque and you say to yourself, by God, I got him out. Makes you feel a little proud.

Ted Kluszewski was one of the most powerful-looking men I ever saw. Like Jimmie Foxx, his arm was just one big club. You could not tell where his wrist ended and his forearm began. And he looked as if he had no ankles; his leg went from the calf right into the shoe. He hit a double off the Ebbets Field scoreboard on a pitch that bounced in front of the plate and when he slid into second the collision was like two freight trains meeting head-on. I think the good lord made guys like Klu, Foxx, Frank Howard, and Boog Powell calm and easygoing to save the world from destruction, because if they were mean and wanted to clean out a room, they could do it in no time.

I pitched against Hank Greenberg when he was winding up his career in Pittsburgh. Tall, handsome, aloof—a superstar all the way. One day he came up with the bases loaded and 2 outs in the ninth. I got a 3 and 2 count on him and threw one of the best curves I'd ever thrown. Everybody in the ballpark thought it was a strike, including Greenberg, but the umpire called it a ball. I'll never forget that pitch. The next day Hank told me it was definitely a strike. Anytime you can fool a hitter like Greenberg, you hate to lose it.

But my greatest memory of Greenberg is a Sunday afternoon in Forbes Field, Hugh Casey pitching. It was a sweltering hot day. Greenberg steps out of the batter's box, calls time and walks to the dugout, and splashes himself with cold water. Casey stands there fuming. When Hank steps back in, Casey calls time, walks to our dugout, splashes water on his face, walks back to the mound, throws strike three past him. It was a great battle of one-upmanship. I'd bet on Casey every time.

Ralph Kiner was a home run threat every time he had a bat in his hands. One of the best power hitters, he hit some memorable shots off me. Ralph couldn't run. Ralph couldn't field. Ralph couldn't throw. Ralph couldn't hit for average. But Ralph could hit home runs as well as anybody in the business.

I pitched against Ted Williams in exhibition games a few times, but I had the rare privilege of being on a train with the

Red Sox when I was broadcasting the Mutual Game of the Day. I had dinner with Joe Cronin and when we went into the lounge car there was Williams with a stick in his hands giving batting lessons to a few players.

Cronin said, "Sit down and watch this." I'm sure he'd heard it a thousand times.

I sat there mesmerized for two hours, watching this man talk about hitting, and talk about pitching, and talk about how the only person who gives him a hard time is a rookie pitcher.

"Once I see him a few times, I got him measured," he said. "Then he belongs to me." Williams believed pitchers are the dumbest people in the world. "If they get you out they follow that pattern, and since I know how they got me out, now I've got them." Then suddenly he said, "That's it. Good night."

Cronin said to me, "You just heard the best in the business."

As I look back at the defensive lineups we faced, the pitcher that hitters dreaded facing the most was not the greatest—his record will tell you that—but for a few years he was as good as anybody: Ewell Blackwell. The Whip. He stood 6-6 and looked like he weighed 125 pounds. When he wound up he turned his back on the hitter, and you could see the ball behind his back. Then he whirled and that arm came around like a snake by way of third base or lower. We were not surprised when he hurt his arm early in his career. He threw hard and never hesitated to knock you down. I would never tease a hitter, especially a right-hand hitter, about facing that guy. He had a natural sinker and a wicked curve. He came within two outs of pitching consecutive no-hitters.

Pee Wee Reese said, "I'd take appendicitis rather than go up against Blackwell." The closest modern pitcher I can think of is Don Drysdale.

Johnny Vander Meer was near the end of his career, but what I remember best about him was a double he hit off me one night in Cincinnati. Reese took the relay and kept the ball and I straddled the rubber on the mound without touching it. Vandy strolled off the bag and Pee Wee said, "John, look what I got," and showed him the ball. Vander Meer said, "You little sonofabitch, if you tag me with that, I'll kill you." Reese ran over and tagged him and kept on running.

Mort Cooper was a big heavyset guy who knew how to pitch, a Rick Reuschel type.

Ken Raffensberger was a cutie, another Preacher Roe; couldn't blacken your eye with a pitch. The ball would come up there looking like a basketball, then all of a sudden it wasn't there.

Schoolboy Rowe was a pain in the ass. Always talking, popping off, with the Phillies after his big years at Detroit. Durocher rode him hard and he'd blow up. He knew how to pitch, all right, but was not much of a human being. He's another one who would throw at Jackie three or four times in a row. I didn't like that.

Johnny Schmitz, left-hand curveballer, owned the Dodgers. I think we eventually got him from the Cubs just to keep him from beating us. I can close my eyes and see that curve; three inches in front of home plate it was up around your head, and the catcher wound up catching it by your feet. Damnedest curve I've ever seen.

Claude Passeau was a respected veteran right-hander whom Leo Durocher held up as an example to us young pitchers. Had a great move to first base and could pick you off just looking at you. Pitched a one-hitter for the Cubs against Detroit in the 1945 World Series.

Hank Borowy was the kind of pitcher who sent batters back to the bench muttering, "He's got nothing. He won't be around the next time I hit." He pitched a one-hitter against us and that's when I learned to be leery whenever I heard batters talk that way.

Harry Brecheen was a crafty lefty with the Cardinals who cheated a lot. (It is one of baseball's linguistic traditions that only left-handers can be crafty. You never hear of a crafty right-hander; it's always "a hard-throwing right-hander" and "a crafty left-hander.") In those days players left their gloves on the field when they came in to bat. Pitchers left theirs on the grass between home and first or third. Not Brecheen. He took his into the dugout. Later Preacher Roe told us he was doctoring the ball. They called him Harry the Cat because he was a good fielder, pouncing on everything he could reach. But we called him Harry the Rat, because he'd throw at you and just before the ball got to your head he'd yell, "Look out!"

Dutch Leonard was a veteran knuckleball pitcher. I've never been enamored of knucklers. I think they're boring as hell to watch. They take so much time and it's the same pitch over and over. I never heard of a championship team that depended on knuckleball pitching. There are too many things that can happen when the catcher tries to hold onto it.

Clint Hartung, the Hondo Hurricane, was going to change the world of baseball: pitch, play the outfield, win 20 games, and hit 50 home runs for the Giants. I remember a headline in a New York paper: "The Ultimate Pitching Battle: Rex Barney v. Clint Hartung." I beat him. He never lived up to the media hype.

The most solid pitcher on the Giants in those days was Larry Jansen. Perfect control, outstanding slider, and a real gentleman.

Red Barrett was probably the fastest worker ever. Grab it and throw. Pitched a complete game against us in about an hour and a half. Once threw just 58 pitches to beat the Reds, 2 to 0. He was not made for the television era.

One day Rip Sewell knocked Joe Garagiola on his back with the first pitch, then hit him with the second. The next time up, Joe pushed a bunt down the first base line, hoping Sewell would field it so he could run up the pitcher's back.

"He tagged me so hard," Joe says, "he knocked me ten feet. I never had a shot."

Sewell developed the "eephus" pitch; it arced like a rainbow coming up to the plate. It was a novelty pitch but he could get it over. A lot of guys swung at it and couldn't touch it, but Ted Williams teed off on one in the 1946 All-Star Game.

Robin Roberts was born a pitcher. One day against the Dodgers he threw nothing but junk the first four innings. The rest of the game he just blew the ball by everybody. He lulled them to sleep, then took over. He had that kind of mind. There are guys who can turn it up inning to inning or hitter to hitter, when they need it. Seaver, Palmer, Ryan come to mind. Baseball players, especially pitchers, have unbelievable memories. They can recall just about every pitch they've ever seen or thrown. Joe Adcock told me he hit two home runs in one game off Robin Roberts, and seven years later he was still looking for that same pitch from Roberts, but he knew he was never going to get it.

I recall a vivid instance of toughness on the field. Ted Wilks was pitching for the Cardinals at Ebbets Field. A line drive hit him in the jaw. He picked up the ball and threw the guy out before he collapsed.

We had a lot of excellent catchers in the National League in those postwar years, and Ernie Lombardi was one of them. If he couldn't reach a wide pitch with the glove, he'd stop it with his bare hand, which was big as a bear paw. When the umpire handed him a new ball it just disappeared in there. And he'd rub it up with the fingertips of one hand. He never stood up to throw to second, didn't have to. Just raise his arm and *whiff*—rifle shot to second. He never even tried to catch most pop fouls, because he knew he'd never get to them. We wondered how he got the mask on over his big schnozz. I think he was very shy and self-conscious, not much of a talker, but well liked.

Andy Seminick was a hard-nosed catcher, completely bald by the time he got to the major leagues. Nobody ever saw his head uncovered. When he'd throw off the mask we used to swear the cap was nailed to his head. One time he was running to first base and the wind blew his cap off; that bald dome turned as red as red can be. A big, burly guy, he was a nonstop chatterbox behind the plate.

Clyde McCullough was another talker—broken nose, tough-looking puss, like a catcher should look—but a delightful guy.

Clyde Kluttz was a very good catcher who remains little known and underrated. He later became an executive with the Yankees and an assistant to Hank Peters at Baltimore.

I remember Mickey Livingston as a loud bench jockey, always firing salvoes at Durocher, and a constant talker behind the plate.

Walker Cooper, a big lumbering right-hand hitter with tremendous power, was a better defensive catcher than he is given credit for. Pitchers told me he was an excellent receiver. Another talker. He'd needle us pitchers when we batted: "You bush bastard, you don't have anything. You won't be around by the time I hit." To the hitters he might say, "You can't hit anything this guy throws." He knew who it would bother; on our team that was Reese and Furillo.

Joe Garagiola was an excellent caller of the game, but hitting was his problem, as he is the first to admit. Still, he had one big World Series with the bat. You have to be pretty good to do that.

I was always an Al Lopez fan. He was a player-coach with the Pirates in '46. In Forbes Field the bullpens were separated by a screen and we would visit. You knew he was going to be a manager; he studied the game closely and was the type of guy who would help anybody. He taught Preacher Roe the slider and spitter and made a winner out of him. I did not hesitate to ask him for help. But unfortunately he couldn't make a winner out of me.

Some slick-fielding first basemen stand out in my memory. Ray Sanders was as classy as you'll ever see, but he is not remembered because physical problems and injuries hampered him. It's a shame nobody ever saw the complete Ray Sanders.

Eddie Waitkus was a very, very good fielder with the Cubs and Phillies who is best remembered for being shot by a lady he did not know in a Philadelphia hotel room. A tall, lanky guy with a great sense of humor. I saw him upset only once, when Ralph Branca knocked him down, then hit him with a pitch. That was almost good for a brawl.

Phil Cavarretta was the best hustler I saw, because he went all out all the time despite playing on losing teams. He ran as hard as he could on every little pop-up or ground ball back to the pitcher. If the catcher dropped the third strike, you'd think it was a World Series the way he'd go down to first base. The Cubs played at one-thirty and they were home by five o'clock. It was an easy life, but you'd never know it by him. He was a favorite in Chicago, but Phil was a mean, surly guy. As a manager, he never gave any credit to anybody for anything, and nobody liked playing for him.

I remember Bert Haas because he was a rough, mouthy jockey. If we got on him, he gave it right back. Most guys would just pretend they didn't hear you, but not Bert. There was seldom much conversation at first base, maybe a "How lucky can you get?" if I got a hit or a walk. But Bert Haas would start in on me. "Christ, you haven't got a thing out there. Who're you trying to fool with that crap you're throwing?"

Babe Young is one of the few guys who caught Pee Wee Reese in a mental lapse. Reese was on first and Dixie Walker was up. Dixie swung and missed. The bat flew out of his hands and landed between home and first. Pee Wee picked it up and handed it to Walker. Young got the ball and tagged Reese. Time had not been called. As a hitter Young was always on himself; he'd swing and miss and stand there muttering, "You dumb sonofabitch." One day he swung and missed and the ball got away from catcher Bruce Edwards and rolled a few feet away. As Bruce retrieved it, Young stepped out, admonishing himself, and took a big practice cut, just missing Bruce's head by inches. That was scary.

Elbie Fletcher was a good guy who took a lot of ribbing, which in his case was a sign of popularity. Elbie hated to hit against me. When the Pirates almost went out on strike in 1946, he was one of those who voted to play and helped prevent the walkout.

I guess these things have their cycles, but there was not a lot of talent at second base in the postwar National League. Red Schoendienst was an excellent infielder who deserves his Hall of Fame honor. He had a peculiar habit: between pitches he took the glove off his hand and held it, and we used to bet that he wouldn't get it back on in time for the next pitch. But he always did.

I remember Jack Lohrke because they called him "Lucky"; in the minor leagues he was called off the team bus just before it went on a trip that ended in disaster. The bus went over a cliff and eight players were killed.

Danny Murtaugh was just flat-out tough. One day he tagged Sid Gordon hard on a play and Gordon went back to the bench yelling, "You little Irish bastard, I'll kill you." Murtaugh called time and walked right over to the dugout. "You want to do something about it? Come on, let's do it right here." Gordon never moved. One day he hit a home run off me that hit on top of the fence and bounced over. Gene Hermanski got a glove on it. But the way Danny told it, he hit it over Greenberg Gardens, over three rivers and two states. A true tobacco-chewing Irish leprechaun he was, and everybody loved him.

Murtaugh reminds me of another point I want to make about ballplayers. You hear a lot of swearing around a clubhouse or dugout, and some of them would be struck mute if four-letter words were banned. But there were—and are today—plenty of pugnacious, aggressive guys like Danny Murtaugh who never used any profanity at all. He hated that kind of language, and his biggest hatred was for the m-f- word. When he managed the Pirates, he had an automatic $100 fine for anybody who said it. That doesn't sound like much money these days, but back then it was enough to cause some players to clean up their act. One day Danny took pitcher Dock Ellis out of a game. Ellis stormed into the dugout. "Murtaugh, you're a no-good m-f- sonofabitch."

"That'll cost you a hundred," Danny said.

After the game Murtaugh went into the clubhouse and found a check for $200 with a note from Dock: "I m-f-'d you again after I got in here."

There was an abundance of outstanding shortstops at that time. After Pee Wee, I thought Marty Marion was the best. Part of the fascination of Marion was his physique. A tall, skinny guy, he moved like a cat, played shallow, and had tremendous range. Some guys preferred Buddy Kerr. Kerr had great hands. He scouts for the Mets and loves to tell everybody how he was with the Giants when I pitched my no-hitter and he hit four line drives that night and had Snider's back against the fence all night. So one day he's telling this story and I happened to have the newspaper account of the game that showed he was taken out for a pinch hitter in the eighth. I thought he was going to die. "My son still doesn't know," he said. "Don't ever tell him. He thinks I wore you out." Now the truth is out. Reese's favorite was Eddie Miller: great arm, didn't cover a lot of ground, but knew how to play the hitters, and anything he got to was an out. He used a tiny glove with nothing in the middle of it. I mean he actually cut the leather right out of the palm.

Connie Ryan was a tough, feisty bench jockey. He'd call you everything in the world right to your face and then punch you out. Always in the middle of a fight. One day in the Polo Grounds Whitey Lockman hit a double and slid into second. Ryan said, "Whitey, would you step off the bag a minute? It's loose and I want to kick it straight." Whitey took his foot off and Ryan tagged him out. Ryan had tipped off the umpire that he might try something like that. All hell broke loose, but Whitey was still out. Ryan was that type of player, always thinking, making the most of what talent he had.

Billy Jurges was a complete player who played a very shallow shortstop, but he had a very short temper. He caused many a fight. Somebody would slide into second and the next thing you knew there was swinging and cursing and rolling in the dirt and a mob scene. Players called him "Bulletproof" because he got shot by some woman but was not seriously wounded.

Roy Smalley was an excellent fielder with a great arm, but more than that, he owned Rex Barney. He was Gene Mauch's brother-in-law, so maybe he felt entitled. All I know is he hit .216 in 1948, all of it against me. I took a lot of riding on the bench because of him.

Bill Rigney was an infielder who thought he was a second Leo Durocher. Just an average player, he fit the description: "He's a good ballplayer, but he's not as good as he thinks he is."

The National League was a little thin on outstanding third basemen, outside of Billy Cox, that is. Whitey Kurowski was a very good glove man and a timely hitter. He had one arm shorter than the other but it did not bother him at bat. Boy, he was tough. And mean. He'd cut you in half sliding into you if he had the chance. Made a lot of noise and pepper on the field.

By the time I saw my hero, Stan Hack, his range at third had shrunk. But anything he got to, he caught, with one of those palm-sized gloves. I doubt that he ever made a mental mistake. A good hitter, he knew the strike zone perfectly. One of the nicest people who ever lived, he smiled all the time, even with a jaw full of chaw. Too nice a guy to be an effective manager. I think he belongs in the Hall of Fame.

I remember a pair of beauts on the Cubs: a hot dog named Lou Stringer; and a character named Billy Schuster who thought nothing of running to the mound instead of to first base when he hit a little nubber and sliding into the pitcher, or running to third instead of first if he was out by a mile. He didn't last long.

The Phillies had a third baseman, Jim Tabor, finishing up after some good years with the Red Sox. A heavy drinker, he died young. I wouldn't mention him at all except that he's the subject of one of the funniest—and hardest to write—stories I ever heard on the banquet circuit. And I wouldn't repeat it if Jim Bagby, Jr., had not been the source. You have to understand that Bagby, a big, fun-loving guy, had a hairlip, which I can imitate more effectively in person than in print. Nor do I feel I am making fun of him, because he assured me that he did not mind my repeating the story the way he told it himself. So here it is.

Bagby and Tabor were rookie roommates with the Red Sox in the late thirties. In those days the manager or a coach made sure that all the players were in by midnight, especially the young guys. They checked by calling the room and talking to both players, or by going around knocking on doors. Bagby was always covering up for the carousing Tabor.

One night at midnight manager Joe Cronin called the room. Bagby answered the phone. "Yeah?"

"This is Cronin. Just checking to make sure you're in."

"Yeah, we're here. Everything's okay."

"Let me talk to Tabor."

"Aw, Jethuth Chritht. He'th thleepin', thnorin' away. He'd beat the thit out of me if I woke him up."

Cronin said, "I want to talk to him. Wake him up."

"You can take my word for it. I wouldn't lie to you. I tell you he'th thleepin', been in bed a long time."

"If you don't wake him up, I'm going to come up there and make sure he's there."

Bagby said, "Well, all right. Goddamn, he'th gonna be mad."

There was a pause, then Cronin heard, "Yeah, thkip, thith ith Tabor. Whaddaya want?"

Talented, smart outfielders were plentiful in those days. One of the best was my Legion ball opponent from Tilden, Nebraska, Richie Ashburn. Before our first game against the Phillies in 1948, Durocher held a meeting.

"Anybody know this kid leading off, Ashburn?"

I said, "I know him. We played against each other as kids. He was a catcher then."

"What do you know about him?"

"Well, he can get down to first base as fast as Pete Reiser, maybe faster."

That brought a big horse laugh from everybody.

"You asked my opinion," I said. "He will bunt, go to the opposite field, good contact but no power, and he'll fly."

During the game he hit a routine grounder to Pee Wee at shortstop, and I can still see Reese catching the ball, coming up to throw, and standing there with his mouth open. Ashburn was already across first base. Leo looked down at me on the bench and said, "You were right."

People ask me if I think Ashburn should be in the Hall of Fame. I hate that kind of question. The standards for the Hall have gone down over the years. There are a lot of guys in there who I don't think should be, some one-dimensional players. Mr. Rickey maintained that an all-around player should be able to run, throw, field, hit, and hit for power. Ashburn was great in three of the five. He did not have much of an arm, but he made up for it by playing very shallow, cutting off many a base hit that way.

I remember Marv Rickert, a left-hand hitter, because he had a strange way of twisting his fanny just before he swung. He was a fun-loving guy, good hitter, and had a great arm. He got into the 1948 World Series because of Jeff Heath's injury.

Peanuts Lowrey was very popular on the Cubs, a fiery, peppy little guy who dreaded batting against me. "I never want any part of you," he told me. "If I ever got one hit off you, that would do me for the rest of my life."

A fellow Nebraskan, Johnny Hopp, came from a family of speedsters. His brother Harry helped Nebraska win the Rose Bowl one year. One of the quickest men I've ever seen, he helped every team he played for. I saw a photograph in his house that should be a lesson to every headfirst slider in the game. In it he's sitting with both hands in casts. Playing for Rochester, he had slid headfirst into second base so hard he jammed both hands and broke both wrists.

You knew Andy Pafko was something special first time you saw him. He could run and hit with power, a good glove man who played hard and could not be intimidated. And a gentleman with it all.

I'm always talking about Carl Furillo's strong, accurate arm. There was a journeyman outfielder, Ron Northey, who had just as strong an arm, but he was a little wild like another hard thrower I won't mention. I saw Northey throw a ball from the outfield halfway up the screen in a lot of ballparks. A short, stocky left-hand hitter, Northey was with the Reds when I relieved Roe one day. My first pitch to him blew between his head and his cap as he went down. Bruce Edwards came out to me and said, "God almighty, Rex. I thought you'd knocked his head off." The next pitch was a foot outside and low. Northey reached out and hit a little tapper to third. Later he told me, "I didn't give a damn where you threw it. I was going to swing and get out of there with my life."

I remember Johnny Wyrostek because he wore me out and he was a pleasant, friendly guy who visited with the pitchers in the bullpen behind his outfield position. He could do it all.

Del Ennis is one of the really super human beings in the world. A stand-up, strong power hitter. I had pretty good luck against him. Ennis was one of the hitters who were always hoping to see a curveball from me, because it was a little slower than the fastball. I think Ennis was at bat when I threw the fastest pitch of my life. I swear he swung at it while the catcher was throwing the ball back to me. Ennis was a much better outfielder and had a better arm than people gave him credit for. I think playing in his home town, Philadelphia, hurt him. They seemed to be on him a lot, and he did not deserve it.

Another super gentleman was Bill "Swish" Nicholson. I think I had more success against him than failures, although I recall some crucial hits and home runs he hit off me. I also remember striking him out in a tight spot with one of the best curves I ever threw. After the game he said to me, "From you, I'm looking fastball. And I'm still looking. I haven't seen it yet." Like many of us, he never visited with the opposition. Just "Hey" and keep on going. But a good guy.

I saw Terry Moore make this catch: playing in right center when Pete Reiser hit a screaming shot toward left center, Moore took off in a dead run and dove flat out, stretched out parallel to the ground, and caught the ball in his bare hand. He could not have reached it with the glove.

I said, "My God, what a catch."

Somebody on the bench said, "Aw, he's been doing that for ten years."

Nuff sed.

Country Slaughter could do it all and do it aggressively, but I never forgave him for intentionally spiking Jackie at first base.

Harry the Hat Walker never stopped talking, on the bench, on the field, as a manager. Came from Leeds, Alabama. I can hear that accent to this day, a carbon copy of his brother Dixie.

He got his nickname from his habit of taking his hat off between pitches and fitting it and adjusting it 'til it was just right, driving everybody crazy. Harry the Hat wore a helmet in a tank just like I did during the war.

Wally Westlake looked the prototype ballplayer: big, strapping, fierce-looking, busted nose and all. But he was very soft-spoken and kind.

Mel Ott played in a few games in 1943 and took batting practice every day. I used to think his peculiar stance was a lot of baloney until I saw it. He really lifted that right leg high, but he got it down at just the right instant, which is the trick in that kind of stance. I remember he was smaller than I had imagined.

Bobby Thomson, the Flying Scot, really could fly. You never saw anybody quicker on the bases. He was a fine outfielder. One day Duke Snider came running in from the outfield carrying Thomson's glove. It had a big webbing attached to it, extending the fingers, which was illegal. Today probably two of them would fit inside an outfielder's glove.

And then there were always the guys who looked like naturals, like ballplayers should look if they were sculpted out of marble, but who somehow never made it. The "can't miss" types. One I recall was Hal Jeffcoat. He had it all: the physique, speed, arm, and swing. But he just couldn't get the job done. The Cubs made a pitcher out of him, with fair success.

It is customary in books of this type to pick all-star teams, but for this review of the postwar National League, I am going to limit mine to an all-defense team which will include the Dodgers. These are the players from my time that I would most like to see on the field if I was on the mound.

Catcher: Roy Campanella
First base: Gil Hodges
Second base: Red Schoendienst
Third base: Billy Cox
Shortstop: Pee Wee Reese
Right field: Carl Furillo
Center field: Terry Moore
Left field: Pete Reiser

If I had a one-run lead in the ninth, the guy I would want to see coming in to save it: Hugh Casey.

If I needed a left-hander to pitch to one batter: Alpha Brazle.

Those are some of my impressions of the guys in the other uniforms that remain in my mind after some forty-five years. It's not all-inclusive, but one's memory never is.

SEVENTEEN

On the Air

I HAVE BEEN in the broadcasting business for forty years now, but I still hear people say, "The only reason Rex Barney has that show or that job is that he's a former player."

Well, in the first place, you don't last as long as I have if that's all you have going for you. And second, or maybe first, I've worked as hard as anybody to get where I am. In fact, I worked harder and longer to be a broadcaster than I did as a player.

A long time ago Joe Garagiola told me, "Just be yourself on the air. That's all I've ever done. And don't worry about what anybody else says."

Good advice. I have tried to follow it.

Red Barber was the first to suggest to me that I should consider radio work when my playing days were over, which seemed like a million years away at the time. When he interviewed me in 1943, he commented that I had a good radio voice.

Players are very aware of the announcers for their team, even though they don't get to hear them very often. I was always an intense and observant listener, absorbing ideas and techniques long before I ever thought of using them. In Brooklyn we used to stand in the outfield during batting practice and imitate Barber as if he were describing the B.P. play by play. Red Barber and Connie Desmond were our radio team. They each did half the game, and all the commercials live. The early broadcasters—Barber, Mel Allen, Russ Hodges, and others—helped to sell the game to the public, especially to women and young people who seldom went to games. Barber ended every half-inning by giving the score, then saying, "Hurry back, heah?" The people in Brooklyn fell in love with that southern accent and the phrases he coined: the flock, the catbird seat, rhubarb. A nut for preparation, he had learned early to describe just what he saw and everything he saw, but without editorial comment. He introduced the egg timer into the booth as a reminder to give the score often.

Connie Desmond was one of the best pure play-by-play men I ever knew. A graduate of Notre Dame, he used to tell us tales about Notre Dame football. And Ernie Harwell began his career with the Dodgers in the middle of the 1948 season. We sure had the best while I was there.

Barber and Desmond were the first to travel with a team and do the road games live. They and the writers were like part of the family. There were a dozen papers in the New York area covering us. They played cards with us and sometimes roomed with a player. Media people rarely came into the clubhouse after a game, unlike the stampede that turns the manager's office into a zoo every night these days. We saw them before a game and they got their background stories then. The newspaper accounts described the game itself and what the writer saw, not the manager's explanation or a player's view.

It was family, but like any family it was not always one big happy one. Some players feuded with some writers, but there was an overriding trust. Writers did not pry into players' private lives looking for dirt. If they stumbled on some, they did not write it. There was no conspiracy or cover-up. They believed, accurately, that the public was not interested.

A lot of players called Dick Young of the New York *Daily News* "Poison Pen," and he got punched out a few times. I thought he was one of the very best writers, because he called things as he saw them, good or bad, and he worked harder than anybody. If we had a secret meeting for players only at 8 A.M., he found out about it and was waiting outside. The next day he'd have the whole story of what went on in the meeting. We knew which players were giving him the scoop, but we didn't do anything about it.

In 1950 when I worked out early in the mornings at Ebbets Field, I was never surprised to find Dick Young watching me. He was on the job at all times.

We even had a full-time photographer, Barney Stein, who traveled with us. It was an interesting collection of characters, and a great experience for me.

There were no pregame or postgame shows from the ballpark when I started. Interviews were done earlier. Later, the first television from Ebbets Field was Happy Felton's Knothole Gang. A player got $25 for being on the show, but Jackie Robinson and Pee Wee Reese were on so often they made all the money.

CBS radio had a football roundup on Saturdays in the fall. Red Barber anchored it, and his correspondent covering the East was a Fordham student, Vin Scully. Scully played baseball for Fordham, but he says the only time his name ever got into the game accounts in *The New York Times* was when Lou Effrat wrote, "After Scully fanned . . . "

Barber liked Scully and brought him to the Dodgers. Scully was gung ho but terrible on the air, full of cliches. He practiced during the winter and studied recordings of Barber and others. His voice is magnificent and he is a great storyteller and fanatic about preparation, as Barber was and as I learned to be. Scully was in the clubhouse, around the batting cage, listening, asking, learning. In more than forty years I have never ever known a player, coach, or manager who did not respect Scully's credibility; with all that he heard and saw, he always knew what to use and what not to use.

Scully leans toward the Dodgers on the air, and why not? He's been with them since 1950. But he is not an out-and-out homer, like Bert Wilson in Chicago, who used to say, "I don't care who wins, as long as it's the Cubs."

Today Vin Scully is far ahead of all the rest of us in this business. He'll quote something from Shakespeare or Homer, and he is not working from notes. You can't go on the air thinking, "I'm going to use this quote or this phrase." It just doesn't work that way. If he is working a World Series on the radio, turn down the sound on the television while you watch, and listen to him.

One of Scully's most memorable lines came during the 1986 Mets-Red Sox Series, and Scully was doing TV. Rich Gedman had just been called out on strikes in a crucial spot and Scully said, "The pitcher jumps for joy and the umpire is very emphatic about the called strike and Gedman walks away muttering something about fertilizer."

That takes a quick mind. Most guys on the air would just lay off something like that. In an instant my phone rang and it was Chuck Thompson. "Did you hear what he said?"

It's almost worth moving to Los Angeles just to be able to listen to him every day. Almost.

I was always interested in listening to broadcasters around the league and later when I was in the business.

Jim Britt in Boston and Jack Brickhouse in Chicago had it made for a while; they did the home games of both teams in their cities and did not have to travel.

Waite Hoyt in Cincinnati and Byrum Saam in Philadelphia were giants. Reds fans used to hope for rain delays because Hoyt filled them with stories from his playing days.

In Pittsburgh Bob Prince and Jim Woods were a great team, and before them there was the inimitable Rosey Rowswell: "Open the window, Minnie, here comes a home run!" Then you'd hear the sound of crashing glass. "You forgot to open the window, Minnie!" Corny stuff, maybe, but it was a big hit with the fans.

Mel Allen was an institution with the Yankees. He rooted for them openly on the air, but he was a creative, distinctive personality.

Russ Hodges had a strange occupational hazard: he was afraid of heights. Most ballpark radio booths are pretty high. He had to tie himself to a brace with a belt or strap to keep from jumping out as he looked down on the field.

Jack Buck started out as the number two man to Harry Caray in St. Louis. Another thorough preparer, when he worked with an unfamiliar team on network broadcasts he asked a lot of questions before a game. Not every broadcaster would do that.

I don't know that the players liked Hodges or Allen, who did not seem to move as easily among them as Buck and Scully and Harwell.

There was a radio in every clubhouse and pitchers got to listen more than anybody else, when they got knocked out of the box or were due to pitch the second game of a doubleheader. I had both kinds of opportunities. I was pitching the second game in St. Louis one day and I lay on the training table listening to Dizzy Dean. Bob Ramazzotti was an infielder with the Dodgers.

Dean said, "The next hitter is Bobazzotti. I don't know if I'm pronouncing that right, but he's gotta be a good player."

Gabby Street, his partner, said, "Why do you say that?"

"Cause he's got two z's in his name like ole Diz so he oughta be good."

The next day Dean said to me, "Kid, I saw you pitch yesterday."

"Yes, sir."

"You throw hard, but not as hard as Ol' Diz."

He was probably right, but I loved that, when one of my idols told me he saw me pitch.

Later I took my first helicopter ride with Diz and Buddy Blattner at the Cleveland airport. "Doggone, this is like riding in air," Diz said, and it was. He told us about betting on games while he was broadcasting, and how he had stiffed some bookie in Chicago and the commissioner called him in and warned him about it.

Frankie Frisch worked behind the mike in Boston for a few years and for the Giants in 1947. He was from New York so could do no wrong, but he was always knocking the players on the air. "These guys are nothing . . . they couldn't play when I did . . . " Then he'd talk about Dean and Hubbell and the stars from his time.

I don't buy that. There are players today who could have played anytime in the past, and there have always been great players on the field in every era. There may have been more stars during some decades than at other times, but a lot of players could have made any team, anytime, past or present.

Baseball is more difficult to broadcast than football or basketball because you have so much more time with no action. That's where preparation helps, not with stats, which I think are overdone, and not with inside jokes about the engineer's necktie or who ate what in the coffee shop, but with background information and anecdotes about the players and the game. The veterans—Hoyt, Harwell, Scully, Barber—excelled at that.

As a play-by-play broadcaster, Chuck Thompson is tops. You know exactly what's going on in the game. He doesn't get behind the action telling stories; he just does the game. When Jon Miller does baseball, he's as good as anybody in the business. A lot of fans like that comedy hour stuff during the games, but I'm not one of them. I can't stand that.

Chuck Thompson has got to go into the Hall of Fame in Cooperstown, and I hope it's soon, but not as a mechanic. We go on the road to do a lot of banquets together. One winter's night he and I went to Cumberland, Maryland, for an annual event. He drove his new Cadillac. On the way home we were going through the mountains and it was after eleven and cold out and a big band tape is playing; we're having a ball and *pow!* Flat tire.

We sat there and looked at each other, two absolute idiots when it comes to mechanical things.

"Do you have a spare tire?" I asked.

"I don't know."

We looked and there was one.

"We need something to take the hubcap off."

"They're locked on."

"Where's the key?"

"In Baltimore."

He had some kind of emergency phone you plug into the cigarette lighter. "But I don't know how to work it."

We fiddled with it and figured it out and got onto the state police with our sad story. A trooper showed up and offered to fix it for us, until we told him we couldn't get the hubcap off. Now it was near midnight, but the trooper had a friend who owned a garage. He roused the poor guy out of bed and got us towed in. The mechanic broke the lock on the hubcap and put a new tire on and Chuck said, "How much do I owe you?"

"I have no idea," he said. Chuck gave him something and when we were back on the road he said, "This is the last Cadillac I'll ever own. They're not supposed to have flat tires." And it was.

About the time I had abandoned all hope of making a comeback as a pitcher, I began doing some radio work in Omaha with Jack Sandler, a local broadcaster. I had grown to like Vero Beach, Florida, during our spring training visits, and I had made some friends there, so I decided to go down there to start a new life.

In Vero Beach, which counted about 2,500 inhabitants, I tried selling cars to pay the rent, worked part time for a 250-watt radio station, WNTM, "Where the North and Tropics Meet." It was the first station in the town.

I did a sports show, a late-night musical scoreboard, high school football and basketball, and every spring I did some Dodgers exhibition games. Daytona Beach had a team in the Class D Florida State League and I did some of their home games. I loved it. I was back in the game.

In the spring of 1955 I got a tip that Charleston, West Virginia, in the American Association, was looking for a play-by-play broadcaster. I sat in the studio and made up three innings of a game between the Yankees and Dodgers for an audition tape and got the job. But I had a lot to learn.

For two seasons I worked the home games live and the road games sitting in a studio at WCAW. Most of today's broadcasters never did a recreated game and they missed a real experience. I sat in a windowless room with a teletype machine beside me. A Western Union operator at the ballpark transmitted the basic information of each pitch and play. (In some cities there was another Western Union operator in the studio, receiving the reports by Morse code and translating them.)

The message might read: "b o os" (ball one outside) . . . "lfb rf" (long foul ball to right field) . . . "go 2b" (ground out to second base). From that we had to describe the action as if we were sitting at the ballpark. On a base hit, I'd rap a pencil against the table to simulate the sound of bat meeting ball. A tape of crowd noise played in the background.

I learned to seek out colorful angles to add to the effect. For example, Lou Skizas, an outfielder who had a brief big league career, was with Kansas City. He had a habit of sticking his right hand in his back pocket before every pitch. I asked him about it and he said he had a rabbit's foot back there. So I'm doing a teletype game and I say, "Skizas steps up to the plate and there's his hand going to his back pocket the way he always does."

People thought I was a genius, but it was all in the preparation.

Rain delays were deadly on those recreations. There was nobody to send the program back to in the studio, because I was the only one in the studio. I filled in with stories from my playing days.

I took some speech lessons and met a professor at Morris Harvey College when I did their basketball games. He offered to help me, and sat in the radio booth with a big yellow pad taking notes. I had broken a tooth jumping out of a tank in the army and it made a slight hissing sound when I spoke, so I got that fixed. I was using too much baseball slang and overusing some phrases. Everything was "real good" or "real great" and he told me to get rid of the "real." We are often not conscious of our speech habits until someone points them out.

One thing that may not occur to fans is that most players do not know how to keep score. They've never done it. Those who go into broadcasting have to learn. I did. Later I taught Phil Rizzuto and Jim Palmer my system and they adapted it to their own methods.

I had a friend with Mutual Broadcasting System, which was doing a game of the day from different ballparks. They were expanding and needed a second broadcasting team. When they asked if I was interested, I jumped at the chance. I finished my stay in West Virginia by doing four games of the state high school basketball championship in one day, then drove to Pittsburgh, where I was snowed in overnight, flew to Florida the next day, and worked the first spring training game, which happened to be the Dodgers and Yankees.

St. Louis was as far west as the major leagues went. I was based in Chicago, and covered the western cities for two years, working first with Art Gleason, then Bob Neal. We were in a different city every day and on an airplane almost every day. It was hectic, but it was the big leagues and I loved it.

Every winter I returned to Vero Beach and worked for WNTM.

I remember one goof I made on a game of the day. I called a triple play a double play to end an inning. Off the air the engineer reminded me that it had been a triple play. It's hard to apologize for something like that when you come back on the air; it just makes you sound dumber. But, red-faced, I acknowledged the error and went on from there.

When the Giants and Dodgers went west in 1958, WOR-TV brought National League games into New York when the Yankees were out of town, and I did them with Al Helfer for a year.

When the game of the day folded and the Mets were born in New York, all that came to an end. I applied for a few jobs around the National League, but there were no openings. So I remained in Vero Beach. I was making a living, but I was out of baseball and feeling low.

I had known Lee MacPhail since he had greeted me and Hal Gregg as an office boy in Brooklyn. Now he was the general manager of the Baltimore Orioles. He had offered to help me if I ever came to Baltimore. So I made the move in 1965.

I started in Baltimore with WAYE, a daytime, 500-watt station, where I did a two-hour sports talk show; I also managed the Pimlico Hotel bar on the side. When the rights to the Orioles games went to WFBR, my call-in show moved to that station, and since then I have worked for the station that carries the games.

Late in 1969 there was talk that the American Federation of Television and Radio Artists might go out on strike. I had never joined the union. It was late in the season when Al Burke of WBAL called me and asked me to come to the station on Sunday morning, "so you won't be seen." I should have smelled a rat. But I went. Burke told me, "If AFTRA goes on strike, Chuck Thompson and Bill O'Donnell will not be able to work the Orioles games." Would I fill in for the rest of the season? He assured me that I would have no problem with the union if I decided to join later. When they went out on strike, I filled in. I did all the games and the pregame, the postgame, and scoreboard shows all by myself. I worked seven Baltimore Bullets basketball games, too.

That winter the Orioles owner, Jerry Hoffberger, wanted me to do the Orioles games in 1970. But I had to join AFTRA. The head of the union, Evelyn Fryman, crucified me for filling in during the strike and told me I would never get into the union. They told Hoffberger if he hired me they would take the teamsters off the brewery's trucks. That was the end of that.

In the spring of 1970 the newspapers were shut down by a strike, and WBAL asked me to cover spring training and phone in reports from the various camps. I was still outside the union, so I did it.

WBAL lost the rights to the games for five years. When they got them back, they still wanted me to do the games. But I had to join the union. Ron Shapiro set up a meeting for me with Ms. Fryman, advising me to keep my mouth shut and be agreeable to whatever she said. She told me off pretty good at the meeting, then gave me a union card. Then the Orioles GM, Frank Cashen, told me to see Bill Costello at the ad agency representing National Brewing. I was slated to be the third man with Thompson and O'Donnell. But when I got there, Costello said, "We've decided to go with a younger man." I had heard so many lies and was so angry, I was ready to pitch him out the window. But I probably would have missed the window, high and inside this time.

When WFBR, a nonunion station, regained the rights in 1982 and 1983, I filled in for O'Donnell and did some television coverage of that year-end Milwaukee series in 1982.

But I ate my heart out for ten years because I should have been working with Chuck and Bill.

EIGHTEEN

The Call-in Show

I'M A NUT ABOUT PERFECTION. They make fun of me at WBAL for showing up two hours before my call-in show begins. But when I sit down and push that button and I'm on the air, I know what I'm going to do. I can't stand that rushing in at the last minute.

When I get up in the morning, I'm thinking out my entire schedule for the day, checking my calendar. I like to get things done right now, instantly, and know at all times what's next.

I enjoy doing the call-in show and I think it is easy, as long as the calls keep coming. Call-in show hosts really sweat if they aren't getting any calls, but I do not generally have that problem.

The producer screens the calls and asks for the callers' names, where they're calling from, and what their question is, and they put all that information on a screen in front of me. They weed out calls if they recognize a caller who has been on within the past week, or spot somebody who is obviously drunk or spaced out.

I expect some callers to be out to stump me; they sit there with the baseball encyclopedia in front of them and pitch questions at me. I do not keep the book at hand. If I don't know the answer, I say so.

My favorites are the ones who call in and ask for my opinion, and when I give it, they say, "Oh, you're wrong."

I say, "Wait a minute. You asked for my opinion; it can't be wrong, it's just my opinion. It may not agree with yours"—it usually doesn't—"but it is what you asked for."

They try to set me up, but I don't mind that.

190

I take all calls from young people and from women. Some call-in shows don't. I think I have a feel for young people, who often know as much if not more than older ones. And they are eager to learn; their opinions have not yet hardened in concrete.

One night close to midnight a little boy's voice came on. "Mithter Barney?"

"Yes, sir."

"I'm so glad I finally got through to you."

"I can't quite hear you. You'll have to speak up. What's on your mind?"

"I'm twelve years old and I have a question about tonight's game."

He asked me the question and I answered it, then I said, "Can I ask you a question? What are you doing up so late?"

"The reason you couldn't hear me very well is that my parents are in the next room sleeping and I'm calling you with the phone underneath the blanket with a flashlight."

I identify with that kid, because I would have done the same thing if we had had that kind of radio show in Omaha when I was twelve.

I said, "Will you do me a favor? Tell your parents tomorrow what you did."

Hesitation, then, "Okay."

About a week later he called me again and said, "I did what you told me to do. My parents gave me the devil, but they understood and said don't do it again."

Michael from Pikesville is a sharp young man of fourteen. One night I asked him, "Where did you learn so much about baseball?"

"Ever since I was young I've been reading about it," he said.

I get to know some callers by their voices. A couple years ago a young girl called in, Karen from Hunt Valley. The second I heard her voice I knew she had a disability of some kind. She had some good questions and I drew her out and answered them and thanked her for calling. I few days later I got a letter from Karen's mother, thanking me for taking the call. She explained that Karen loved the Orioles, especially the Ripkens.

"My husband was listening to you in the car," she wrote, "and almost drove off the road. He did not think Karen would have the courage to make a call like that. We cannot thank you enough for the way you treated her."

I make mistakes sometimes, or my mind goes blank. A guy called and asked what I thought about the Orioles' bullpen for 1992. "It looks okay to me," I said, "with the right-handers Frohwirth, Williamson, and Olson, and the two left-handers, Flanagan and—" and I could not think of the other pitcher, so I said, "and that guy we got from Texas."

Sure enough, next call: "Jim Poole, Rex." Oh, yeah. Thanks.

I marvel at fans who criticize players by saying, "He looks like he doesn't even care," and stuff like that. My answer to them is, "Do you think maybe he has a sick wife or child; do you think he might not feel well; do you think maybe his mother or father, 5,000 miles away, might be dying of cancer? Do you think baseball players have those problems, the same as you do?"

That's one reason Cal Ripken's playing streak is so unbelievable to me. No player can be totally ready, mentally and physically, to play every day, year after year, with no distractions on his mind.

WBAL reaches the entire East Coast, and I get calls from old-timers and I can relate to them when they ask about players from the 1940s and 1950s as well as the modern players. Some of them tell me they saw me pitch. There must be millions of them out there. I sound skeptical, but then they'll recite the date and the other team and the lineups. It's amazing how people remember those things. One guy came up to me and said, "I saw you pitch your first major league game."

"No way," I said.

But then he reeled off all the details.

Some regular callers know it all. I've been preaching for years that baseball is 85 percent defense and pitching. Good defense makes winning pitchers. I mention examples such as Pat Dobson; when he came from San Diego to Baltimore he became a twenty-game winner. Why? In San Diego every ball went for a hit; in Baltimore they went for one out or two. There's always somebody who will call and say, "I'm sick and tired of your preaching pitching and defense. That's not the game at all. It's home runs and offense." I try to explain that if you can't keep the other team from outscoring you, all those home runs won't win for you. Look up the heaviest-hitting home run teams in the record books and see where they finished. "You're wrong," they'll say.

My pitching form. Sometimes I pumped once, sometimes twice, to disrupt the hitter's timing. (Photo courtesy Street & Smith and the Cleveland Public Library)

This is how we celebrated clinching the pennant in 1947. Burt Shotton shares the piano bench with Bobby Bragan. Seated at left: Spider Jorgensen and Phil Haugstad. Grinning behind Bragan is Al Gionfriddo. Standing, from left: Gil Hodges, Danny Comerford, Dixie Walker, Arky Vaughan, me, Ray Blades, Ed Miksis, Stan Rojek, Elmer Sexauer, Vic Lombardi, Dick Whitman, Joe Hatten, Duke Snider, Jack Pitler; Clyde King. The guy with the derby is John Griffin. Dan Bankhead is in back by the window. (Photo courtesy AP/ Wide World)

1947 National League champions. From left, bottom row: Joe Hatten, Ed Stanky, Hugh Casey, batboy Stan Strull, Carl Furillo, Jackie Robinson, Al Gionfriddo. Second row: Spider Jorgensen, Cookie Lavagetto, Ray Blades, Clyde Sukeforth, Burt Shotton, Jake Pitler, Stan Rojek, Vic Lombardi, Hal Gregg, road secretary Harold Parrott. Third row: Doc Wendler, Pete Reiser, Ed Miksis, Gil Hodges, Bruce Edwards, Ralph Branca, Hank Behrman, Harry Taylor, Danny Comerford. Back row: Gene Hermanski, Bobby Bragan, Clyde King, Pee Wee Reese, Tom Sunkel, Tommy Brown, Dixie Walker, Arky Vaughan, me, and John Griffin.

We visited Post cereals, one of our radio sponsors, in the late forties. Front row, from left: Clyde Sukeforth, Bruce Edwards, Milt Stock, Pee Wee Reese, Burt Shotton, a Post executive, Doc Wendler, Roy Campanella, Bobby Morgan, and broadcaster Vin Scully. Back row, from left: Carl Furillo, Joe Hatten, Jack Banta, Bud Podbielan, Wayne Belardi, Jackie Robinson, Tommy Brown, me, and Ralph Branca.

The odd-shaped Polo Grounds, where I pitched my no-hitter. Note the clubhouse is back of center field. It was a long walk to the showers, especially on the day in 1951 when our season ended abruptly.

All aboard for Florida, February 1949. Suits and ties were the standard dress code in the big leagues in those days. From left, front: Jake Pitler, Roy Campanella, Buddy Hicks. Back: Jackie Robinson, Gil Hodges, me, Gene Hermanski, and Branch Rickey, Jr. (Photo courtesy the National Baseball Library)

The Dodgers All-Stars, 1949. Our home court was the stage of the Brooklyn Paramount Theater, where we played between showings of a Bob Hope movie. Eddie Miksis and Ralph Branca are in front, with me, Gil Hodges, and Don Newcombe in back.

Borneo Barney...Rickey Riddle Since '43

Mahatma Won't Swap Rex
for Fear He'd Hurt Brooks

Righthander Believes That Hard Work This Spring
Will Help Him to Overcome Base-on-Balls Habit

By JOE KING

VERO BEACH, Fla.

Rex Barney is the pitcher who puzzles even Branch Rickey, but the Brooklyn no-hit righthander believes he has the recipe to ease the wrinkles from his boss' brow. Oh, it's simple. Just hard work.

Barney came here two weeks before training opened to run his legs into condition. Since camp opened he has been throwing, throwing, throwing. He will work in batting practice, then retire to one of the strike-zone mounds for another hour of throwing. The idea, of course, is to master control.

That's the trouble, control—no doubt of that. Rickey knows it, but Barney will have to show him the fault has been corrected.

"I do not know what to expect of Barney," the president expounds. "I do not know whether I can expect anything. His trouble is the base on balls. Two walks, then two balls on the hitter, and there it comes, the home run pitch."

Branch, conscious of second-guessing criticism charging mishandling of the fire-baller last year, points out that the pitcher was encouraged "with the rat on the back," and also given "the goad of the bullpen" for treatment.

Well, why not trade a man who has "exhausted" the resourcefulness of the Brooklyn masterminds?

Set Through '51 on Flush of '48

There is no chance of that. "I will not trade Barney because I cannot get the high price I believe he is worth," says Branch. "I would not trade him for little because I would be very much afraid of the bounce. He has such pitching potential that he might bounce back and hurt us dreadfully. I would not trade him under the same circumstances next year, I believe."

That would maintain the pitcher on the Dodger roster into 1951.

"Here is a point I will allow," Rickey pursues. "No doubt the boy was hurried and did not have the benefit of training in the minors. But he has never had an outstanding record anywhere, except for that lightning flash the latter part of 1948."

True enough. Barney was rushed from Class B through Triple-A into the majors in one season, 1943. When

REX BARNEY

20 GAME WINNER

Masterpiece -- or Phony?

MAYBE I AIN'T NO LEONARDO DA VINCI... BUT I'LL BE DOUBLED UP AT SECOND IF THAT AIN'T A ENIGMATIC GRIN ON HIS PUSS JUST LIKE ON TH' MONAR LISAR.?

Always Wild in New Togs

VERO BEACH, Fla.—Rex Barney was in a group in which speed-ball pitching was being discussed. One of them told a story about a ball that got away from Walter Johnson, broke through the netting protecting the press box, and hit a telegrapher on the head, knocking him out.

"I'll tell you a funny thing that happened to me," Barney said. "In my first game of professional ball my first pitch got away. I was with Durham in the Piedmont League and the pitch went over the first batter's head and through the netting and hit the local sports writer in the eye. I was only there a month—"

"I'm surprised," one of the listeners said, interrupting, "that, after you beaned the local sports writer, you lasted a month."

"Well, they sent me to Montreal," Barney said. "The first pitch I threw there to the first batter—the batter was Goody Rosen, incidentally—went around the back of his neck and up the backstop. Then they brought me up to Brooklyn and the first pitch I threw to the first batter in the majors hit Eddie Stanky in the ribs. Stanky was with Chicago then, but at least I was improving. I wasn't as high as I'd been."

"I should think," another of the listeners said, "that more ball players would get hurt. I don't mean just by wild pitches, but I mean pitchers that, oh, yeah, Barney said. "Especially in batting practice. Shagging flies in the outfield you almost get beaned. And when you have 'to pitch to Carl Furillo nobody wants it. It's not his fault, but he's got me so nervous that I worry about it and I try to space my turn so I'm not pitching when he comes up."

Barney, as Swinger, Hits Rickey for $3.90 in Cash

VERO BEACH, Fla.—Rex Barney is sure he has the answer to Branch Rickey's riddle this spring, but so far he has grabbed only some of the Mahatma's loose change, and not yet impelled him to tab his problem boy a 20-gamer.

The money mentioned wasn't the salary deal, in which Barney was cut, but not the full 25 per cent first offered. The dough came in this way: Rickey was directing his experimental six-man infield defense against the bunt which is designed to move a man to third, and Barney was the hitter. Branch said via loudspeaker: "With this particular hitter, I will bet one dollar to a dime he cannot beat this defense." Barney took him up. A moment later the pitcher nearly picked the runner off second. "Of course," Rickey clarioned, "the hitter loses if the runner is picked off."

Barney nevertheless won four out of five bets with Rickey for a grand total of $3.90 cash, paid on the spot.

Burt Shotton. I think I went 'bad last year because of that broken ankle I suffered sliding into second in the last game of 48," Barney reminisces. "When I came down here last year, my ankle wasn't long out of a cast, and I couldn't do any training for two weeks. I tried to hurry it, and never did feel right all season.

"I have no gripe against the Dodgers," he says. "I wasn't doing a job last year. The only time I hoped for another starting chance was after I one-hitted the Cubs in late August. I thought I was natural that day, loose and free the way I used to be. But there wasn't room for me as a starter the rest of the season."

Regains 'Feeling of Assurance'

By that time Barney had lost the confidence of his boss. He didn't win as a starter until his seventh attempt, and won only one of his next four as a starter. Two wins in 11 starts, and both against the Cubs, didn't inspire Shotton that he had an ace.

The pitcher who puzzles the Mahatma is sleeping well these nights, because he believes he has regained the touch.

"There was many a night last year when I was so restless after a bad day that I would stay up trying to figure what I did wrong, and why I could not come out of it," Rex relates.

"Don't have trouble sleeping now, and I don't think I will have. I remember when Cookie Lavagetto told me when I first came to Brooklyn. 'I never pitched,' Cookie said, 'but I know it has to be the same as with everything else. The secret is the same, and that's getting the feel of your job, and knowing you have found the right way to do it.' I thought I had the secret in '48, because I felt assured. Last year I was confused again. This spring I have that feeling once more."

Well, Rickey will see, beginning in mid-April. In the meantime, Branch may have found the hydrogen bomb before the Atomic Commission. In Barney he has such a weapon in prospect that he has to hope it will explode sometime against the foe, yet dares not let go of it for fear that it will go bam in his face.

---

through August and September, but then pulled an el floriperoo last term. In 20 starts he completed only six games and gave 89 walks in 141 innings.

Blames Broken Ankle

What is the Barney story?

"If I were old," he picks up, "I would have to fear I was through after a bad year. But I am still young (at 25) and know hard work will get me up there. I also know I can do it because I have done it.

"I first knew I had the stuff in that World Series game in 1947 when I struck out DiMaggio and those other guys with three on base. I thought I was all set after 1948. I'll say one thing for Leo Durocher: he surely gave me the chance to prove I could do it. At the beginning of '48 he told me, 'I don't care how bad you are, I am going to start you every four days.' I was bad at the start, but I won four in a row for Leo just before he left for the Giants, and kept going under

---

The Sporting News *played me up as the biggest mystery since the disappearance of the dinosaurs. (Clipping courtesy The Sporting News)*

My son Kevin at 14, and daughter Christine, aged 16.

A Dodger reunion in Brooklyn. From left, front row: *Steve Lembo, the notorious Dick Young of the New York* Daily News, *Clem Labine, Joe Hatten.* Back row: *Gene Hermanski, George Shuba, Al Gionfriddo, Cookie Lavagetto, and me.*

Maryland Treasurer Louis Goldstein presenting me with a proclamation on Rex Barney Day in Baltimore, July 6, 1983.

Four former pitchers now pitching behind mikes at a World Series. From left: *Lefty Gomez, Johnny Murphy, me, and Sandy Koufax.*

Larry King was an occasional visitor to the broadcast booth at Memorial Stadium.

An avid fan, George Will visits before an Orioles' exhibition game in Miami.

My pal, Yogi, reminding me that I never gave him the collar in Norfolk, no matter what the old box scores show. (Photo courtesy Irving H. Phillips, Jr.)

My longtime pal, Chuck Thompson, and me at Camden Yards, 1992. (Photo courtesy Scott Wachter)

Three generations of pitchers from Omaha: me, Gregg Olson, and Hall of Famer Bob Gibson. (Photo courtesy Gene Sweeney, Jr.)

Physical therapist Robin Korotki, who brought me back to life following my stroke in 1983, accompanied me on my first day back to work after my leg amputation in 1992.

I wouldn't be standing in this photo if it weren't for these two good men, Dr. Sheldon Goldgeier (left) and physical therapist Dr. Bill Neill. (Photo courtesy Scott Wachter)

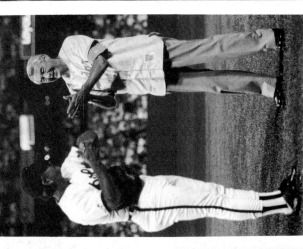

On September 9, 1992, the 44th anniversary of my no-hitter and 15 weeks after my "bad cut," I walked out on the field at Oriole Park unaided on my new leg for the first time. Wearing a replica of a 1948 Brooklyn uniform shirt, I threw the ceremonial first pitch to my old pal, Rick Dempsey. True to form, the pitch was high and outside. (Photo courtesy Scott Wachter)

One night Orioles manager Johnny Oates was listening on the way home. "I felt sorry for you," he told me. "Everybody in baseball agrees with you and I was wondering how you were going to get out of that, and you didn't do too well because the guy never listened to you." I know there are some anti-Rex Barney callers out there, no matter what I say. But I don't mind.

I rarely meet any of my callers, but once in a while it happens. I was in Sabatino's one night and a man came over to me and said, "My son, Eric, calls you from time to time. He loves talking to you, because you talk to him and give him a chance to say what he thinks." Then the kid came forward and we shook hands.

"Meeting you is a big thrill for him," the father said. What he didn't know is that it did more for me than it did for his son. I see myself in all these youngsters.

A girl named Karen from the Eastern Shore called me for years, starting when she was about thirteen. An avid fan, she kept score while listening to the games. One day I was leaving Memorial Stadium and a lovely lady called out my name. I stopped. "This is my daughter, Karen, who calls you from the Eastern Shore," she said, and introduced me to Karen, a beautiful girl, then eighteen and a student at Washington College in Chestertown. Again, that means more to me than it ever will to her.

Maurice called me one night during the 1991 season. A bright, articulate man, he asked, "How many real major league players do the Orioles have?"

I said, "One."

He agreed, then asked, "How many do the other American League teams have?"

I admitted I hadn't thought about it that way. I figured they were all in the major leagues, and I know what it takes to get there, although it is less than it used to take.

I said, "Oh, three or four."

Then one night an hour before game time a security guard in the press box came to me and said, "Rex, there's a guy here who wants to see you."

I went out and looked around and noticed a black man with a cane and two little boys guiding him. I continued looking for the man who wanted to see me.

"Who wants to see me?" I asked.

The black man said, "I do. I'm Maurice."

He was blind and worked for the Library of Congress translating things into braille, and was a real baseball freak.

You'd think people would want to talk about what's going on today, but the question I get asked most on the show is, "Why didn't you have control? Why were you so wild?"

My answer is usually, "If I had control the way I should have, I probably wouldn't be sitting here talking to you. I had every instruction, some say too much. To this day pitching coaches and managers say to me, 'I wish I'd had a chance to work with you.' They all believe they would have cured me. I also think back to what if I had signed with the Yankees or Detroit; I may have been much better or I may never have gotten to the major leagues and accomplished what little I did."

What I don't tell them is that I still don't have control. At home I'll sit and crack walnuts and eat them and toss the shells at the wastebasket, and I still miss high and outside.

I go to all the football and basketball games I can, and I work as the ring announcer at the fights. But even during the winter, when I try to talk about those sports, people want to talk baseball. When the producer tells the caller, "Rex is talking about football," they say okay, and when they get on the air they may ask a football question, but what they really want to know is something about the Orioles.

Whenever a player is in a slump, that's a big topic, and everybody has the solution. Managers draw plenty of comment; in 1989 Frank Robinson was a genius, in 1990 he was a bum.

In the spring of 1992 the hot topic in Baltimore was about the Orioles signing Cal Ripken, who would become a free agent at the end of the year. Everybody kept saying that the Orioles should have signed Cal Junior after the 1991 season. You think Cal was that dumb? Why not wait until all the awards were in and all the other stars had signed big contracts? That made him smarter than all the writers and broadcasters and fans who said he should have been signed at the end of '91. Sure, he could have, but not should have.

I predicted in the early spring that the Orioles would announce they had signed him around opening day, for a big publicity gimmick to go along with all the hoopla over the new ballpark. Well, they didn't. For weeks after that, I was reminded of that and had to admit I made a mistake. But I believe as I write this that they will sign Cal. I watched his agent, Ron Shapiro, whom the Ripkens have the utmost confidence in, huddling during spring training with Roland Hemond and Larry Lucchino. I think the chances of Cal going elsewhere are slim and none. People who predicted it did so just in case it happened, and they could tell everybody, "I told you so."

After Cal signs, callers will find something else to get on. Two years ago, when Cal was slumping, every caller said he should miss a few games and take a rest. The next year he had a big one. Then callers said the only reason Bill Ripken was playing was because the Orioles were waiting for Cal to make a move. I don't buy any of that stuff.

Some calls are touchy, like dynamite. Toward the end of the 1991 season a woman called and announced that she was black.

"Don't you think that Frank Robinson was a scapegoat for the Orioles?" she asked.

"No, I don't. He had his chance as manager for a few years and he failed."

"I don't agree." Then she started in on the black-white business and I knew she was baiting a trap for me. The producer was telling me on the earphones, "She's trying to get you."

I tried to explain why I thought Johnny Oates would be a better manager, emphasizing my great respect for Robinson as a player, but not as a manager.

Then she said, "What about Don Baylor?"

Now I knew I was in trouble.

I said, "Don Baylor has done nothing to be a manager."

"Well, he's been a coach."

"Frank Robinson managed for three years in winter ball before he got a major league job. Johnny Oates has managed in the minor leagues for years and won pennants."

"Baylor is being pushed out of baseball because he's black."

I said, "He is not out of baseball at all; he's a coach with Milwaukee," which he was at the time.

She did not know that, but she still insisted I was wrong and Frank was a scapegoat and Baylor should have been the Orioles' manager. For the rest of the show, black and white callers alike agreed with me. They knew she had been trying to make it into a racial situation, and it was not. Baylor has his chance now with the Denver Rockies.

Some of the most interesting calls I've received came after the show as a result of it. I did a television call-in show once and we had calls from all over the country. At one point I stated that club owners who meddle with their managers are losers. The next morning I got a call from the Orioles' owner, Edward Bennett Williams.

"Rex, I heard your show. You are wrong about club owners."

"How am I wrong?"

"George Steinbrenner."

"Mr. Williams," I said, "I know you are his lawyer, but the only time the Yankees won with him was when Gabe Paul and then Al Rosen was the general manager. Once he decided he knew the game and put those caddies in to work for him, they've won nothing, nor will they as long as he meddles."

"Well, what about Charlie Finley? He won three world championships at Oakland."

I said, "He was not a meddling owner. He was his own general manager. When he was in Kansas City, he had a general manager, and when he moved to Oakland he wanted to take that man with him. But the GM told Finley, 'You know enough about the game now and you work on a small budget. Listen to your scouts and you can be your own general manager.' Incidentally," I added, "do you know who that general manager was who taught Finley everything he knew? It was your own GM, Hank Peters."

And EBW hung up on me.

I don't consider myself an expert on the game. I have an opinion, and I may know a little bit more than the next guy. But I know enough to admit that you never know this game. When somebody buys a ball club and assumes that ownership makes him an instant expert, I cringe. When EBW first bought the Orioles, he and I rode down in the elevator together after every game and he'd ask questions about why this or that happened. Good questions. But by the third year, there were no more questions. He was telling me. He knew it all.

EBW criticized Eddie Murray severely. One day Eddie said to me, "What I don't understand is this: if a man owns a big company or is the world's greatest lawyer, what gives him the right to criticize me as a ballplayer? If the manager gets on me, or the general manager, they are baseball people, and I understand that. But somebody who owns the team for a few years? I don't tell them how to run their business."

When Hank Peters wanted to sign Fred Lynn to a two-year contract, and Lee Lacy and Alan Wiggins to short-term contracts, EBW overruled him and offered them long-term deals. Toward the end of that season, Hank told me he'd be gone by the end of the year, and he was relieved at the prospect. It is tough to work for somebody who knows less about the business than you do, but thinks he knows it all.

You can't know this game. Mr. Rickey used to say, "I've dedicated my life to baseball and I can't figure it out."

Ask Sparky Anderson if he knows this game and he'll answer, "No, but I'm trying to learn."

But I hear guys among the press and broadcasting who have been around for a few years say, "Oh, I know baseball."

One time I was working with a very pompous broadcaster for the Orioles and we were in Texas. The engineer for the visiting radio team had been around for fifty years and seen thousands of games. My partner made a statement on the air that I knew was incorrect. But I let it go. We broke for a commercial and the engineer said, "On that last play, I think it should have been . . . " and he explained what he thought had been an error on the air. My partner took off his headset and said, "Let me tell you something. I've been in this game four years, and I know the game."

At that time I had been in the game only about forty years, but I knew the engineer was right. He looked at me and I winked and he understood.

I enjoy talking to people on the air, and mingling with them at sports banquets, and meeting them, and signing autographs. I love it when a kid comes up to me and says, "Mr. Barney, I called you the other day. Remember me?"

And once in a while fans will apologize for giving me a bad time when they called. I tell them, "Don't apologize. That's what it's for. If we all agreed, there wouldn't be any talk show."

NINETEEN

"Your Attention, Please . . ."

IF A PUBLIC ADDRESS ANNOUNCER ever gets to thinking that nobody is really listening, all he has to do is make a mistake and he'll find out. Like the night I announced Bill Ripken as Cal, for some unknown reason. To this day I hear people say, "Oh, yeah, you're the guy who's been here twenty-five years and still don't know one Ripken from another."

One night I was getting to the end of a promotional announcement and I felt a sneeze coming on. I've got all I can do to rush through the last lines, hit the shutoff button, and sneeze. But I missed the button, and 40,000 people heard this amplified sneeze come out of the loudspeakers. Of course, my friends Jon Miller on TV and Chuck Thompson on radio had to let everybody else in the world know that I had just sneezed for the fans. Everybody in the press box was laughing. I told them, "The only reason I did that was to see if you guys were listening. I never make mistakes."

The next day wherever I went people were God blessing me. That didn't bother me. I consider it a compliment to be recognized.

One day the ballpark was filled with boys and girls from the schools' safety patrols. I closed my welcome with: " . . . and please do not throw any 'deebris' (accent on the first syllable) on the field." I've said that word, debris, correctly many times. Why I said 'deebris' that day I'll never know. Instantly the phone rang. I picked it up and heard somebody laughing so hard he could hardly talk. It was Jim Palmer, calling from the bullpen where he was warming up to start the game.

I said, "What do you want, fool?"

He said, "Does deebris rhyme with zebras?" and hung up.

Just make a mistake and you'll find out quick who's listening. To this day I hesitate whenever I see that word, debris.

Before there was Diamondvision, I used to make the routine announcements: Would the owner of car with license plate so-and-so report to their car . . . Will the parents of Johnny Jones report to the Red Cross room . . . Will Johnny Jones report to the Red Cross room . . .

We used a printed form with the names or numbers written in. One night they handed me one and I started reading, "Will the owner of automobile with Maryland license tag DCG—" and I paused; oh, my God, this is my number, I thought. I turned off the mike and you could have heard that press box going crazy all the way out in the bleachers. My friend Chuck Thompson had jotted down my license number and slipped the message in with the others. They were yelling at me, "Aren't you going to report to your car?"

My worst goof went all over the country. I know, because my family called me from California, wanting to know if it really happened.

In 1977 the Orioles acquired outfielder Elliott Maddox from the Yankees. Milwaukee was in Baltimore for a doubleheader and Maddox made his debut in the second game. Between games is a hectic time for me; I have to get the lineups, write them on a slate for the press box, and make some announcements.

Ten years earlier an ax-swinging racist named Lester Maddox had been elected governor of Georgia. His name was still associated with racism.

I began giving the lineup for the Orioles. "Batting first, playing center field, number 24, Lester Maddox." I had written, "Elliott." I said "Lester." Do you know what that did to that black player? Talk about all hell breaking loose. I couldn't tell you what the next eight names were that I read off. I went through them amid the uproar in the press box and switched off the microphone, picked up the phone, and called the Orioles' dugout.

Earl Weaver answered.

"Earl, can I talk to Elliott?"

"You better talk to him."

Maddox got on the phone. "Elliott, I apologize to you as much as I can. I know it's over and done with, but I am really sorry."

"It's okay," he said. "It's happened before, but never in front of so many people."

In the bottom of the first inning, he was the first to bat. I came on: "Batting first, center fielder—" and I can sense everybody holding their breath "—Elliott Maddox." Phew. Great sighs of relief. And the little rat took off his hat and bowed to me.

A few days later in the clubhouse Maddox said to me, "Hey, Lester Barney, come here."

I said, "Boy, don't you ever call me Lester."

He said, "Don't you ever call me 'boy.'"

I think I got in more trouble calling him "boy" than Lester Maddox.

I did the press box announcing for the Colts' games for fifteen years. One day I announced a Colt catching a punt on the pitcher's mound. I corrected it when somebody pointed out to me that it was the twenty-yard line. And I once called the Bengals' wide receiver Isaac Curtis "Isaac Hayes," the rock star.

Another sure way to tell that players are listening is to mispronounce their names, or go by the book and not by the players' wishes. The first time Cleveland came to town in 1970, John Lowenstein was a rookie with them. The league publishes an information book that lists the players' names phonetically. The American League book showed "Lowensteen" so that's the way I said it. The next day he asked me, "Would you mind saying Lowen*stine* when you announce me? My parents pronounce it that way and I prefer it."

That taught me a lesson: don't go by the official book; go to the player and ask him how he wants it.

I announce "Cecil" not "Ceecil" because that's the way Fielder prefers it.

Some names are tongue twisters, like Mike Pagliarulo. The first time I saw that name on a lineup card, Yogi Berra had written, "Pags." He said, "I don't know how to spell it or pronounce it, so just call him Pags."

When I first saw Felix Jose's name, I thought it must be Jose Felix, but it wasn't.

I've know Bill Ripken since he was a baby. Like everybody else, I called him Billy. But when he made it to the Orioles he asked me to please call him Bill on the PA, hoping that others would pick it up from there. From then on he was Bill as far as I was concerned.

When Tim Raines came to the White Sox from the National League, he decided he wanted to be known as Rocky. On opening day in Baltimore, I told him, "The first time I announce you, I'm going to call you Tim Raines, because you're new in the league and people won't recognize Rocky Raines."

That was okay with him, but later he dropped the Rocky himself.

Rene Gonzales is known in the clubhouse as Gonzo. One day he said to me, "Rex, I bet you'll never say Gonzo on the PA."

The next time he went into the game I announced, "Now playing third base, number 88, Gonzo Gonzales."

He looked up at me and almost fainted. Afterward, he said that was okay, but Gonzo was an inside nickname and please don't use it again.

I study players' names very closely and if I find it is difficult or I'm uncertain I ask the player. Somebody started calling the White Sox shortstop Ozzie Guillen "Gidgen" on radio and TV while I was announcing him as "Gueeyen." When a broadcaster corrected me, I said, "Maybe you're right, but I asked Ozzie and I'm doing it his way."

Ozzie told me, "You one guy pronounce it right."

Whatever they want is what I do.

We have a few traditions in Baltimore. Oriole fans always boo whenever I mention New York. It doesn't matter what the message is. It could be a car with New York tags or a promo about the Yankees coming to town. I always stress *New York* because I know it'll draw a rousing reaction. And when I announce the temperature at game time, for some reason I get booed if I report anything under 70 or over 80.

One of my traditions is "Give that fan a contract" and here's the story of how that began. In the early 1970s, before an opening game, Jack Dunn of the Orioles had a meeting of the stadium workers. He asked for suggestions on how to get the fans more involved.

When it was my turn to speak, I said, "When I was a player in the Piedmont League in 1943, I heard a guy in Raleigh say 'Give that fan a contract' whenever a foul ball was caught in the stands. And they would give the fan a small token contract of some kind."

The rest of the people in the meeting laughed and called it corny and that was that. But afterward, Dunn said, "The only idea worth trying is Rex's suggestion, so let's do it."

They wrote up a format that I kept in front of me: "Give that (man-lady-boy-girl) a contract."

This was before the executive boxes were installed in Memorial Stadium and there were seats adjacent to the press box. A few weeks into the season a foul ball came up near the press box and I glimpsed the back of an individual who made the catch. I said, "Give that lady a contract." The ugliest, toughest-looking guy I have ever seen, long hair down his back and a long straggly beard, turned around and showed me the ball and gave me the dirtiest look and some sort of threatening gesture. And I thought, am I going to get out of this place alive? And of course the guys in the press box are having a ball. I tore that prompter right out of the book and from then on, it was "Give that *fan* a contract."

We used the gimmick all year and the next spring we had another meeting. "What are we going to do about the fans' contracts?" I asked.

"Scratch it," they said. "We got enough out of it."

So I quit doing it. And the fans started calling and writing, asking what became of the fans' contracts. So it went back in and has never been out.

People ask me how I know if a ball has been caught when it's hit out of my view. The ushers give me a signal, then they get the fan's name and address and the Orioles mail them a form that looks like a contract with the date and who the hitter was, signed by the general manager and me. We have some problems with the sight lines at the new ballpark.

If a ball bounces or somebody else touches it first, it is not a good catch. One day somebody said to me, "I deserve a contract. I caught a home run ball but you never give contracts for that." He was right. But maybe it would not go over so well if Cecil Fielder hit a home run against the Orioles and I'm giving a fan a contract because he caught it.

The players pay attention to that stuff, too. Some who have told me they listened for it include Kelly Gruber, Alan Trammell, Don Mattingly, and Rod Carew. Carew said to me, "I've never heard you give a fan an error." It happened that day that a fan with a glove dropped a pop foul and I gave him an error and there was Carew at first base waving to me.

One day Reggie Jackson made a sensational catch and the next day he told me he should have gotten a contract from me. I told him he's supposed to catch them.

Ruben Sierra, one of my favorite players, was on the Texas Rangers team bus going to the hotel in Detroit one night. The bus stopped at a red light. There was an empty billboard on a building. From the back of the bus Sierra called out, "Give that billboard a contract!"

A few managers have commented about it to me, too. When Don Zimmer was fired by the Cubs and came back to the American League as a coach with the Red Sox, he complained to me, "You mean I gotta listen to your 'give that fan a contract' stuff again?"

In 1989 JoAnne Russell, the tennis pro, was a TV commentator at the Wimbledon tournament. Russell, who grew up in Florida, used to come to Baltimore every summer to visit her sister and take lessons from a local coach. She was a big Orioles fan and went to games at Memorial Stadium. During one of the Wimbledon matches, a player hit a ball into the stands where a man caught it. And JoAnne Russell announced, "If we were in Baltimore, Maryland, they would give that fan a contract."

Later she told me, "We picked up on that when we were kids and went around yelling it all the time."

My other trademark is "THANK Youuuu."

When I was young, my mother always stressed the importance of respect and courtesy and I've never forgotten. Her favorite words were "please" and "thank you." About fifteen years ago I read a promotional spot at the ballpark and instead of saying "Thank you" as usual, I put a little spin on it without really thinking and said, "THANK Youuuu."

Later some friends remarked on how nice it sounded, so I did it now and then but forgot about it more often than not. But as more people commented on it, I became more conscious of it and made it a point to emphasize the "THANK" and draw out the "Youuuu" every time I said it. And the rest, in a minor way, is history. Today the people I do radio commercials for insist that every one end with it, and I hear people imitate it wherever I go. That's very rewarding to me. I consider it a compliment.

One night I was leaving the ballpark and this tiny little kid with his father came up to me and said, "Are you Rex Barney?"

"Yes, I am."

He was staring up at me, his eyes as big as two boiled eggs. "Would you say thank you for me?"

I said, "Thank you."

"No! No! Not like that!"

I thought the kid was going to start bawling.

"Oh," I said, "you mean THANK Youuuu."

"That's it," he grinned.

I like that. Kids are learning politeness. Nothing wrong with that.

I'm in the Pimlico Hotel restaurant one day and I go to the men's room and this little kid, all dressed up, follows me in and his eyes are glued to me and I know exactly what he's thinking and what he wants. But as he continues to stare at me, I begin to think maybe I don't know what he wants. Now I'm washing my hands and the kid is still staring, and not a word has been said.

Finally the kid says, "THANK Youuuu."

"Where'd you learn that?" I ask.

"Aren't you Rex Barney?"

"Yeah."

"That's where I learned it. Can I have your autograph?"

He pulls out a paper napkin and a pen.

"Why didn't you ask me for this when you first came in here?"

"I've listened to you all my life and I just wanted to make sure it was you. But I knew it was you all the time."

I knew he knew.

Even some players imitate me. My fan, Ruben Sierra, had a contest in the Texas clubhouse when they were in Baltimore: which player did the best "THANK Youuu." I was the judge, and I declared Ruben the winner. No point in taking a chance on losing my best fan.

Every year members of the Maryland Professional Baseball Players Association visit the Johns Hopkins Children's Center for terminally ill kids. I go there with the players and it tears me up to see little girls who have lost all their hair, boys who listen to all the games and know every player. Invariably some kids say to me, "Say thank you," and when I do, others chime in with, "Oh, you're the guy!" and I hear, "Give that fan a contract" from these kids who are never going to get out of there alive.

The MPBPA honors the best in baseball at a Tops in Sports dinner every winter to raise money for the center. One or two of the kids are there, but they usually don't say anything. In 1991 two boys came wearing tuxedos; one had lost his hair and wore an Orioles cap. They both wanted to say something to the audience.

The first one got up and thanked everybody for their support and sat down. The second was a real extrovert. This was his second year at the dinner, and he had already outlived the time the doctors had given him. He said, "Maybe you noticed last year that Cal Ripken, Jr., sat next to me. Well, I told him what he was doing wrong and you see what kind of year he had." He looked down at Cal. "And if I were you, Cal, I'd sit next to me again tonight and I'll make you have a better year." That brought down the house.

Then he said, "In closing—THANK Youuu," just the way I do it. That brought tears to more eyes than just mine.

I am the only former player doing the public address announcing at a major league ballpark. But even in my playing days we were always aware of the announcers. In those days they sat on the field beside the dugout.

The three most memorable announcers from my time were in Brooklyn, Chicago, and New York. All three were just right for where they worked: Tex Rickard, a little round guy with a gravelly voice, famous for his malapropisms, was the essence of Brooklyn; Bob Shepard, whose magnificent enunciation fit with the regal Yankees of the forties and fifties (he also did the Giants' games in those days); and Pat Piper, who sounded like a gangster, everybody's image of Chicago.

In Ebbets Field, people in the front seats often draped their jackets over the left field wall, where they might interfere with the ball. Tex Rickard would announce, "You people in left field, take your clothes off."

These days there is a separate sound system in the press box and the writers get a lot more information than the fans hear. But in the old days the PA man on the field was the whole show. One day Preacher Roe was pitching and he became ill and had to leave the game. Rickard announced, "Preacher Roe is no longer pitching because he doesn't feel good."

The bullpens were on the field just outside the foul lines in right and left field. When a pitcher got up to start throwing, Tex would look into the dugout and ask, "Who's warming up?" We'd make up some screwy name, like "Joe Traspashek." Tex didn't know the difference. He'd announce to the fans, "Joe Traspashek warming up." You never knew what you might hear at Ebbets Field.

We enjoyed imitating Pat Piper of the Cubs. He snapped out everything he said like a character in a gangster movie, and I don't mean one of the good guys. I can't imitate him in print—I can on the radio—but he would put things this way: "You fans throwing things on the field better stop or they're gonna throw you out of here."

We were all intrigued by Bob Shepard's delivery. An English professor, he leads us all in longevity and eloquence. I like to think I have been influenced by him.

With the Orioles, one of my primary duties is to get the day's lineups as early as possible. Some PA guys show up just before a game. Not me. If I arrive four hours before game time, people say, "Where you been? You're late." I get the Orioles' lineup first and take it to the visiting manager, pick up his and bring it to the Orioles manager. If there is a change later—and I keep a supply of Wite-Out on hand—they call me and I pass the word along. Then I call the public relations office and give them the lineups, so they can print them in the programs. Next I write them on the blackboard in the press box, then fill in my own scorebook. Later, when the umpires show up, I get their positions.

Being a former player gives me some advantages. I am welcome in the clubhouses and accepted, even by the younger players, as one of them. I knew many of the managers when they were players, and some of the younger ones have read about me. They also know that I'm not in there looking for a scoop, and if they're discussing a player or a trade, whatever they say won't show up in the newspaper the next day. And I never ask why somebody is playing and somebody else is not.

I get to know which managers will arrive early and who will be late and give me a problem. Most arrive around 3:00 P.M. for a night game. Very few take the team bus. They are all very cooperative but they have their idiosyncrasies.

Ralph Houk would make out his lineup on the team bus and hand it to me immediately.

Tony LaRussa takes more time than most.

Gene Mauch had a reputation for being the worst manager to deal with. "He never wants to give you the lineup," they warned me, "and he'll change pitchers five minutes before the game, and keep you guessing."

Oh, really?

They had no idea that Gene and I had roomed together at Ma Gregory's boardinghouse in Durham in 1943. I'd go in to see him and we'd talk about the good old days, then I'd ask him for the lineup and he'd hand it to me. When I'd bring it to the Orioles manager I'd be met with disbelief.

People warned me about Alvin Dark, too. When Alvin managed Oakland, he had to wait until the A's owner, Charlie Finley, called him. It was the same when Dick Williams was there. Not that they paid much attention to what Finley had to say, but they had to wait for his call. That gave me a problem, but Dark was not the cause.

They said the same about Bobby Valentine, the Texas manager: "You'll never get it from him until the last minute."

What they didn't know is that Valentine is married to Ralph Branca's daughter, Mary, and I'm her godfather.

Sure, I use those connections, because they just happen to be there.

Billy Martin often got to the ballpark a half hour before game time. And he would not answer his phone at the hotel. That created problems for me, but when I explained the situation to him, he would take my calls and give me the lineup.

The press guys would ask me, "How'd you get that?"

"Never mind how. Here it is."

Sometimes I'll use the Nebraska connection. Darrell Johnson, who managed three clubs in the league, was born in Horace. He was a buddy of Pat Santarone, the Orioles grounds keeper. One Sunday morning I was in the clubhouse to pick up Earl Weaver's lineup and Santarone was in there, all hung over.

"If you're going over to the Texas clubhouse, Johnson won't be there," he said. "I dropped him off at five-thirty this morning." An hour before game time I called Johnson at the hotel. No answer. I waited and tried again and heard this growl.

"What do you want?"

"We got a game in less than an hour," I said. "Can you make it?"

"Yeah, I'll make it."

"How about doing me a favor? Give me the lineup so I can get my work done."

He gave it to me, and showed up about five minutes before game time.

One of Earl Weaver's superstitions was that he would not give his lineup to anybody but me. And he would not accept the other team's lineup from anybody else.

Some managers like to study and analyze and pick apart the other manager's lineup. Others, like Billy Martin, don't even want to see it. All they want to know is whether the righty or the lefty is pitching.

I've never had a problem working with managers, except once. Jim Fregosi, now the Phillies manager, was in his second year with the California Angels. He'd been a fair player, not good enough to be traded for Nolan Ryan and three others, which he was in 1971.

Now it's 1979 and the Angels and Orioles are in the AL Championship Series. I'd dealt with Fregosi all year; he came across as arrogant, but I'd had no problems with him. He often played cards in his office before a game with his coaches and the Angels broadcasters, Don Drysdale and Dick Enberg.

It's the first game of the playoffs in Baltimore and I go in to get the lineup. They're playing cards around his desk.

"I suppose you want the lineup."

"Yeah, if I can get it." I hand him Weaver's.

"Didn't you see the papers?"

"Yeah, but sometimes they're wrong."

"Okay, here it is."

He gives me the lineup, but no pitcher.

"Who's the pitcher?"

"Oh, put down Lefty Gomez, Mose Grove, Bob Feller, anybody you want."

"Really?" I say. "They wouldn't even help your ball club."

I don't know to this day why I said that. There is dead silence. I turn and walk out.

Enberg and Drysdale follow me out. "That was the greatest thing you could have said," they tell me. "He needed to be put in his place in front of his own people."

Two years later Fregosi was fired; it took him five years to land another big league managing job. Then in 1986 he was back in Baltimore as the White Sox manager. I was working for Home Team Sports, and I asked him to do a fifteen-minute interview. As we walked out on the field he said, "I owe you an apology."

"What for?"

"Do you remember that little confrontation we had?"

"Yeah."

"I was being a smart ass and you put me in my place. But you taught me something. You won't hear any more of that out of me."

I dearly love my job as the Orioles PA announcer. As a player and a spectator, I never thought it seemed very difficult. It isn't physically hard, unless you have to go to the bathroom in the middle of an inning. But when I first got into it, it took some time to get used to it.

I have always been comfortable at a microphone; I've done PR work, radio and TV game broadcasts, pregame and postgame shows, and I even did some Blast soccer games for cable TV. The PA job doesn't pay like broadcasting, but with my baseball pension and radio work and another small pension, I have no financial problems.

It all began one night in 1967 when I was sitting in the stands at Memorial Stadium before the game and Phil Itzoe, the Orioles road secretary, came over to me.

"Bill Bolling is ill," he said. "Would you do the PA tonight?"

I agreed and, with Phil at my side guiding me through it, I had no problems. During the next few years I filled in for Bolling, and by the early 1970s I was doing most of the games. I officially became the Orioles regular PA announcer when Bolling left in May 1973.

One of the things I had to adjust to was the five-second delay between my speaking and the fans hearing the words. I can hear what I have just said while I am saying something else. That can be disconcerting to politicians and others who are called upon to participate in pregame ceremonies and are not accustomed to it.

I always start with, "Your attention, please," which I learned from listening to Pat Piper in Chicago. Then I say, "Ladies and gentlemen, welcome to Memorial Stadium," or at least that's what I said until 1992. I practiced for weeks saying, "Welcome to Oriole Park at Camden Yards," and was apprehensive about stumbling over it, or inadvertently saying "Memorial Stadium" the first time. But I got through it okay.

We had some small crowds at Memorial Stadium in the early 1980s, but it never got as bad as the day in 1905 when the Oakland Oaks and Portland Beavers played a Pacific Coast League game before a paid attendance of one. In those days the home plate umpire announced the lineups to the fans. On that day he addressed the crowd, "Dear Sir . . . "

My job requires constant concentration on the game. I never know how long a batter will be at the plate and when I will have to announce the next one. I have to be alert for lineup changes and pinch hitters, and be careful not to announce them until the umpire points to me, which makes the change official. If I announce a pinch hitter prematurely, that can lead to big trouble if a manager decides to make a switch before the man gets into the batter's box. Some umpires signal with an emphatic gesture; others do little more than flick a thumb at their side. I have to be aware of those mannerisms. It all forces me to become more involved in the game, and I like that.

Occasionally there are distractions. Back in the 1970s, when streakers were the fad, we had a rain delay one day at Memorial Stadium. Chuck Thompson is sitting beside me and suddenly he says, "My God, look at that." We see this little round fat guy taking his clothes off in the stands near the third base dugout. He runs onto the field wearing nothing but tennis shoes, goes up to home plate and acts like he's hitting the ball. Then he starts around the bases, falling into second, and sliding into third, and heading for home plate while the crowd is going berserk. He crosses home plate and heads for the first base dugout, but he must have seen a policeman there, so he jumps the gate and runs behind the dugout and comes out the other end, right past a lady sitting there holding a big umbrella and reading a newspaper. She does a classic double take as he dashes by her. When the guy ducks into the dugout, Nestor Chylak, the umpire, is standing there. He comes out on the field and holds his hand up with his thumb and index finger about a half-inch apart and the crowd goes wild.

Later I asked Jack Dunn what they did with the guy. He said, "They made him put his clothes on and he was fined $100, but he did all right."

"What do you mean, he did all right?" I asked.

"His friends had put up $500 if he'd do it, so he came out $400 ahead."

That was the only streaker that I can remember.

On August 19, 1992, I had the thrill of announcing the major league debut of Bret Boone. The Seattle second baseman, the son of longtime catcher Bob Boone and grandson of 1940s infielder Ray Boone, was the first third-generation player in the big leagues. It was doubly meaningful for me, and gave me a sense of my own longevity in the game, because I had pitched against his grandfather.

I never think of what I do as work. Many nights I leave the ballpark thinking, "Boy, that was the greatest game I ever saw." But it wasn't really. I still remember a 1–0 pitching duel between Nolan Ryan and Jose Mesa. What a game. But it doesn't have to be 1 to 0. It could be a high-scoring game. I just love to watch the way players execute. I remember a night

211

when Mike Flanagan came in against California, bases loaded, 2 outs, Orioles ahead by a run, Wally Joyner, a good hitter, at bat. It must have taken Flanagan 20 pitches before he struck out Joyner, who kept fouling them off. I get a big thrill out of a confrontation like that. When I go home, I mull over what I've seen for a long time, after almost every game.

My friend Broadway Charlie Wagner, who has been with the Red Sox for more than fifty years, asked me once, "What keeps you going?"

"The same as you," I said. "Love of the game."

Neither of us feels like he's ever worked a day in his life.

TWENTY

Living High and Running Low

IN 1968 I MARRIED Carole Bennett, a teacher in the Baltimore
City schools and great baseball fan who worked part-time in
the Orioles' ticket office. She was a good worker until the
game began, then she'd disappear with her scorecard into the
stands.

When I was fifty, I went for an insurance exam and they
discovered that I had diabetes. I have given myself daily insulin
shots ever since and never missed a game until 1983. The
doctors told me to cut out all sugar and alcohol, but I figured,
well, maybe I could get away with just cutting out the sugar
and the insulin would take care of the rest. I found that I liked
hanging out at bars, talking with fans, or sitting up until all
hours after a game, swapping stories and matching drinks with
visiting managers and old baseball pals. I enjoyed being one of
the guys, and kept up with the best of them. I never passed out,
never got violent or belligerent, never fell down or went to sleep,
never embarrassed myself, never needed anybody to take me
home, never had a hangover. I mean, I was invincible. The
drinking got heavier around 1979, and it was partly responsible for my divorce in 1981, although Carole and I remain
friendly to this day.

In 1982 I did some Orioles games on radio when Bill
O'Donnell was ill, and worked twenty games with Ted Patter-
son on Supertelevision. I was single, could come and go as I
pleased, sit up all night with my buddies if I felt like it. It never

213

affected my work. I was feeling no pain. On into the next year I continued to fly high, until one day I slammed into a mountain.

The Yankees were in town on June 22, 1983. I was sitting in Orioles manager Joe Altobelli's office gabbing. Joe said, "Rex, after the game, how about bringing Yogi down to Sabatino's in Little Italy and we'll get together?"

"Sounds great."

Yogi and I drove downtown and, as any Baltimorean knows, there is no such thing as a parking space in Little Italy. As we drove around, Yogi said, "A guy can get dizzy trying to get someplace around here."

We finally found a space and went inside. Billy Martin was upstairs with some friends and we found Altobelli with some guys he knew from Rochester and joined them. As the night wore on, those who couldn't keep up with us seemed to evaporate. Billy came down and we sat around throwing the bull and tossing down the sauce until four or five in the ayem. Then I took Yogi back to Cross Keys and went home.

I wasn't feeling so hot and couldn't sleep, so I decided to do some paperwork, pay some bills and stuff. I got everything out and put it on the table and started to write, but my arm was way out here somewhere, not over the paper. That's dumb, I thought. I pulled it over and started to write my name, and left nothing but wavy lines on the paper. I gave that up, went into the bathroom and started to shave; little cuts began bleeding all over my face. So I took a shower and that braced me.

I had an appointment with Brooks Robinson and Ron Shapiro, the agent, that morning in Ron's office in the Rotunda; I had been scouting minor league players they might want to represent. I dressed and went out to my car, but I could not line up the key with the lock. I mean, I was wild high, just like my fastball had been. I finally made it fit and got in, then had the same trouble with the ignition. So I switched hands. Ever try to put the key in the ignition with your left hand? It's not easy. Somehow I started the engine and drove away.

I stopped at a newsstand and got out and bought some newspapers; every few feet I dropped them. Going into the bank to cash a check, I bumped into people. Through all this, nothing was registering upstairs. Maybe I had one drink too many. I'll get over it.

I was still not feeling very well when I got to Ron's office. The Orioles team doctors, Dr. Leonard Wallenstein and Dr. Sheldon Goldgeier, had an office on the same floor, so I stopped in there and told them I was not feeling right. "I have a meeting with Brooks and Ron," I said. "Can you give me some vitamins or pills or something to perk me up? I drank pretty heavy last night and I guess I'm feeling it today."

"It isn't that," Dr. Wallenstein said. "Don't you know what's happening?"

"No."

"Do you notice how your arm keeps dropping?"

"Yes."

"And you're having trouble with some words?"

"Yes."

"You're having a stroke."

I started to get up. "Oh, no," I said.

"How'd you get here?"

"I drove."

"No, you didn't."

"Yes, I did."

"Well, you're not driving anymore."

They sent a nurse down to Ron's office, where they found Brooks's son, Michael, who offered to drive me to North Charles General Hospital. They asked me if there was anybody I wanted them to notify; I said, "Carole, Chuck Thompson, and the Orioles."

On the way to the hospital I could feel myself sinking lower by the minute. Soon after we got there, Carole and Chuck arrived. A nurse wheeled me into a room where a doctor said, "Unbutton your shirt." I fumbled with the buttons. Nothing happened. Frustrated, I just yanked it open.

"Open your hand and close your eyes."

He put something in my hand but I could not identify it. My head ached violently, and I heard some doctors murmuring, "He's in bad shape. I don't know if we can bring him back or not." Right through the pain I heard all that. I begged them for something for the pain and they gave me some pills.

Suddenly Jim Palmer and Al Bumbry appeared in the room, and the next thing I knew was when I woke up four days later.

215

What happened during those ninety-six hours I lay in a coma I can only relate as it was told to me. The rest I can tell you as I remember it. It may be a little more dramatic than a doctor would describe it, but that's because I was the guy it was all happening to.

I went in on a Thursday. Every day Carole and Chuck Thompson were there, although I didn't know it at the time. I was still out. Somewhere along the line, the doctor told Chuck that if I did not come out of it in a day or two, they might have to operate on my brain. That might save my life but leave me like a vegetable. Chuck knew I would not want to live that way; he couldn't make the decision, but he fervently hoped it would not be necessary.

On Saturday, Chuck was waiting outside the room when Dr. Goldgeier came out, his clothes all torn and disheveled.

Chuck said, "Boy, somebody must be giving you a bad time."

"Yeah. Rex."

"What? He's as pugnacious as a rocking chair. He's never been violent in his life."

"Well, he is now. He's knocking interns around, throwing nurses against the wall."

Apparently I had been hit by diabetic shock, cardiac and respiratory arrest, and violent seizures from alcohol withdrawal, and I don't know how many other things. They told me later Dr. Goldgeier worked feverishly on me for a couple hours and almost lost me.

I also learned later that the day I conked out, the Tigers had come to town. Sparky Anderson was on his way to the ballpark when the cab driver told him I was in the hospital. Sparky said, "Turn around and take me to the hospital first." But of course he could not see me, and I was seeing nothing.

And then I woke up. I heard a voice say, "What day is this?"

I said, "Friday."

"No."

"Well, I came in here on Thursday."

"You've been in a coma for four days. It's Monday."

I still hadn't made out the source of the voice. I was staring at my black and blue arms.

"We've been sitting on you," he said, "trying to get a straitjacket on you to control your thrashing around."

I looked up and said, "Dennis, what are you doing here?"

It was an intern, but I could have sworn it was Dennis Martinez of the Orioles standing there. Shows you where my mind is all the time.

I'm here to tell you I was in bad shape. No strength at all. My entire right side was paralyzed. I couldn't speak clearly, just mumble. When Carole came in and saw my face land in the mashed potatoes on the tray, she knew I was in trouble.

The therapy started immediately. Carole told them to work me hard; I could take it. Physical therapist Robin Korotki drew the assignment. She told me later that she had seen me while I was still out of it and decided, "I can't help him. He's too big for me." But she took my case.

Every time they came to take me to therapy I cried, "Please don't take me." It was hard work and they never let up. Robin worked with me every day, and even came in on weekends. The first few days I felt like a hero if I could move a finger on my right hand. Gradually I began to see some progress and my attitude changed. Now I wanted to do all the daily therapies—speech and physical and occupational—twice a day. We worked and worked, and I cried a lot and anguished a lot and threw things against the wall out of plain frustration.

Players and friends came to see me. Billy Martin called from the dugout wherever the Yankees were. I received hundreds of cards and letters and calls. When Phil Pepe wrote something about me in the New York *Daily News,* I got mail from Brooklyn and New York, from fans thanking me for the many thrills I gave them. I gave them thrills? Pee Wee gave them thrills. Jackie gave them thrills. Furillo gave them thrills. But me? Well, if seeing a guy throw a ball a hundred miles an hour by a hitter or over his head or behind him gave them thrills, then I guess I did. They wrote things like, "Old Dodgers never die," and if that doesn't make you feel good, nothing will. For a while I could not read, but when I could those messages were as good therapy as anything.

But I have always been uncomfortable when I am on the receiving end of attention. I prefer doing things for somebody else. I was embarrassed when people came to see me, and when a nurse cleaned my feet or bathed me.

"This bothers me," I said one day. "Can't we get somebody else to do that?"

"It's my job," she said.

It didn't mean anything to her. I was just another collection of parts.

Some of the therapy involved working with kids' coloring books, and blocks and things. I'd say, "How old am I?"

"Well, you're about five. If you work hard, next week you'll be six or eight."

I worked as hard as I have ever worked on anything, doing whatever they asked. One day Robin said, "Turn over on your stomach and do three push-ups."

"I know what that is, but I don't know how. Baseball players do not do push-ups."

She demonstrated by whipping off about ten of them. "Now you do it."

The first one I tried, my arms just collapsed. On the second try, I lifted myself a few inches.

"You really don't know how, do you?" she said. "But you'll know before you're finished here."

Before I left I could do ten, rest a few minutes, do another ten, rest, and then do another ten.

Now I was really putting those kids' blocks together and working those exercise books. One day Chuck was there and the therapist showed us a page in a book and said, "How many animals are in this barnyard picture?"

I said, "Seven."

Chuck said, "God, I hope he's right."

"Why?" the nurse asked.

"That's all I can find," Chuck said. "If it's wrong, you'll have me in the next bed."

When she checked the answer and it was seven, you never saw two more relieved men in your life.

Little things like that meant a lot to me. When I could place a circle in another circle, that was progress. It made me feel good, and a little weepy, too. I could feel everything coming together. I was working with a speech therapist, too, but I had not yet tried to write anything. I think I was scared. The young aides kept bringing me stacks of mail every day. One day a bunch of them came in and said, "Mr. Barney, can we have your autograph?"

I said, "Sure."

She handed me a pad and pen and I signed the first one and started to cry.

"Are you all right?" she asked.

"This is the first time I've been able to write something legible for weeks," I said. I was overjoyed.

When the Orioles had left on a road trip I had made little progress. I missed working four games on Super TV. Chuck Thompson juggled his schedule and filled in for me and never took any money for it. I hadn't seen him for a few weeks, and when the team returned home and he came to see me, I never even said hello. First thing I blurted out was, "Hey, Charlie, come here. I want to show you something," and I wrote my name for him.

Later Chuck said, "I've never seen anybody so proud and so happy that he could write his name."

Once I had a four-hour pass. Chuck drove me to Cross Keys and to the ballpark and back to the hospital.

And then another shock lay in ambush for me. Or so they thought.

One day Dr. Goldgeier came in and said, "You won't be able to drive a car or go back to work for at least a year and a half."

Tears streamed down my face.

"Can't you take a swing at me," he said, "hit the wall or do something, instead of just sitting there and taking it?"

Inside I have always been very competitive, and I was fighting mad. But I don't show it. My two wives used to say, "Don't you ever yell or scream?" That's not my way.

I said nothing, but when the doctor left I told Chuck, "That's not going to happen. Ill be out of here and back to work in a couple months. And I'll be driving sooner than that, too." It was August, and I was not about to miss the rest of the season and maybe the playoffs and World Series. Didn't they know they were dealing with one stubborn Irishman?

When it came time for me to be released from the hospital, I needed full-time care. Carole's mother, Mrs. Lydia Bennett, and grandmother, Carolina Briglia, who is now 104, had an extra room and offered to take care of me. I owe them everything. They weighed my food portions and made sure I took my medications on schedule and nursed me well. I could go out for a while in the afternoon, but not at night. Friends would take me to the ballpark where I hung around for a few hours.

By mid-August I could stay out at night but still not drive. Elrod Hendricks lived nearby and he offered to bring me to the ballpark and take me home at night after the game. Sometimes his son, Ryan, was with him. One night when they took me home, the porch light, which had always been on for me, was out. Ryan said, "Mr. Rex, are you getting a message here?" It turned out the bulb was burned out.

One day Carole took me to the doctor's office for a checkup. She told Dr. Goldgeier that I had a strange idea about going back to work.

"Well," he said, "maybe by September you'll be able to do a few innings."

I pulled out a schedule. "I've been studying this," I said, "and I have it all figured out. The Orioles play Kansas City a twi-night doubleheader on Friday, August 19, and day games Saturday and Sunday. I could work the first game on Friday and be home before dark, then do the games on Saturday and Sunday."

"Whoa," he said, "not so fast."

He was skeptical but I was adamant. Finally he relented.

"But you'll have to have a nurse there with you."

Feeling chipper, I asked, "By the way, can I have a beer or a martini or something?"

"Sure," the doctor said, "you can drink all you want. You'll die, but go ahead and drink."

I have not had a drop of alcohol since June 23, 1983.

On August 19 Robin Korotki went with me to the ballpark to check my pulse and blood pressure every few innings. Let me tell you, before that game was over, her blood pressure was higher than mine. The Royals' Gaylord Perry had a no-hitter and a 4–0 lead going into the eighth inning. An avid fan, Robin was getting more excited by the minute, and she couldn't understand why everybody in the press box was so calm.

When the Orioles got 3 hits and 2 runs in the eighth and the writers were tearing up their stories and throwing the crumpled paper in the air, Robin checked my pulse. Mine was still normal, but hers was racing like crazy. She could not understand how I remained so calm.

"There is an unwritten rule," I told her. "No cheering in the press box."

She said, "I don't understand that. I could never work here."

The Orioles won the game with 3 runs in the last of the ninth, and Robin became an island of excitement in a sea of restrained but frenzied reporters rewriting their stories again. All in all, it was a rousing return to work for me.

I worked that weekend and the rest of the season, including the playoffs and then the World Series in Philadelphia and Baltimore. Sure, I may have been doing it all from memory, or habit, but I did it.

The stroke taught me a lesson in how lucky I am, and it gave me a dose of humility, too. I can remember doctors looking at the records in my room and shaking their heads in disbelief. I know how far I've come. To this day people come up to me and I can see they've had a stroke and never fully recovered. They say to me, "You had a stroke? I did, too, and I was never in a coma," and they shake their heads, because they were left worse off than I was and it tears me up, but I try to say something encouraging to them.

The following winter I was in the Prime Rib restaurant and a guy was staring at me. He came over and introduced himself.

"Do you remember somebody asking you to unbutton your shirt?" he asked. "I was the one. I never thought I'd see you alive again, much less working."

The doctors had told me that if I worked, I could beat it. When it was over I said to them, "I owe so much to so many people."

They said, "Yes, you do. But you did it."

I say it's the will to do what you want to do. That sounds corny, but I could have quit and lived on Social Security and my pension and not worked so hard to come back. Not me. Not as long as there was a ball game.

TWENTY-ONE

The Lost Weekend

THE LAST WEEKEND at Memorial Stadium in 1991 was the most lavish promotion event ever staged by the Orioles, and I missed it.

All during that season, there had been a series of nostalgic events marking the farewell to that grand old ballpark before the move to Camden Yards in 1992. From time to time, the Orioles brought back popular players of the past, such as Don Baylor, Doug DeCinces, Bobby Grich, and Harmon Killebrew, a fan favorite despite the damage he had done to us with his bat.

One of the highlights of the year for me was when the four 20-game winners of 1971—Dobson, Palmer, Cuellar, and Mc-Nally—came out. Being a big dumb Irish sentimentalist, I can shed a tear, and I did that night.

And one night they brought back Tippy Martinez and Len Sakata. I had been there in 1983 the time Tippy picked off three men at first base in one inning; when Sakata, an infielder, had volunteered to come into the game and catch for the only time in his life, and then hit a home run to win the game. What a thrill it was for me to introduce that pair again. I get choked up just thinking about it now.

Detroit was in town for that last series, which was to culminate in a Sunday afternoon game, followed by an elaborate show, including the digging up and transporting of home plate to the new park, and a stream of former Orioles taking the field until the whole place was awash in memories and emotions. Then decked out in a tuxedo, I was to walk out to where home plate had been, and say, "Ladies and gentlemen, for the very last time at Memorial Stadium, THANK Youuuu."

I had not been feeling well for several months. I had always had high arches in my feet; one had collapsed and was flat as a pancake. The bones shifted and my foot spread. It was not painful, but it affected my walking. My leg had been swollen and I had to keep it propped up. Toward the end of the season I had felt drained by fatigue. But I was pumped up for that last series.

On Friday night they introduced all the old announcers. Ernie Harwell was there, and it was also his last series after thirty-two years with the Tigers. I did not know they were going to introduce me as part of that ceremony, and it was a big thrill when they asked me to stand up in the press box and take a bow.

The game that night went extra innings and it was after midnight when I walked out of the press box. A fireworks show was beginning and the crowd was still in their seats. As I walked toward the elevator, I noticed a smashed paper cup on the ground. When I tried to step over it, I slipped and fell to my knees. I got up, stood there a moment, walked another few feet, and collapsed. I never fainted, never lost consciousness, but I could not move.

The elevator man said, "Rex, are you all right?"

"No, I'm not. I have no strength."

He went for a wheelchair and took me to the first aid room where one of the team doctors checked me over.

"We've got to get you to the hospital," he said.

They put me in an ambulance and took me to Sinai Hospital and gave me all sorts of tests. My heart was okay, and they finally determined that I was suffering from exhaustion, dehydration, and anemia.

Once the news got out that I had collapsed and was in the hospital, the place became a three-ring circus. Fans and players kept calling, insisting that I had to be there for the last weekend. Poor Dr. Goldgeier had to deal with them and tell them there was no way I could be there.

Orioles owner Eli Jacobs was determined that I have the last word on Sunday, so they sent a camera crew to my room to tape my part. You can imagine that scene, with the lights and cameras and people maneuvering around the furniture that fills a hospital room. The club president, Larry Lucchino, wrote my closing line: "I'm very sorry I couldn't be with you today, but on behalf of the entire Baltimore Orioles organization, ladies and gentlemen, THANK Youuu."

It took me four takes to get it right; I kept breaking down. My head and heart were at Memorial Stadium; my body was in a hospital bed. To this day, Jim Palmer and Brooks Robinson accuse me of doing all that just to upstage them and the other old Orioles who were on the field that day.

I watched it on television on Sunday, that last inning when Mike Flanagan walked in from the bullpen. We all knew that was going to happen, but he was still not ready for it. Like any triumphant but traumatic event in your life, you get ready for it, but you're never really ready.

It took him longer to make that journey to the mound than I had ever seen him take. Later he told me, "I'm walking and thinking: what does this mean? With all the things I have accomplished here, and all the fans' support, I can't let them down now."

He didn't get any help from the umpire. Every close pitch was a ball. I looked up to heaven and said, "Dear God, please take care of this man. He's the nicest, dearest man I've ever known. Please help him."

Then he ends up striking out the last two guys. I said, "My prayer was answered. God took care of you, pal."

Jim McKay had called me on Saturday, and I did not know that he was going to lead into me from Camden Yards the way he did on Sunday. As I watched it, I thought: Boy, it's a good thing I taped my part ahead of time, because this guy McKay is so revered and respected in Maryland, I would have broken down for sure after the introduction he gave me.

Robin, the therapist after my stroke, and some of the nurses and doctors who had been on duty during that siege, came in to see me. I received hundreds of cards and letters and calls from my friends and from people I do not know. That gave me a wonderful, gratifying, and humbling feeling. You're rushed to the hospital and you feel very alone and then you find out that you're wrong: there are more people who care about you than you can imagine.

As I lay there, I thought back over the years I had spent at that brick palace on 33rd Street, and the many important people I had met and introduced there. The list included six presidents: Johnson, Nixon, Ford, Carter, Reagan, and Bush.

I replayed some snapshot memories:

Lyndon Johnson came up to the press box and walked around pressing the flesh, but had nothing to say.

Richard Nixon was congenial.

After the last game of the 1979 World Series, when the Pirates beat the Orioles, I was in Earl Weaver's office commiserating with him and Jimmy Carter came in. Carter was a little shorter than Earl, so I could see Earl really liked this guy.

Ronald Reagan knew who I was from his broadcasting days. He was booed in Baltimore because the Orioles lost every time he was there. The crowd is usually polite to visiting politicians, but harder on local ones. Nancy Reagan came with the president once, but I don't think she cared much for being there.

Bobby Kennedy threw out the first ball one year and I met him. He seemed a little standoffish to me.

The biggest fan and the friendliest of the bunch was George Bush. The first time he came to Memorial Stadium, Commissioner Bart Giamatti was with him. Giamatti asked one of the Secret Service guys to escort me over to their booth. Bush was standing there with his jacket off. Mrs. Bush, a warm, gracious lady, and one of their sons were there. Giamatti said, "Mr. Bush, this is Rex Barney, the PA—"

"Oh, I know all about him," the president interrupted. "He pitched for Brooklyn when I was at Yale, and he was pretty wild," he went on, telling me about myself.

From then on, whenever he came to the ballpark, he'd wave to me. I know this all sounds like "Celebrities who have met me." But that all means a great deal to me. I consider it an honor. I am constantly amazed by the people who turn out to be baseball fans and who remember me from my playing days.

When Eli Jacobs introduced me to Alan Greenspan, the chairman of the Federal Reserve Board, Greenspan said, "Oh, I watched you pitch in Ebbets Field."

One time Edward Bennett Williams called me into his box. When I went in I saw Danny Kaye sitting there. EBW said, "Rex, I want you to meet—" and that's as far as he got.

"Oh, I know him," Kaye blurted out. "That's Rex Barney." He knew me from the days when he hung around the Dodgers' clubhouse in Brooklyn.

Sure, I like all that, a little bum from Nebraska being treated that way. It never dawns on me that they may be looking at me with any admiration—or what, envy maybe?— because I was a big league pitcher at one time. I find all that hard to believe.

Tom Selleck has worked out with the Orioles a few times, and Kevin Costner. Selleck looks like a ballplayer swinging the bat. A left-hand hitter, he hit a few into the stands during batting practice.

In 1991 the Orioles met Queen Elizabeth. She came with Prince Philip and President and Mrs. Bush to see her first baseball game. Ordinarily, the security arrangements for a presidential visit are very tight. On that occasion they were doubly so. A few weeks beforehand, security people swarm all over the place, looking at everything and deciding where to station sharpshooters: on the roof, up in the light towers, in the stands. A half hour before the game they kick everybody out of the press box and go through the place with dogs and scanners. Everybody is frisked. There is a lot of commotion, and guys in suits everywhere with those little wires going into their ears.

The Oakland A's were in town when the queen visited us. A loose, loud bunch, they were laughing and joking about it, but they got very quiet when it came time to line up and file into the Orioles' dugout to shake hands with the queen, who wore white gloves and took every hand. The players were not supposed to remove their caps, but a few did.

The queen was then supposed to go back up to Eli Jacobs's booth, but she asked Bush if she could walk out onto the field. The security people were aghast, but they walked out on the field and the crowd cheered.

They stayed at the game for a few innings and I introduced her again from the booth and she stood up and waved. When they left, I am certain that Bush would have preferred to stay. He takes off his jacket, loosens his tie, and enjoys the game for its own sake.

One year he was to throw out the first pitch and he was down under the stands warming up with Elrod Hendricks. "I want to make sure I reach home plate," he said.

Over the security men's objections, he ran out to the mound when I introduced him, wound up, and threw a strike. He went out to the mound when he opened the new ballpark at Camden Yards in 1992. The fans knew he was breaking the rules and they appreciated it. He enjoyed what he was doing and it showed.

Those were good times, the years after my stroke. Until 1991, my health was good, and I did hundreds of banquets and appearances every winter, speaking before all kinds of groups. Older fans knew me from my playing days; younger ones knew me only from "THANK Youuu" and "Give that fan a contract" and the call-in show. When I am not watching a ball game, I enjoy talking baseball, and they gave me many opportunities.

In the summer of 1989 I was elected to the Brooklyn Dodgers Hall of Fame. The Dodgers museum is located in the Long Island Historical Society, 128 Pierrepont Street in Brooklyn Heights. Governor William Schaefer declared June 13 Rex Barney Day in Maryland, and off I went to the induction ceremony at the Dodgers museum. The other inductees that day were Clyde King, Eddie Stanky, and the longtime batboy, Stanley Strull.

As we approached in a bus, we could see crowds of people walking toward the site. It was a sea of Dodger blue and white, but not a single cap with LA on it could be seen. Everything stressed Brooklyn. We were their beloved Bums, the real Dodgers. As far as those people were concerned, the Dodgers did not exist anymore, anywhere.

The Sym-Phony band was playing as people lined up for autographs. I must have signed a thousand of them. It always gives me a feeling of pride, to see people standing in line for blocks just to meet me.

They were mostly older people, with kids staring at us who had never heard of us. Their fathers and grandfathers were telling them, "Do you realize you're looking at a real Brooklyn Dodger?" I mean, it made you feel like some kind of fossil, like a dinosaur in a museum.

One youngster about fifteen said to me, "Are you Rex Barney?"

"Yes, I am," I said, feeling ten feet tall.

"Did you really pitch a no-hitter for the Dodgers?"

"Yes, I did." Now I'm really feeling all puffed up.

He said, "I don't remember you, but my father does."

His father had told him what to say. I didn't mean a thing to the little bum. Deflated me on the spot.

The announcer read telegrams of congratulations from baseball people, then got to this one:

"I want to thank you for being part of the Brooklyn Dodgers and for all that you accomplished for the fans there. I, too, am one of those fans. Signed, Peter O'Malley."

When the name was read aloud, the crowd booed like crazy. You'd think after thirty years they'd forget. No way. Peter O'Malley was just a little kid when the Dodgers left Brooklyn. He had nothing to do with it. That made no difference. I know one thing: if my name was O'Malley and I moved to Brooklyn, I'd change it, quick.

They gave each of us a blue and white Brooklyn Dodgers pin. When it was my turn to stand up and say a few words, I heard people saying, "THANK Youuuu" and "Give that fan a contract." In Brooklyn! Some of those people had never set foot in any other ballpark except Ebbets Field in their lives. Many of them had sworn never to go to another National League game, and they kept that vow.

I said, "I never thought I'd be with all the great Dodgers in the Hall of Fame. To a guy like me, from Omaha, Nebraska, being accepted in Brooklyn the way that I was, and still am, is a great honor."

They had a party for us and some of the other Dodgers—Erskine, Branca, Reese, Shuba, Gionfriddo—who were there, and if you don't shed some tears at a get-together like that, there's something wrong.

Later I learned that they had an original seat from Ebbets Field that they were going to present to me in 1993.

Every winter the Baseball Assistance Team has a dinner in New York to honor a current player who has contributed to the community through charitable activities. Glenn Davis is one of the past honorees. Ralph Branca is the chairman and Joe Garagiola the president of BAT, which raises money to help former players who were not eligible for any pensions and are in need of help. Many former players avoid events of this kind, but they pay their own way to this one to help BAT, which has tried without success to get help for needy old-time players and their families from the current pension plan. The sad truth is, the young players of today just don't care. In January 1992 I represented the Orioles at the dinner, where Dale Murphy was the honored guest.

I always look forward to seeing guys I haven't seen for some time and reminiscing. It is very rewarding to me to be accepted among them, and to remain a part of the exuberance that is so much in evidence when we get together and swap stories, most of which are self-deprecating. Nobody talks about how great they were; we all know that.

Ballplayers' thinking never changes. Hitters who had heard about the new Oriole Park at Camden Yards were intrigued by the short right field wall. I've seen them at old-timers' games come out on the field and first thing they say is, "I see it's a pitcher's wind." That's just the way they think.

I arrived in New York before noon and it was raining, so I went down to the hotel coffee shop. I was sitting there alone for a few minutes when I heard my name. It was Clyde King, who had been my roommate in Havana in 1947. He and his wife, Norma, sat down with me.

A few minutes later I heard, "Number 26." It was Ralph Branca and his wife, Ann. Branca had worn number 13 and I was double 13.

It was a genuine family reunion; when teams use that term "family" today, I have to laugh. They don't know what it means, and never will.

At the dinner, Mantle, Mays, and Snider were special guests. Can you imagine, those three playing at the same time in New York, plus Joe DiMaggio at the end of his career? Snider reminded the audience that the song, "Mickey, Willie and the Duke," would never have been written if the composer had had to work with Edwin, his real name.

Seeing that trio standing there, I realized that none of them had made any money. Mantle reached $100,000 one year and then took a cut. The money and the long-term contracts have destroyed what we had. Nobody knew or cared what anybody else was making in our time. We all knew the ones who deserved the most made the most, however little it seems by today's standards.

I saw a lot of players I did not recognize. One man came over to me and said, "Do you know who I am?"

"No, I don't," I confessed. "I'm sorry."

"I'm Willard Marshall."

"Willard! I've been wanting to thank you for forty years. You grounded into a double play in the first inning of my no-hitter in 1948 and from then on the Giants did nothing."

He said, "Oh, why did I even bother to say hello to you?"

Warren Spahn was sitting at the table just behind me. You know what that meant to me, to be sitting and visiting with the best pitcher I ever saw? And he remembered my hitting a double off him. That not only made my day, but it reminded me of how ballplayers' memories constantly amaze me.

I was leaving the next morning at eight o'clock, but the old Dodgers wanted to meet for breakfast. So at six A.M. there was Snider, Erskine, Branca, King, Podres, Zimmer, and me at the table, and who comes walking in but Rachel Robinson, Jackie's widow.

"Jackie would want me to look out for you guys," she said. "You know, when Jackie was playing, he probably couldn't even sit at this table, but I can sit here now."

There is a lot of camaraderie among players of the 1940s and 1950s, but I believe it is even more pronounced among former Brooklyn Dodgers. The extinction of baseball in Brooklyn may bind us closer; we are part of something that is gone forever. The Dodgers are still a very close-knit organization; they send out newsletters to former players and keep in touch with us. But if the Dodgers had been in Los Angeles already when I signed with them, it wouldn't be the same. It's Mr. Rickey, it's Leo the Lip Durocher, it's Jackie, it's Ebbets Field, it's the holy wars against the Giants, it's every other team loving Ebbets Field and the fans, but wanting to kill us on the field.

All of that, the intensity and the ardor, disappeared when the two teams went to California.

To this day, fifty years later, I still see that gleam in people's eyes when they see each other, and it tells me there was something special between us that has never died, and I am proud to have been part of it for all these years.

A Bad Cut

PEOPLE WHO HAVE DIABETES can do everything to keep their blood sugar stable, but other things can happen to them. If they get a sore or an open wound and it does not heal rapidly, they can be in trouble.

In 1985 I had just such a sore on my left foot and it landed me in the hospital. The doctors talked about amputating the foot, but they cut a hole through it instead. It took months for it to heal, months I spent in the tender loving care of Carole's mother, Lydia Bennett, and grandmother, Carolina Briglia. During all that time I had to take antibiotics every two hours around the clock. That kind of routine is debilitating in itself.

I know one thing for sure: I am the luckiest guy in the world to have such saints for in-laws. And I'm glad that, contrary to the country music song, all my exes are not in Texas.

From 1985 to 1991 I was in pretty good shape. The problem with my left foot recurred and they had to remove the tip of a bone. In November 1991 I had a cataract removed, but that was a breeze. I was awake, talking baseball, for the entire thirty-minute operation.

But from time to time during those years I had some down days when I just felt all washed out. Infections in my legs and feet were probably draining me of energy. I was taking good care of myself and could not understand why this should be happening. But I fought it and stuck to my schedule, sometimes running like a madman to make two appearances during the day, then working a game that night and maybe doing the call-in show until midnight. I was a hardheaded Irishman who played hurt and never complained; and I was wrong and it cost me.

All through May 1992 my right leg and foot were hurting, but I was toughing it out. Why, I don't know. On Friday, May 22, the Angels opened a series at Baltimore. I can't tell you how much I hurt while I worked that game. I didn't sleep much that night and, the next morning at six, I decided, "That's it. I'm going."

I called Dr. Goldgeier's office and spoke to Dr. Marshall Levin. "I'm hurting. I'm in trouble."

He said, "I'll meet you at Sinai Hospital."

"You better get me a room," I said.

"You're that bad?"

"I'm that bad."

I wrapped my swollen, discolored foot in bandages and a big heavy sock and took a cab to Sinai. In the emergency room I was surrounded by doctors looking at my foot, shaking their heads, muttering among themselves, and looking very serious. They hooked me up to an IV and a surgeon came in and took a look and said, "I hate to tell you this, but we should amputate this immediately."

"Whoa," I said. "Wait a minute. I want to talk to my own doctors."

When Dr. Goldgeier and Dr. Charles Silberstein, an orthopedic surgeon and close friend, got there, I asked them for their opinions.

"We really can't tell you what to do," they said. "It's up to you. But if we just do something partial, you'll still hurt and you'll probably be back here next month."

"What are you talking about doing?"

"We're talking about amputating below the knee, which is the good news, because you'll recover a lot quicker than if it was above the knee."

I can't say I was surprised, because I'd heard that these things can happen to diabetics. But it's still a shock to confront the words. And as far as the good news part of it was concerned, I was not exactly flooded with feelings of good fortune at that moment.

When I did not show up at Camden Yards on Saturday, there was no way to keep it a secret that I was in the hospital. But I did not want to see or talk to anybody. I mean nobody. I could not handle another circus like the lost weekend in October. I took no calls.

All Saturday and Sunday I lay there just thinking and talking to doctors. They wanted to talk more about baseball, and I had to keep reminding them to talk medical stuff to me. Everybody kept telling me I would feel better than I had in years if I had the operation.

I said all the prayers I knew and asked for all the help I could get. But I don't believe in messages coming down and telling you, "Yes, have the operation," or "No, don't do it." I knew the answer had to come from me. I thought and I cried and I wondered how in the hell I would function. I thought about Sandy Amoros, one of the Dodgers from the 1950s. Sandy had an artificial leg. I had seen him in Los Angeles in 1991 at a Dodgers' reunion, but I never thought anything about it at the time, because you don't think anything like that will ever happen to you.

I considered having the partial operation, weighing whether I could tough my way through that way, like an idiot. On Monday Dr. Jeffrey Kremen, the top surgeon in this field, assured me that after the operation I would have no more pain, no more apprehension hanging over me, no more wondering what if this and what if that. The "what if" would have become reality, and I could deal with that a whole lot better.

I still can't tell you exactly when or why I made the decision. I think the part about still having the knee had something to do with it. Sometime Monday evening or Tuesday morning I said, "Let's go. Let's do it." It was May 26, my daughter's birthday.

I asked Dr. Kremen, "What time will you do it?"

"About five this evening."

That afternoon about three o'clock I called WBAL and taped my 4:15 radio show. I was probably destroyed and didn't sound very good, but I did it. I did it the next day and the next and never missed one, and it was good therapy for me.

So, late that afternoon, they put me on this gurney and start wheeling me to the elevator and I'm rolling along thinking, "What am I doing? God knows what my life will be like after this. Should I get up and get out of here some way?" And I'm lying there waiting and a couple people—visitors, not nurses or doctors—come over to me and say, "Are you Rex Barney?"

"Yes."

"What's the matter?"

"Oh, I just have to have a minor little operation."

And the guy who's driving the gurney went, "Mmmmm." He knew. Here I am stretched out on this stretcher thinking God knows what and these people ask me, "Can we have your autograph?"

I thought, "Now, what do I do? I mean, why should I upset them?" They ran and got napkins or some such thing and I signed them. And one guy says, "Will you write 'THANK Youuuu'?" and I'm thinking, "What am I going to write 'thank you' about?" But I laughed; what else was I going to do?

Then you get down to the operating room and they talk to you and the next thing you know you're asleep and you're out of it.

I kept a journal during my hospital stay, and here are the entries for three days:

May 26: GONE

May 27: GONE

May 28: GONE

But I managed to do my 4:15 show every day. I can imagine what I sounded like.

Then I woke up on Friday morning and thought, "Dummy. Let's go. Enough of this." I thought about the men I had known in baseball who had gone through the same thing. Bill Veeck, whose war wounds as a Marine cost him a leg, was the most energetic club owner and showman in the game. He'd mash out cigarette butts on his artificial leg and it never slowed him down.

Harvey Kuenn was playing golf one day and the golf cart flipped over on a hill and crushed his right leg. It couldn't be saved. He went on to manage the Milwaukee Brewers, and made jokes about his wooden leg. I remembered sitting in the dugout with him in Milwaukee one night with mosquitoes as big as horses flying around. One landed on his propped-up leg. Kuenn looked at it and said, "That sonofabitch is in for a rude awakening when he tries to bite that leg."

Harvey told me, "No matter how slowly I walk out to the mound, no umpire can make me hurry. That's why my pitcher in the bullpen will always be ready by the time I get out there."

Bob Uecker said he tried to get Harvey to put the leg on backwards and walk out on the field with one foot pointing ahead and one the other way. Kuenn tried, but could not fit it to his stump backwards.

I thought of Monty Stratton, a pitcher for the White Sox in the thirties, who lost his leg in a hunting accident and came back to win eighteen games in the minor leagues in 1946.

And Bert Shepard, a P-38 pilot in World War II, who lost his right leg below the knee when he was shot down over Germany. In 1945, Shepard, a left-hander, actually pitched five good innings in relief for the Washington Senators on an artificial leg, then played and managed in the minors. (I also pictured myself with a peg leg, like Long John Silver or Pegleg Bates, an old-time tap dancer. But I guess those are out of fashion now.) And I figured if those guys could do it, there was no reason why I couldn't, too. It was time to get on with my life. I began my physical therapy and rehab that day and I've never looked back.

You've heard of phantom pain and itching? Let me tell you, they are real. I had those things for weeks. Middle of the night my toes itched and I reached down to scratch them and said, "You dummy, there's nothing there." When I told the nurses my foot hurt, they laughed. They're used to that stuff. For a while, when I went to slip a sock over the stump, I reached all the way down to where my foot had been. And sitting in a wheelchair with my half-leg straight out, I still instinctively but needlessly pulled it back out of the way when someone walked by.

It took a while to get used to the sounds of the alien words that were being applied to me. When Dr. Kremen stood over me, admiring his handiwork, and said, "That's one of the most beautiful stumps I've ever seen," I cringed. I still hate the world "prosthesis"; I prefer to call it my leg and let it go at that. And it took me a while to stop choking on the word "amputation."

No word about my condition had been leaked to the media. When Mark Hyman of the morning Baltimore *Sun* approached me for a statement, I discussed the wording of a press release with people at WBAL and Rick Vaughn of the Orioles. I resisted the use of "amputation"; it sounded terrible to me. I just wanted to call it an operation. But Mark said I would have to call it what it was and I gradually but reluctantly came around and agreed, and now I use it all the time and it doesn't bother me anymore.

I began to eat like a horse to regain my strength and went at the physical therapy all out. I knew something about that routine from my stroke nine years earlier, but this was different. With the stroke, I had mental capacities to regain. One day I could understand orders but could not do them. The next day I could not understand but could do the things. That had been a mental roller coaster. This was all mechanical. I knew what I was doing at all times, and I didn't fight it.

The hardest thing to overcome was the loss of balance, the tendency to want to use that leg to steady myself when I began to totter or fall. But of course I didn't have a leg to stand on. Using a walker, I had to climb up and down a curb, and go up and down a short flight of steps. It sounds simple, but I can tell you, it took me some time to stand there peering down at that step before I felt the strength and confidence and balance to lift myself to the next one.

Nobody can imagine what it is like until they are in those shoes—or shoe. It's like being Jackie Robinson or pitching a no-hitter or huddling in a foxhole under enemy fire. You can't describe it. People can try hopping around on one foot, but it is not the same thing. When part or all of one leg is gone, the imbalance in the weight of your two sides throws you off. You have to guard against slipping or falling and relying on a leg that isn't there to stop you.

Another important part of the therapy was building my upper body strength to do simple things that would now be more complicated, at least until I had a replacement leg. The things you normally take for granted and do without thinking, I now had to stop and think about: getting out of bed to go to the bathroom with my leg off, taking clothes from a closet, getting dressed. I lifted weights while sitting in a wheelchair, and pulled on tension cables, and held a bar over my head while rolling up a one-pound ball of lead on the end of a string five times with each hand. That's tiring, especially when you get to the last few.

"One more to go, Rex," the therapist would say. And I imagined that "one more to go" was Whitey Lockman at the plate with 2 out in the last of the ninth of my no-hitter and I put all I had into it.

I had to pull a taut cable twenty times up, twenty times straight ahead, with each arm. And I remembered Mr. Rickey saying a good pitcher will finish as strong as he started, and I kept pitching, pulling, stretching, beyond the twenty times.

I worked hard, and I guess my attitude was contagious. The therapists told me I had brought four other people out of their doldrums without my realizing it. There were some older, some younger than I was, and apparently they had not been making much progress. When they heard me saying, "Take that, Whitey Lockman," as I pulled and stretched and lifted, they said, "What's with him?" The therapists answered, "He wants to get back the way he was. Don't you?" And I guess they figured, "If that fool can do it, I can do it."

I had my own sources of inspiration. One day some friends brought a man named Elmer Lynch to see me. Lynch walked in like anybody else and I never would have guessed that a year ago he had had the same kind of amputation as I had. He showed me his leg and demonstrated the things he can do, and he assured me that he had asked all the same questions I was asking. I asked him how he went to the bathroom in the middle of the night and he said, "You could strap the leg on or use a crutch. You'll learn to hold onto the sink when you wash your hands, like I did."

Lynch was impressed with my progress and figured I would be walking as good as he did in about three months; it had taken him about six. His visit was very encouraging to me and I thanked him. He said he was glad to be there to help me.

When the doctors told me to expect a lot of requests to appear before groups of amputees and be a spokesman for them, I assured them that I would do so gladly.

One day a man knocked on the door and came in and told me he had a daughter who listened to me on the radio. He asked if he could bring her in and I said sure. Her name was Laura; she was about nine years old. I asked her, "How did you get to be such a big baseball fan?"

"From listening to you on the radio," she said. "Can I shake your hand?"

We shook hands and she asked for my autograph, signed with a " THANK Youuuu." Then they left. A few minutes later Laura returned alone. "Can I ask you one more thing?" she said.

"Sure. What is it?"

"Can I give you a kiss?"

Now, why would you lie there and waste your life away when you have something like that to come back for?

I discovered that the doctors were correct: I had no pain, except for the phantoms. I felt better than I had in a long time. I was healing ahead of schedule. Within a few weeks I was wearing a shrink bandage to help reduce the swelling, and they began measuring me for a temporary leg to practice with. I would have to learn to walk again, and drive a car differently. I knew my life had been altered. I would have to adjust. Could I do all that? I knew damn well I could.

Doing my radio show every day forced me to read and pay attention to what was happening in the world of baseball, and that helped. But nothing meant more to me than the calls and letters I received from baseball people and fans. The first call that came through to me a few days after the operation was from Orioles manager Johnny Oates in Oakland. "I had to talk to you," he said. "But I didn't know what to say. I called my wife and asked her and she said, 'You have to say what you feel.' I've been sitting here thinking about it and now I know what I want to say. I love you. Now you can tell me how to run the ball club."

What could I say? "Well, you goofed up a game in Seattle." Not that he had, but I had to say something.

And Oates said, "Well, now I know you're better already."

He called me almost every day after that. Other players— Flanagan, Storm Davis, Elrod Hendricks, Cal Senior, the trainers—called from California. And the radio guys—Joe Angel and Jon Miller and Chuck Thompson and Dr. Paul Eicholtz—called often. Those calls meant a lot to me. Players from other teams called, too. Sparky Anderson called from the Detroit dugout one night. And I began to get it through my head that maybe I do mean something to those people.

Then the old Dodgers checked in. Buzzie Bavasi, the general manager in Durham back in 1943, now retired after a long career in baseball, called several times. Ralph Branca, Sandy Koufax, Peter O'Malley, Clem Labine, whose son had undergone a full leg amputation. Clem said I would adapt to it with no problem.

Carole was there almost every day. Gary Davis, a producer at WBAL, was invaluable to me, doing many things that I asked of him. Friends brought me food, and sent baskets of fruit so big it took two men to carry them. Jon Miller brought me a print of a 1955 World Series scene at Ebbets Field. I don't know how many hundreds of pieces of mail went to WBAL and the Orioles for me.

One of the first to visit me was my personal psychiatrist, Jim Palmer. He came busting in one Saturday morning about ten o'clock, closed the door, all but hung out a 'Do Not Disturb' sign. He's telling me he'll do anything I need or want, and all the time we're talking, he's fooling with his hair, patting it, arranging a few errant strands, and fussing with it.

"What's wrong?" I said.

"I got the world's worst haircut," he said.

"It looks fine to me. Didn't Linda cut it?" She's been cutting our hair for about twenty years.

"Yeah."

We go on talking and he's still fretting with his hair. Then he jumps up and heads straight for the little mirror in the corner of the room that I hadn't even noticed was there.

"It's too short on top," he says, studying himself. "And I have to go on television tonight."

"You look fine. Go home and get dressed and go do the game. There's nothing you can do about it now."

"I know, but it's a bad cut."

"Come over here, pal," I say. I point to my stump. "Now, there is a bad cut. Forget about your haircut. This is a bad cut."

We both laugh. "You're right," he says. "I'll never complain about a bad haircut in your presence again."

Then he says, "You know, I think you ought to make a comeback."

"What the hell are you talking about?"

"With your artificial leg you'll probably have great control. You won't overthrow anymore."

Vintage Palmer, that.

The next day, Sunday, nine o'clock at night, no knock, no nothing, here comes Rick Dempsey bursting in with his mother and sister and he's carrying a pizza as big as a cartwheel. I told him I couldn't eat the pizza and he disappeared down to the nurse's station and you've never heard so much confusion in your life for the next fifteen minutes. They're having a pizza party and he's signing autographs and having a ball.

I was beginning to think about going back to work, figuring maybe I could manage it by August 1. I knew there would be no steps to conquer at Camden Yards, and getting around in a wheelchair would be no problem. I could not have done the same at Memorial Stadium.

One day Dr. Goldgeier came in and said, "I've been thinking about when you could go back to work. How does July 1 sound to you?"

I said, "Please don't tease me about that."

"I'm serious. It's a day game. You can get to the ballpark early and not cause as much commotion as you would at night. Of course, you'll need a few people with you to help you."

I said, "Let's do it."

He told me it would be up to me if I felt like working after that. You know what the answer was to that. I had missed seventeen games. I did not miss another one from then on.

A few minutes later in walked Robin Korotki, the therapist who had worked so diligently to bring me back from the stroke. "I'm volunteering for duty July 1," she said. "I wouldn't let anybody else be with you on that occasion."

Exactly four weeks after I had gone to the hospital I was released, back in the care of Carole and her mother, her sister, Patricia, and Patty's husband, John Szczecinski. There is no way I could have come back the way I have without them, and there is no way I can ever repay them. They have been there to help me from chair to walker, up and down steps, in and out of cars, to the therapist five mornings a week, to the ballpark, to WBAL, waiting on me hand and foot. Robin has chauffeured me and assisted me at the ballpark more than once. Gary Davis and others have pulled that duty as well.

During my absence the Orioles had used someone different to fill in for me at each game, from Baltimore radio and TV personalities to game show host Pat Sajak. One night John Patti of WBAL used my line, "Give that fan a contract," and the fans booed the poor guy.

As I got closer to Wednesday, July 1, I started to question if I was truly ready. Not about handling the PA; I had been studying the Milwaukee Brewers' box scores to become familiar with the names. But I was apprehensive about losing my balance and falling. I knew people would be very solicitous and try to do things for me and I still resisted that. On Saturday Linda came to the house and gave me a haircut. It was a good haircut.

By Wednesday morning I was ready to go, but when I got to the ballpark I was not prepared for the reception I found there. I was astounded by the outpouring of affection. Sure, I knew all about the calls the hospital and the Orioles and WBAL had fielded for me, and I read all the cards and letters from fans and players and players' wives.

That day, surrounded by all that adulation, Robin said to me, "Just accept it. Don't try to explain it." The doctors told me I didn't belong to myself anymore; I belonged to the people. I've never gotten that through my head.

People of all ages came up to me to welcome me back and shake my hand. That was better therapy for me than anything. One of them was the president of the wheelchair softball league. Two years earlier I had thrown out the first ball to start their season. Now he wanted to know if I'd pitch for them. They brought me baskets of fruit and pots of flowers grown in their yards. Fans streamed constantly up to the front of the press box to greet me and ask for autographs. I had to put some of them off by promising to stay after the game and sign for them.

There were more hugs and kisses than at an Irish wake, just about everybody who works at the ballpark, from Lt. "Uncle Phil" Ferace, the grizzled, white-haired head of security, to the young blond Beth Plecker, the assistant director of the Home Team Sports television crew. I know one thing: I've never been kissed by so many men in my life. I think I broke the record for one day.

I had made an appointment to meet with Johnny Oates in his office at nine to get the lineup, then I rolled over to say hello to Ernie Tyler, one of the few people who have been with the Orioles longer than I have. I was up in the press box by ten o'clock, writing the lineups on the slate as far up as I could

241

reach. Do you know what a thrill it was for me just to write the umpires' names on there? You can't know.

I got upset because my scorebook had not been kept up the way I liked it. And Robin, who can be a real Marine drill sergeant when she has to, got on me for letting such a little thing upset me. She was right, and I thought: "Two of a kind, Palmer and me—his bad haircut and my messed-up book. Two perfectionist pitchers. But he had better control."

Then I turned on the mike and said, "Testing." That's all I said. There were no fans in the place yet, just ushers and the grounds crew. And I heard shouts and applause, and all those guys were looking toward me and waving. Somebody hollered, "What do you say?" And I said, "THANK Youuuu." It felt good.

For an hour before the game the press box was swarming with radio and television guys and cameras and writers and photographers and you'd have thought Princess Di had shown up. They were out in the seats in front of the press box, up on tables, following me and preceding me wherever I went, which wasn't far. It was overwhelming, and it began to sink in that maybe I am more than just an anonymous voice coming out of a loudspeaker to a lot of people.

If you'd been in that ballpark, from the second I said, "Good afternoon," I don't think you could have heard anything else, the noise was so deafening. I choked up only once. I was proud of myself for that.

As I began my opening announcements, four ball girls stood at home plate holding up signs that read, "THANK YOOOUUUU."

And wouldn't you know, with 2 outs in the ninth, the Orioles leading, 7 to 4, Gregg Olson pitching with a man on second and a 2 and 1 count on the hitter, the lightning and thunder crashed and the skies dumped a downpour on us that held up the game for more than an hour. When the game finally resumed, Olson threw one pitch and Pat Listach hit a fly ball to Mike Devereaux in center field and the game was over and I had completed my first day back on the job just five weeks after my bad cut.

Thanks to Carole's sister Patricia, who is a nurse, I was lucky to get to work with therapist Dr. Bill Neill at Kernan

Hospital. The longtime trainer for the Baltimore Colts, Bill is the best in the business. I worked with him for three hours a day five days a week in June and July. He assured me that, come August, I'd be walking so well that nobody would suspect I had an artificial leg. But he stopped short of promising me that I would have better control on the mound.

While I was in the hospital I had kidded the doctors and nurses, telling them we lacked a dramatic finish for this book, so I had agreed to provide one. And there it is.

No encores, please.

By the first week of August I was ready to try driving a car. I did not think I would like using hand devices, so another amputee let me try driving her car, which was equipped with a gas pedal attachment on the left side and a large brake pedal. Dr. Neill warned everyone to move their cars from the parking lot, telling them, "Rex Barney is going to be driving a car for the first time." I tried it out and didn't hit anybody, which is more than I can say for my big league pitching debut. I ordered a car with similar equipment and knew I would soon be behind the wheel as well as on my feet.

A few weeks later I was able to desert the wheelchair and walk with a cane, but it was another month before I was fitted with my final leg.

I mark September 9, 1992, as the completion of my recovery. For years I have been introducing people to throw out the ceremonial first ball before each game. Aware that it was also the anniversary of my no-hitter, the Orioles gave me the honor of introducing myself in that role before the Yankees game that night.

I went down to the Orioles' dugout with Robin and Dr. Neill and made my preliminary announcements from there. Charles Steinberg, the Diamondvision wizard and my PA coordinator, surprised me with a replica of my old Dodger uniform shirt, number 26, which I put on. Dr. Neill told me, "If you fall on your face out there, I'm out of here. Don't let on that you know me."

True to form, I choked up as I announced:

"And now, ladies and gentlemen, if you will permit me, I'd like to take just a moment to give you a personal message. I must tell you how grateful I am to all of you for the help and encouragement you have given me this summer in my recuperation and rehabilitation from surgery.

"Tonight is a special anniversary for me. It was forty-four years ago today that I threw a no-hit, no-run game for the Brooklyn Dodgers, and I can think of no greater way to celebrate than to share it with you. So tonight, to celebrate this anniversary and to show you how effective and heartfelt your support has been, I am delivering my own first ball by walking for the first time under my own power since the surgery. And I have asked our favorite catcher, Rick Dempsey, to catch me. I hope I throw a strike.

"Once again I say to all of you who have made me feel so much better—THANK Youuuu."

I put down my cane and emerged from the dugout. The standing ovation from the fans overwhelmed me. Then Rick Dempsey said, "You're going out to the mound."

"No way," I said.

"I won't give you the ball unless you do."

I went two-thirds of the way to the mound. Dempsey rubbed up the ball, then loaded it—made a spitter out of it—and handed it to me.

I'll say this for myself: I am the very model of consistency. The pitch I threw to him was high and outside. But I did it, and Rick and I walked off the field hugging each other.

TWENTY-THREE

If

I'VE OFTEN SAID I'd like to be the commissioner of baseball. What a life. You wake up in the morning and say, well, I think I'll go to Detroit today and watch the Tigers. And there's that problem out in Oakland about the mustard for the hot dogs; I'll fly out there tomorrow. Besides, the Yankees are playing the A's . . .

Of course, it is not that easy, but that's probably the way I would look at it. And it pays well. Sure, you have to make decisions, but I wouldn't mind that. I'd have a bunch of lawyers on the staff and two league presidents for input. I've always believed that two people saved baseball: Babe Ruth and Judge Landis. I like to think I would be a little like Landis, who was tough. He didn't hesitate to kick somebody out of the game, right or wrong. I'm sure I'd be hearing from the players' grievance committee every other day and have lawsuits galore.

So, if I were the commissioner of baseball, what would I do?

First thing, before the seat was warm, I would throw out the designated hitter. I despise the thing. I believe that nine men are supposed to play the game and one of them is the pitcher. People say the DH gives older players a chance to stay in the game. Baloney. Baseball is not intended to be an employment bureau for old semiplayers. Why not give those roster spots to young pitchers or other players coming up? The DH takes away something from the strategy of the game when it comes to pinch-hitting for the pitcher, and robs the fans of a chance to second-guess the managers. At the very least, having it in one league and not the other is an abomination. If I couldn't throw it out altogether, I'd lock both leagues in a room until they decided to have it in both or throw it out. Using two sets of rules during a World Series is ridiculous. It was a mistake to start it in only one league in the first place.

Some pitchers don't like pitching to nine hitters who are a threat at the plate, and some don't like to hit. Rick Sutcliffe claims that most of his arm problems started from hitting; your arm jerks when swinging a bat. I broke my ankle sliding on a base hit. Preacher Roe threw left-handed but batted right-handed to put less strain on his pitching arm. All I know is, a lot of pitchers threw a lot of innings over the years and took their turns at bat. Let them hit. Put down a bunt. Maybe get a base hit.

I predict the DH will go down the drain, even if they don't elect me commissioner. The sooner the better.

Next, there would be no such thing as American and National League umpires. They would all be major league umps working in both leagues with the same strike zone and rules. I would abolish umpire crews and mix them up on assignments, instead of having the same four working together all the time. Players and managers identify umpires by the crew chiefs: that's a good crew, they say, or that's a lousy crew, based on how they evaluate one or two of the four in that crew.

I would get rid of the umpires who are not so good and see to it that all the umps are capable. And I would pick the best six to work the playoffs and World Series without restraints. As it is now, every umpire must work at least one playoff, World Series, or all-star game every fifteen years; he must have six years' experience, and he cannot work the same event more often than once in four years.

I do not think baseball has handled the drug business properly. I would give players one chance and throw them out of the game. If somebody does not abide by the rules, out he goes. Period. If a player is not in the proper condition because of drugs to give the 100 percent he owes the fans who buy the tickets and the club that pays his salary, out he goes. Dick Williams wrote about the evidence he saw of drug use under the stands during games in Montreal, but it was just swept under the AstroTurf.

If

I like Steve Howe, but he should have been out of the game after the first incident. Why should he and others be exceptions while 500 other guys are playing by the rules? They say you can't fire a baseball player. Why not? I have no sympathy for them.

I do not believe there was ever as much of a drug problem in baseball as in other sports, because it is the only one that spans eight months of everyday action. It is tougher to stay up mentally and physically. But when you take a kid and give him all that money, right away he'll attract parasites who say, "Try this, it'll make you feel good," and he tries it and is hooked. But I don't blame the parasites. I blame the athlete who does it to himself. He has to be responsible for his own actions.

The game should be speeded up, but I'm not sure how that can be done. Maybe limit the times a catcher can go to the mound. Maybe require the batter to stay in the batter's box once he gets there—why do they have to step out after every pitch? But I do not favor abolishing the intentional walk or making it automatic. Make the pitcher throw the four wide ones. Things can happen.

I would not have newspapermen act as official scorers. I would hire scorers who, like the umpires, would be employed by major league baseball and travel as the umpires do. They could be former players, who can objectively judge the gray areas between hits and errors and what a fielder should have been able to do. You should hear the calls I get in the press box from dugouts on both sides complaining about scorers' decisions.

One day the Tigers were in Baltimore. An Orioles batter hit a pop fly back of short. Alan Trammell backpedaled, waving everybody off, but he didn't back up far enough and it dropped behind him. The scorer called it an error. The phone rang. It was not the Tigers complaining about the error, but Earl Weaver. "We're supposed to get those things called hits at home," he said. Batting coach Terry Crowley added, "Give the guy a hit. He's in a slump and we're trying to help him." That's being objective?

The biggest complaint I've heard from pitchers in both leagues is that in many parks the mound in the bullpen is different from the one on the field, and they have to adjust when they come into a game. That bothers me; I don't know why it is that way. The mounds should be the same height, diameter, and steepness. I understand there is no significant difference in Oriole Park at Camden Yards.

Mound heights should also be checked more often to see that they conform to the rules, instead of the petty stuff that goes on. In 1991 the Orioles' head grounds keeper Paul Zwaska noticed the grass in front of the mound was worn away. Pitchers are travelers; they circle the mound and take a few steps toward home plate to get the ball from the catcher. So Zwaska cut out about six inches of grass and replaced it with dirt in front of the mound. An umpire supervisor told him it was illegal; he had to replace the grass. Zwaska said, "Show me in the rules where it is illegal and I'll fix it." The umpire insisted, but Paul was adamant, and he was right. The rules "suggested" a sixteen-foot-diameter circle. The next year the rule was changed to "required."

In ancient times when I pitched there was a dirt path from the mound to the plate. Nobody knows why. If we put that in at Oriole Park it would really look like an old-time park.

Being an old traditionalist, I do not like green and yellow and garish uniforms. Give me the old style Detroit, Yankee, and Red Sox uniforms. Home white; road gray. That's what God intended baseball players to wear.

I never saw anything wrong with the reserve clause, and I guess that shows how out of date I am. Clubs spent a lot of money to bring players through the minor leagues, most of whom never made it to the majors. Sure, we were slaves of a sort; we could not play for another team or auction ourselves off to the highest bidder. And we could be traded anywhere without our consent. But, at the time, in our ignorant bliss over just being in the big leagues, we never minded it. Today the system is rent-a-player. We will rarely see a player spend his entire career with one team.

I was out of baseball four or five years before I actually got my release. The Dodgers were worried I might make a comeback and retained their rights to my services. Some players never got an official release notice; they just left the scene.

The controversy over Pete Rose will go on forever, so if I were commissioner I would have to deal with it. For starters, I would have thrown him out for good if there was any evidence that he had bet on his own team or an opponent. I would have suspended him for a specific term for betting on other games or other sports.

Did Rose bet on baseball games? I don't know. I do believe the commissioner's office had a lot more on him than ever came out. And I'll say this: if Rose had said to me, "I agree to be suspended for life but I'm not guilty," I don't buy that. He would have been out immediately and for good. Period.

The Hall of Fame voting is not the commissioner's business. I respect Rose for his ability on the field. He did a lot with little talent. It doesn't matter if I like him or not. Based on his ability alone he probably belongs. A lot of guys in there were no angels. And I think he will get in someday, but there should be some explanation as to what he did and why he was banned.

Bart Giamatti came to Memorial Stadium one day in the midst of the Rose hearings. He said to me, "As I go around the country I like to talk to players who have been in the game a long time and never really left it. What do you think about this Rose business?"

"You put me on the spot," I said. "It's a tough question."

"If it'll make it easier for you," he said, "I've talked to Bob Feller, Hank Aaron, Joe DiMaggio, Ted Williams, a few others in the Hall of Fame."

I said, "I'm not in the Hall, but I don't think he should be in there. What he did or was alleged to have done—and there must be something to it if he agreed to be banned for life—I feel he doesn't think he should be in there, either."

Giamatti said, "All the Hall of Famers I talked to said they would not attend if he were admitted."

I don't blame them.

On the Hall of Fame, there's no doubt in my mind the standards for election have come down. Based on present criteria, I think Stan Hack, Tony Oliva, and Jim Bunning should be there. I also think the voting system should be changed. The 400 or so writers who have belonged to the Baseball Writers Association of America for at least ten years do the voting. I know some of them who never go near a ballpark, never see a game. Why shouldn't the broadcasters who see every game all year be allowed to vote? And the PA announcers, too?

I would have tossed George Steinbrenner out of the game long ago. I probably would not have let him in in the first place. In every book I read about Watergate and Nixon, they nailed Steinbrenner for giving employees big raises they never saw. The money was going to the Nixon campaign. Somebody blew the whistle. I would say goodbye to Mr. Steinbrenner for good, for the good of baseball.

Expansion continues to water down the game. I think we will see some team go into bankruptcy if only to escape from the long-term contracts that are strangling them.

Don't ask me how I would straighten out the scheduling mess. It certainly makes no sense as it is, with teams playing some teams more than others, and teams in one division playing more games against teams in the other division than in their own. That's indefensible. To win your division, you should have to do it against the rivals in your own division.

I would like to see interleague play. I think it would make all the teams a little more competitive. I don't have the vaguest idea how they would draw up a schedule where each team had to play at least twenty-seven other teams during the season. Every team would visit every city for one series, maybe play every other team six games a year. I doubt that it will happen, anyhow; the two leagues love to sell a bill of goods to the fans that one league is better than the other.

I think eventually there will be more divisions, maybe four in each league, and some sort of playoffs with wild card teams, like the NFL. I dread the possibility; it would be awful. I accept the present playoff system only grudgingly, but I can't turn it back. I don't know what I'd do with twenty-eight or thirty or thirty-two or forty teams. Four divisions in each league? Eight divisions? Four leagues? Six leagues? Round robin playoffs? The World Series during Super Bowl week?

The mind boggles. I think I'll resign as commissioner.

Now that I'm no longer the commissioner, I think I'll become president of the Orioles. First thing I would do is have one general manager, Roland Hemond. No assistant GMs. What is an assistant GM? What does he do? I have no idea.

If

Doug Melvin is in charge of the minor leagues. He goes to a ball game somewhere almost every day and is invaluable in providing the general manager with opinions on minor league players. But that is not an assistant GM. I think he'll be a good general manager someday.

Roland Hemond is a very knowledgeable baseball guy. Everybody in the game who knows him thinks the world of him, but his hands are somewhat tied in Baltimore. I don't think he gets his way, and I think that's wrong. A general manager should be able to make all the final decisions, run the club, be left alone to sink or swim. Hire and fire managers. Make trades. Sure, run things by the owner, but a smart owner will say, "You're running it, not me. If you make too many mistakes, we'll get rid of you." It's just a job, after all. But let the guy do the job.

I would try to discourage the big "Oh!" in "The Star-Spangled Banner" when it is sung in Baltimore. But I would lose, because the fans created it. It started with Wild Bill Hagy, the unofficial cheerleader in the 1970s. He sat in section 34 down the right field line in Memorial Stadium and started the forming of the letters that spell out *Orioles*. The fans began screaming out that "Oh!" near the end of the anthem and everybody laughed about it at first. I thought, "Here we are, the city where the national anthem was written, and we seem to be making a joke of it." Visiting players and media people wonder what it's all about the first time they hear it. People call in and ask me how I feel about it. When I say I don't like it, they invariably say they don't like it, either. Many of them are offended by it. If a person who is invited to sing the anthem is not used to it, that "Oh!" can be disconcerting and throw them off stride, so the Orioles sometimes tape it ahead of time and the singer lip-synchs it on the field. I wish the fans would cut it out.

If I was running the Orioles I would not have left the old ballpark. I worked there for twenty-five years and knew every brick and corner and was comfortable there. I loved that old ballpark.

But as long as we were moving, I'm glad it was to a new old-fashioned park and not one of those round plastic places with carpets. I love Oriole Park at Camden Yards, too. How can

251

you not? And I'm especially proud of the right field corner, because I had a part in designing it. Eli Jacobs grew up a Dodger fan in Brooklyn and he wanted something reminiscent of Ebbets Field in the new park. So he asked the architects to talk to me about what it was like, and the results of those discussions is a right field corner as similar to Ebbets Field as we could come. It's not exact by any means; for one thing, the scoreboard is not identically situated. But it's a close-enough reminder for me.

The new press box has heat and air-conditioning, which is okay, as long as they don't have to close us in. I don't like watching a game through a pane of glass. I want it open so I can get the feel and the smell and the sounds of the ballpark.

I have a theory that good hitters should be pitching coaches and good pitchers should be hitting coaches. Who studies pitchers more than good hitters, and who studies hitters more than good pitchers? I would give that a try.

I would not be as secretive as most clubs are today. The worst thing they do is let a player find out he's been traded or released by reading about it or hearing it on the radio. There's no excuse for that. What's wrong with telling a player they are thinking of trading him and are working on a deal that might involve him? Randy Milligan felt hurt when the Orioles got Glenn Davis to play first base. Nobody told him about it before they announced it. The night before, he was at a banquet with some people from the Orioles' front office. They could have said something to prepare him for the news that affected his chances of playing regularly. He had to read about it the next day.

I think all public address announcers should explain technical plays or decisions to the fans in the ballpark, so they are as well informed as those at home listening or watching on TV. Many fans keep score and don't know how to mark such things as interference calls or obstruction plays. They are often not aware of why a runner was sent back to a base or why someone was allowed to advance one base or two. The Diamondvision at the new Oriole Park is doing some of that, but fans everywhere are entitled to be better informed.

Now that I have issued that order, I think I'll resign as the Orioles president and get back behind my own PA mike.

TWENTY-FOUR

THANK Youuuu

T HERE YOU HAVE IT. This will be the only book like this that I will ever write. I did not think I would enjoy doing it when I started, but I have enjoyed it.

When I came out of that stroke in 1983, I said I didn't know how I could ever repay people for their prayers and support. Perhaps sharing my life and thoughts with you is one way I can do that; that is for you, the reader, to decide.

Whenever I look at those team photos of the 1947, 1948, and 1949 Brooklyn Dodgers, I say to myself, "Look at that. You didn't do very well, but you were there. You were part of it. Not many people can say that."

Good or bad, I was in those two World Series. I must have had something going for me. When I see the faces of my old teammates, I still get that old feeling of frustration. Why didn't I get it done? That reverberates in my mind endlessly. I was responsible for my own failure. When I had the chance to correct it, I still didn't do it. Was it physical or mental or both? I still don't know.

I can go through life not thinking one thing about it, and once in a while something will jar me and I'll think, "Why couldn't I do it? Such an easy thing, to throw the ball over home plate."

When you have closed this book, you might say the same thing I've been saying for forty-five years: "I wonder why that boy couldn't get it together?"

It was all such a big part of my life, how can I just discard it? I wouldn't even try. I relive it all, the nightmares and the good times. And one of those good times was the last half of that 1948 season, when I didn't believe anybody would ever beat me. Ever.

Sometimes I dream that I am fifty years old and I'm making a comeback. I'm playing with Pee Wee and Ralph and Duke, and Bruce Edwards is catching me. And I've got it all together. Soon as I wake up, I know it's goofy. But I still have that dream.

And when I look at the faces of those players who stayed up there and achieved so much, I wonder why Rex Barney, who had such a mediocre record, still lives in the minds of so many people. Why is it that, to this day, we can be in Florida during spring training and I call a popular restaurant for a reservation and give them my name and I hear, "Oh, my God. I hate you. I've hated you all my life. I've been a Giant fan since I was a kid and I remember what you did to us." I mean, I still hear that stuff. They give me a hard time, but then they always treat me swell. But do you think that Reese or Snider or Stan Musial ever get a reception like that?

At the Orioles' carnival one winter, a guy came up to me and said, "Rex, I saw you pitch your first big league game. I was a little kid, and you pitched the second game against the Cubs after Hal Gregg pitched the first."

Why do they remember things like that? Why do I get old yellowed newspaper clippings and box scores from fifty years ago in the mail? Why do people hold onto stuff like that?

I was having lunch with my daughter a few years ago and an elderly gentleman came over to me and said, "Are you Rex Barney?"

"How in the world would you recognize me?" I asked.

He explained that he had lived and worked in New York and his whole life had been baseball. "I just want to tell you one thing," he said. "You played when they were the real Dodgers."

And I think that has something to do with it. I guess if I stood on the corner of Flatbush and Atlantic Avenue in Brooklyn for a half hour, somebody would recognize me. That's amazing to me. It's almost as if I have become some sort of mythological greater-than-life character in the minds of those Brooklyn fans, who wondered what I might have achieved with all the stuff I had. I wonder about it myself. Sometimes, as I lie awake in the dark stillness of the night, I tell myself, "Yeah, you should have." People can take "what might have been" and turn it into something as grand as their imaginations will carry them.

What if I had pitched for ten or fifteen years and won 250 or 300 games? Would I still be the same person, with the same personality? I would like to think yes, but I don't know.

I consider myself one of the most fortunate guys in the world, because all my life I have done what I wanted to do. In January 1993 the Maryland Professional Baseball Players Association honored me at their annual Tops in Sports dinner with their Eddie Rommel Award for "meritorious service to baseball over a long period of time." (Rommel, a Baltimore native, pitched for the Philadelphia Athletics, then became an American League umpire. He was behind the plate when I pitched in Game 7 of the 1947 World Series.) I deeply appreciated this honor, but they got it wrong. It is baseball that has given me so much over the years, not the other way around.

After I had the stroke, the doctors told me that most people go back to their old habits, which kill them. Many of my friends expected me to go that route. And some thought I would just fold it up and live on Social Security and my pensions. I think of that now, but it never occurred to me then. Baltimore has been good to me. I love what I am doing and will never quit. Ever. Somebody will have to yell, "You're out!" to get me out of the game.

I have worked hard to achieve whatever I have done. But wait. That's wrong. Work is the wrong word for what I do. Willie Stargell was correct when he said, "The umpire never yells 'Work ball.' He says, 'Play ball.'" I'm grateful that, after fifty years, I'm still playing.

Index